THE CHILLING EFFECT
IN
TV NEWS

THE CHILLING EFFECT
IN
TV NEWS

Intimidation by the Nixon White House

Marilyn A. Lashner

PRAEGER SPECIAL STUDIES • PRAEGER SCIENTIFIC

New York • Philadelphia • Eastbourne, UK
Toronto • Hong Kong • Tokyo • Sydney

Library of Congress Cataloging in Publication Data

Lashner, Marilyn A.
   The chilling effect in T.V. news.

   Bibliography: p.
   Includes index.
   1. Government and the press—United States—History—
20th century. 2. Television broadcasting of news—United
States—History—20th century. 3. American newspapers—
Sections, columns, etc.—History—20th century. 4. United
States—Politics and government—1969-1974. I. Title.
PN4745.L37 1984   302.2'34'0973   84-3148
ISBN 0-03-069662-3 (alk. paper)

Published in 1984 by Praeger Publishers
CBS Educational and Professional Publishing
a Division of CBS Inc.

© 1984 by Marilyn A. Lashner

56789 052 98765432

Printed in the United States of America

To my husband, Melvin

ACKNOWLEDGMENTS

When I chose to pursue the doctorate, the school of communications at Temple University opened its doors to what became the most intellectually invigorating experience of my life. I shall always be grateful to this sprawling "people's university" and particularly to its department of radio-television-film for a brilliant faculty, challenging standards, and, above all, a personalized warmth that I enjoyed from day one.

To Professor Mike Kittross, my graduate advisor and chairman of my dissertation committee, my deepest appreciation for his vast storehouse of knowledge, his enthusiasm for creative logic, his shared devotion to words and language, and even his indefatigable worship of perfection, puns, and red penciling. Ever ready with time, references, and debate, he was the consummate teacher and always a friend.

To Professors Chris Sterling, Tom Gordon, John Roberts, Dennis Lowry, John DeMott, and the sociology department's David Elesh, distinguished members of my dissertation and testing committees, I acknowledge my appreciation and esteem. In his own way, each provided indispensible input and guidance for my graduate study, dissertation, and beyond. A special thanks to Chris Sterling who was never too busy for conversation and problems and who, as an editor and accomplished bibliographer, introduced me to the joys of authorship and publishing.

Thanks also to former and present deans Kenneth Harwood and Bob Smith for special confidence in me; to Professors Ed McCoy, Sydney Head, Gordon Gray, and Jerry Knudson, whose classroom delivered thoroughgoing gratification; and to Bob Roberts, the ultimate librarian, whose seemingly limitless knowledge of the literature was surpassed only by his kindness and talent for creative helpfulness.

Of course I am much indebted to those whose scholarship I used as sources: in particular to Professor Ole R. Holsti who kindly communicated with me to offer direction and help in content analysis methodology; to Professor Terrence P. Hopmann who made research materials available to me; and to Professors Charles E. Osgood, Sol Saporta, and Jum C. Nunnally who developed procedures for evaluative assertion analysis and who, with others, developed the watershed literature on the measurement of meaning.

I am grateful to those distinguished media executives who allocated large blocks of time to rate the events of my chronology: James E. Allen, Barry Bingham, Jr., Otis Chandler, Wallace Dunlap, Paul Duke, Reuven Frank, Daniel E. Gold, Herbert W. Hobler, Robert D. Ingle, Lewis Klein, Richard H. Leonard, Elmer W. Lower, John W. Macy, Jr., Richard S. Salant, William Sheehan, Arthur R. Taylor, Franklin A. Tooke, Gerald E. Udwin, and Vincent T. Wasilewski. While these men are in no way responsible for this book's general thesis, nor its analysis and interpretation, I hope my work does justice to their generous contributions.

Those who helped with coding or gave other technical assistance are also much appreciated: Meryl Udell, Kim Knause, Anne Letizi, Jorge Martinez, Linda Small, Felice Croul; James Pilkington, director of the Television News Archives at Vanderbilt University; and Professor John Flueck of Temple University's Data Analysis Laboratory.

A most appreciative thanks is reserved for editor Michael Fisher, gatekeeper and friend, who believed in this book — and, I suppose, in me. And to editors Barbara Leffel, Rachel Burd, and Beth Wilson whose professionalism, patience, and sharp insights were of inestimable value.

My family has always been a source of joy and strength for me, and this period and this project were not exceptions. I give warm and loving thanks to my parents, Mildred and Jack Auerbach, whose devotion and pride have always been a wellspring for incentive toward achievement. Thanks also to each of my four children — Bret, Jane, William, and Suzanne. Though busy with productive careers of their own, they were an exuberant cheering section, always close, always generous with coding assistance, brainstorming, advice, and, most importantly, with love. And finally, I give thanks to my loving husband, Melvin, for his perceptive input, support, and encouragement, but most of all, for his suffrance through countless readings and rereadings, empty cupboard, restaurants, and a wife's obsessive preoccupation with words, numbers, and academic debate. In every sense he has been my inspiration and champion. I recall that day when — with determination, pluck, and my manuscript in hand — he set out in search of a publisher. Of course he succeeded as he always does. I love you, dear, for that day and for the 13,000 others.

M.A.L.

CONTENTS

Acknowledgments   vii

List of Tables   xiii

List of Figures   xv

Introduction   1

OVERVIEW

1   **A Vulnerable Press**   5
    Serving Two Masters   7
    Life in an Iron Web   12
    Notes   15

BACKGROUND

2   **The Separate Traditions of First Amendment Theory**   21
    The Warp and the Woof of First Amendment Theory   22
    When Is a Right a Wrong?   24
    Glimmerings of the Regulation Snowball   26
    Third Cousins, Once Removed   32
    Notes   34

3   **The Importance of Opinion Journalism**   39
    Three Faces of the Press   39
    A Matter of Terms   43
    Commentary as Trump   44
    In the Beginning   48
    Notes   49

4 **More Than Adversaries: Nixon and the Press** 53
Presidents and the Press 55
The President Who Would Rule Thunder 56
Siesta at Watergate 59
Notes 62

THE CASE STUDY

5 **Research Design** 69
Getting in Focus 69
Methods and Procedures 71
Expectations Revisited 90
Notes 92

6 **Nixon's "WHAMA": Index of White House Anti-media Assault** 99
Finding the Face in WHAMA 100
Raining Daggers: A Frequency Count 103
Charting Storms of State 103
Notes 108

7 **The Newspaper/Television Difference** 109
How, in a Nutshell 111
Index of Vigorousness 112
Dimension by Dimension 114
The Shape of Timidity 121
Notes 122

8 **Chilling Effect** 123
Collision Course 124
The Fact of the Matter 132
Notes 132

OTHER ANALYSIS

9 **Ranking the News Analysts** 137
High Rank, Low Rank 139

Uneasy Lies the Head that Wears a Crown 145
Anatomy of Vigorousness 145
The Television Firmament 148
The Most Vigorous Network 150
Notes 151

10 **Executive Suite** 153
Profiles of High Places 154
Old Questions of Who and How Much 157
Notes 160

IMPLICATIONS

11 **Past, Present, and Holding** 165
Pressures on the Press 166
Timid and Intimidated 167
In Praise of a Festering Sore 168
At Issue 170
New Directions 171
Notes 177

12 **Prime Time Fringe** 179
The Commentary Connection 179
The People, Too 182
Notes 184

APPENDIXES

A **Chronology of the White House Anti-media Assault
During the Nixon Administration** 187

B **Coding Procedures: Step-by-Step Example** 231
Full Text of Commentary 231
Coding Procedures in Brief 233
Thesis Statement-Assertion Sheet 235
Assertion Chart 236

Evaluation Computation Chart: Domestic Problems 237
Evaluation Computation Chart: Minor Issues 238
Evaluation Computation Chart: Nonissues 238

C **Supplementary Tables** 239

Glossary 249

Bibliography 255

Index 289

About the Author 297

LIST OF TABLES

3.1	Three Matched Views	42
5.1	Vigorousness Defined and Redefined	79
5.2	Six Thesis Statement/Commentary Comparisons	82
5.3	Attitude Object-Subject Matter Category Scheme	84
5.4	Modes of Expression: Weights and Indicators	89
6.1	WHAMA	104
7.1	Index of Vigorousness	113
7.2	Television Timidity	116
9.1	The Commentators/Columnists Ranked	140
9.2	Report Card on Style	142
C.1	"Uninhibited?"	239
C.2	"Robust?"	240
C.3	"Wide-Open?"	241
C.4	"Debate?" (a point of view)	242
C.5	"Debate?" (positive or negative emphasis)	243
C.6	Impact of White House Anti-media Assault on Newspaper/Television Vigorousness	244
C.7	Impact of White House Anti-media Assault on Newspaper/Television Blandness	245
C.8	Chilling Effect of the White House Anti-media Assault on Television Commentary, by Vigorousness	246
C.9	Chilling Effect of the White House Anti-media Assault on Television Commentary, by Blandness	247

LIST OF FIGURES

2.1	The First Amendment Family Tree	33
7.1	Criticism of the President	118
7.2	Watergate Commentary	119
8.1	Press Reaction to White House Pressure	127
8.2	Chilling Effect	129
8.3	Reverse Chilling Effect	131

THE CHILLING EFFECT
IN
TV NEWS

INTRODUCTION

chill.ing ef.fect (chil'ing i-fekt') *n*. A significant reduction, in measures over time, and in light of influence by an outside factor, of the vigorousness of journalistic coverage of public issues.

The term "chilling effect" was applied to a First Amendment issue in the 1965 Supreme Court decision in the case of *Dombrowski v Pfister* (380 U.S. 479). Upholding the cause of three civil rights proponents seeking to enjoin Louisiana from prosecuting under the state's anti-subversive act, the Court said:

> A criminal prosecution under a statute regulating expression usually involves imponderables and contingencies that themselves may inhibit the full exercise of First Amendment freedom. . . . The chilling effect upon the exercise of the First Amendment right may derive from the fact of the prosecution, unaffected by the prospects of its success or failure.

Since that time "chilling effect" has taken its place among the phrases most frequently used in First Amendment literature, along with others such as "marketplace of ideas," "uninhibited, robust and wide-open debate," "no prior restraint," "freedom of speech," and "freedom of the press." Through use the term has come to refer to a result that is barely perceptible − if not imperceptible − and that is derived from factors not primarily concerned with the quality of journalism content.

1

Many factors are spoken of as causes of the chilling effect. This study focuses on only one — the power of the White House as derived from broadcasting's regulatory environment. The journalistic form under scrutiny is political commentary in television news programs.

Media watchers have long contended that broadcast regulatory policy contributes in some measure to the chilling effect in broadcast journalism. With increasing frequency bills to modify broadcasting policy as it now stands have been introduced into Congress, and for years there have been calls from many quarters to replace or revise the Communications Act under which broadcasting presently functions.

In *Red Lion* v *FCC* (395 U.S. 367), a landmark decision in broadcasting, the Supreme Court questioned the possibility that broadcast regulatory doctrines were a catalyst for the chilling effect where "coverage of controversial public issues will be eliminated or at least rendered wholly ineffective." Though the Court suggested that "such a result would indeed be a serious matter," it concluded in this 1969 decision that the ability of present regulatory doctrines to cause a chilling effect was "at best speculative." But the Court went on to say:

> And if experience with the administration of these doctrines indicates that they have the net effect of reducing rather than enhancing the volume and quality of coverage, there will be time enough to reconsider the constitutional implications.

Thus the Court has not eliminated the possibility of renewed examination of broadcast regulatory doctrines, should new empirical studies show evidence of the chilling effect. With these comments the Supreme Court has challenged research. This study is a response to that challenge.

consistency, a clear and restless eye, and sometimes thunder or fury, the analyses that television commentators reserved for White House affairs were writ in poetry and balm. No words of Caesar here to stand against the world. Reacting to administration pressure, television's Howard K. Smith, Eric Sevareid, David Brinkley, Frank Reynolds, and Harry Reasoner would tiptoe around White House corners with their own brand of commentary nonspeak: hedging, platitude, and trivia in which controversy was homogenized, euphemized, or avoided. What vigorousness there was in network commentary was reserved for such domestic problems as crime, drug abuse, race relations, and poverty, or for such nonissues as science, invention, history, and art. In these categories, where the targets were nonspecific or sterile, the danger of scorching sensitive White House nerves seemed comfortably remote.

Thus it was that the White House was able to focus its steely precision on the one crucial area of a troublesome press, criticism of administration policies. And here, where it mattered most, network television was handily intimidated. While the newspaper columns were at first nibbling and later clawing at the Watergate story, television commentary studiously avoided it and concentrated instead on spirited discussions of nonissues. While the newspaper columns were expressing judgment and criticism in their commentary on the president, television opted for balance and was reluctant to take a point of view. Newspapers used strong and active rhetoric in their discussions of government; by contrast, television's rhetoric was weak, passive, and qualified.

It was usually the case that in both newspapers and television a decline in the level of vigorousness in one subject-matter area would be compensated for by increased vigorousness in another. So it was in the case of television, where diminished vigorousness in criticism of the administration was normally accompanied by increased vigorousness in commentary on such "safe" categories as domestic problems and nonissues. But according to the analysis to be described in a later chapter, television had a breaking point — a point at which its defenses appeared simply and completely to crumble. In every instance when the White House pressure reached that critical point,[1] television vigorousness slumped in the "safe" subject matter areas as well — not only on White House matters. It was as if the best of network intentions, their integrity, their

OVERVIEW

1

A VULNERABLE PRESS

During the Nixon administration the First Amendment failed. As the target of a White House offensive, the free press was baited, harassed, discredited, battered. And in the end at least one part of that press was manipulated. So far as anyone knows, this kind of surrender on the part of the press could have happened as well in previous administrations. Certainly it could happen in future ones. The First Amendment, that venerable protector of the people's right to know, was designed to insulate the press from government pressure. But during the Nixon presidency the White House succeeded in intimidating the already timid television press.

Richard Nixon was not a man to suffer gamely through the traditional tension of the press-government adversary relationship. Haunted by ghosts stemming from his early political career, he embarked from the very first days on an assault of anti-press maneuvers that was unprecedented in its ardor and intensity. Law suits, tax audits, FBI investigations, threats, subpoenas, license challenges, retaliation, and power plays became the hallmarks of hi dealings with the press. By orchestrating a barrage of anti-medi efforts, the Nixon White House was able to chill dissent in politic commentary delivered on network television evening news progran — a feat it was not able to accomplish in nationally syndicate columns in newspapers.

While newspaper columnists — Tom Wicker, Joseph Kraft, Jan Kilpatrick, Clayton Fritchey, James Reston, Jack Anderson, Da Broder, and more — were focusing on White House affairs w commitment, and their professionalism were no match for an administration that would pull out all stops.

SERVING TWO MASTERS

Network television news programs reach more than 44 million people nightly.[2] For most Americans television is their major source of news, and of all media television is considered to be the most believable.[3] Television news personalities are heroes enjoying more recognition and popularity than most statesmen. And by their ability to slant the news, these journalists have the potential for enormous power. During the Nixon administration television news commentators allowed themselves to be manipulated by White House pressure. Instead of performing with the independence that a free press requires, they tailored their comments in such ways as to satisfy the administration will — or at least to sidestep administration displeasure. As White House anti-media pressure mounted, television commentators avoided criticism and controversy, and concentrated instead on less sensitive areas. This was not the case with newspaper columnists, who became more vigorous in the face of increased White House pressure.

The fact that television and newspapers responded differently to the White house anti-media assault is enormously significant: Television is a medium regulated by government, while newspapers in most respects are not. Though many other factors — economic, historical, technological — characterize the differences between these media, none is more significant than the difference in regulatory environment. It is essential, then, that all evidence concerning the comparative effects of government pressure be considered in light of the differences in public policy under which each medium functions. There can be no denying that these differences are of critical importance in determining the anxiety, tolerance, or fear with which the media may react to government pressure.

As it has evolved, public press policy in the United States reflects two distinct trends of First Amendment theory: libertarian theory supportive of laissez-faire policy for the printed press and sometimes for the broadcasting press, and social responsibility theory supportive of affirmative policy for the broadcasting press alone.[4] Variously described as "the almost press," "the half-opened media," "distant cousins," and as having second-class status under the First Amendment, broadcasting has been denied the level of economic and editorial independence traditionally accorded the printed press. Instead, broadcasters have been forced to straddle the divide between the two conflicting lines of First Amendment interpretation. On the one side is the laissez-faire commitment by which government maintains complete separation from editorial functions of the press; but on the other side is the government-supervised affirmative approach by which government licenses, oversees, evaluates, requires, and punishes.

The laissez-faire interpretation — rooted deep in the libertarian philosophy of Milton, Locke, Mill, and Supreme Court Justices Holmes, Brandeis, Black, and Douglas — gives trust to man's reason and to his ability to seek out truth in the marketplace of ideas. In this context — which we shall call the "journalism tradition" — freedom of the press means no governmental restraint prior to dissemination; however, in the event that the press is found to have committed transgressions, post-dissemination punishment is permitted. Under this regime the press enjoys full editorial autonomy. It gathers what information it can and publishes what it will, and the government, except for such reasons as "national security," is powerless to interfere in advance of publication. Afterward, if the press is accused of crime or violation of rights, it is for the courts to decide. Here is the arena where broadcast journalists march side by side with print journalists to fight the battles of prior restraint, subpoenas, gag rules, defamation, invasion of privacy, obscenity, newsman's privilege, contempt citations, and government secrecy.

The printed press functions entirely within this journalism tradition, but broadcasting is required additionally to function within a newer affirmative interpretation that sanctions government involvement in the editorial process. Grounded in fear of the technological revolution, in a less optimistic view of man and society, and in doubts about the efficacy of the libertarian philosophy, this affirmative interpretation reflects the twentieth-century commitment to social responsibility and a new perspective on First Amendment theory that identifies the people's right to know as the paramount guarantee. Under this interpretation the rights of broadcasters are secondary to those of the public. Here the government asserts its social responsibility to "maintaining and enhancing"[5] free expression commitment, and their professionalism were no match for an administration that would pull out all stops.

SERVING TWO MASTERS

Network television news programs reach more than 44 million people nightly.[2] For most Americans television is their major source of news, and of all media television is considered to be the most believable.[3] Television news personalities are heroes enjoying more recognition and popularity than most statesmen. And by their ability to slant the news, these journalists have the potential for enormous power. During the Nixon administration television news commentators allowed themselves to be manipulated by White House pressure. Instead of performing with the independence that a free press requires, they tailored their comments in such ways as to satisfy the administration will — or at least to sidestep administration displeasure. As White House anti-media pressure mounted, television commentators avoided criticism and controversy, and concentrated instead on less sensitive areas. This was not the case with newspaper columnists, who became more vigorous in the face of increased White House pressure.

The fact that television and newspapers responded differently to the White house anti-media assault is enormously significant: Television is a medium regulated by government, while newspapers in most respects are not. Though many other factors — economic, historical, technological — characterize the differences between these media, none is more significant than the difference in regulatory environment. It is essential, then, that all evidence concerning the comparative effects of government pressure be considered in light of the differences in public policy under which each medium functions. There can be no denying that these differences are of critical importance in determining the anxiety, tolerance, or fear with which the media may react to government pressure.

As it has evolved, public press policy in the United States reflects two distinct trends of First Amendment theory: libertarian theory supportive of laissez-faire policy for the printed press and sometimes for the broadcasting press, and social responsibility theory supportive of affirmative policy for the broadcasting press alone.[4] Variously described as "the almost press," "the half-opened media," "distant cousins," and as having second-class status under the First Amendment, broadcasting has been denied the level of economic and editorial independence traditionally accorded the printed press. Instead, broadcasters have been forced to straddle the divide between the two conflicting lines of First Amendment interpretation. On the one side is the laissez-faire commitment by which government maintains complete separation from editorial functions of the press; but on the other side is the government-supervised affirmative approach by which government licenses, oversees, evaluates, requires, and punishes.

The laissez-faire interpretation — rooted deep in the libertarian philosophy of Milton, Locke, Mill, and Supreme Court Justices Holmes, Brandeis, Black, and Douglas — gives trust to man's reason and to his ability to seek out truth in the marketplace of ideas. In this context — which we shall call the "journalism tradition" — freedom of the press means no governmental restraint prior to dissemination; however, in the event that the press is found to have committed transgressions, post-dissemination punishment is permitted. Under this regime the press enjoys full editorial autonomy. It gathers what information it can and publishes what it will, and the government, except for such reasons as "national security," is powerless to interfere in advance of publication. Afterward, if the press is accused of crime or violation of rights, it is for the courts to decide. Here is the arena where broadcast journalists march side by side with print journalists to fight the battles of prior restraint, subpoenas, gag rules, defamation, invasion of privacy, obscenity, newsman's privilege, contempt citations, and government secrecy.

The printed press functions entirely within this journalism tradition, but broadcasting is required additionally to function within a newer affirmative interpretation that sanctions government involvement in the editorial process. Grounded in fear of the technological revolution, in a less optimistic view of man and society, and in doubts about the efficacy of the libertarian philosophy, this affirmative interpretation reflects the twentieth-century commitment to social responsibility and a new perspective on First Amendment theory that identifies the people's right to know as the paramount guarantee. Under this interpretation the rights of broadcasters are secondary to those of the public. Here the government asserts its social responsibility to "maintaining and enhancing"[5] free expression

OVERVIEW

1

A VULNERABLE PRESS

During the Nixon administration the First Amendment failed. As the target of a White House offensive, the free press was baited, harassed, discredited, battered. And in the end at least one part of that press was manipulated. So far as anyone knows, this kind of surrender on the part of the press could have happened as well in previous administrations. Certainly it could happen in future ones. The First Amendment, that venerable protector of the people's right to know, was designed to insulate the press from government pressure. But during the Nixon presidency the White House succeeded in intimidating the already timid television press.

Richard Nixon was not a man to suffer gamely through the traditional tension of the press-government adversary relationship. Haunted by ghosts stemming from his early political career, he embarked from the very first days on an assault of anti-press maneuvers that was unprecedented in its ardor and intensity. Law suits, tax audits, FBI investigations, threats, subpoenas, license challenges, retaliation, and power plays became the hallmarks of his dealings with the press. By orchestrating a barrage of anti-media efforts, the Nixon White House was able to chill dissent in political commentary delivered on network television evening news programs — a feat it was not able to accomplish in nationally syndicated columns in newspapers.

While newspaper columnists — Tom Wicker, Joseph Kraft, James Kilpatrick, Clayton Fritchey, James Reston, Jack Anderson, David Broder, and more — were focusing on White House affairs with consistency, a clear and restless eye, and sometimes thunder or fury, the analyses that television commentators reserved for White House affairs were writ in poetry and balm. No words of Caesar here to stand against the world. Reacting to administration pressure, television's Howard K. Smith, Eric Sevareid, David Brinkley, Frank Reynolds, and Harry Reasoner would tiptoe around White House corners with their own brand of commentary nonspeak: hedging, platitude, and trivia in which controversy was homogenized, euphemized, or avoided. What vigorousness there was in network commentary was reserved for such domestic problems as crime, drug abuse, race relations, and poverty, or for such nonissues as science, invention, history, and art. In these categories, where the targets were nonspecific or sterile, the danger of scorching sensitive White House nerves seemed comfortably remote.

Thus it was that the White House was able to focus its steely precision on the one crucial area of a troublesome press, criticism of administration policies. And here, where it mattered most, network television was handily intimidated. While the newspaper columns were at first nibbling and later clawing at the Watergate story, television commentary studiously avoided it and concentrated instead on spirited discussions of nonissues. While the newspaper columns were expressing judgment and criticism in their commentary on the president, television opted for balance and was reluctant to take a point of view. Newspapers used strong and active rhetoric in their discussions of government; by contrast, television's rhetoric was weak, passive, and qualified.

It was usually the case that in both newspapers and television a decline in the level of vigorousness in one subject-matter area would be compensated for by increased vigorousness in another. So it was in the case of television, where diminished vigorousness in criticism of the administration was normally accompanied by increased vigorousness in commentary on such "safe" categories as domestic problems and nonissues. But according to the analysis to be described in a later chapter, television had a breaking point — a point at which its defenses appeared simply and completely to crumble. In every instance when the White House pressure reached that critical point,[1] television vigorousness slumped in the "safe" subject matter areas as well — not only on White House matters. It was as if the best of network intentions, their integrity, their by implementing measures designed to neutralize the potentially tyrannizing effects of scarce resources, big business, new technology, depersonalized living, and monopoly. Freedom of the press in this context — which we shall refer to as the "regulation tradition" — means governmental oversight where, in the name of consumer protection, the economic and editorial freedoms of the press are compromised by an authoritarian system of rules and regulations enforced by a hierarchy of punitive sanctions.

We speak, then, of two traditions under First Amendment theory: the journalism tradition and the regulation tradition — the former governing the affairs of both broadcasting and print, and the latter governing only broadcasting. Each has been upheld by the Supreme Court as clearing the barriers of the First Amendment. At times the basic assumptions of these traditions coincide. Both profess a commitment to First Amendment values of "uninhibited, robust, and wide-open" debate on public issues.[6] In ideal, if not in practice, both are rooted in the principle of localism — newspapers by historical accident, broadcasting by design. Both are committed to the profit motive. And both profess commitment to self-regulation and to professionalism.

But there are five major areas in which the assumptions of these separate traditions clash, in which the values inherent in one tradition deny the values inherent in the other. Essentially grounded in economic theory, these differences are the following:

1. Concept of unlimited resources vs. doctrine of scarcity

2. Resource allocation by market controls vs. resource allocation by government decision

3. Laissez-faire vs. government licensing

4. Private ownership vs. public-trustee principle

5. Editorial autonomy vs. government management of information.

It is at these tension points that the assumptions of the regulation tradition articulate what amounts to the essence of broadcast public policy in the United States. Consequently it is here that the widespread criticism and concern regarding broadcasting's eroding First Amendment rights are focused.

Concept of Unlimited Resources vs. Doctrine of Scarcity

The essential natural resource in publishing is paper, whereas the essential resource in broadcasting is the electromagnetic spectrum. In economic terms these essential resources are similar, in that each is limited in amount and has the potential for scarcity. But spectrum space is obviously and immediately limited and scarce, whereas the finiteness of paper is less evident. In an effort to deal with the scarcity issue made abundantly apparent by intolerable interference, Congress in 1925 passed a resolution declaring the ether to be "the inalienable possession of the people of the United States,"[7] and embarked on a policy of controlling and limiting its use. Though economists criticize the premise that scarcity is a phenomenon unique to spectrum space,[8] and even though in practice there are today more broadcasting stations than newspapers in this country,[9] the doctrine of scarcity as the reason for licensing remains the keystone of the regulation tradition.

Resource Allocation by Market Controls vs. Resource Allocation by Government Decision

The printed press operates according to a free-enterprise system in which the ordinary pricing mechanism of supply and demand determines the economic value of essential resources (what things cost) and, ultimately, resource allocation (who owns what). On the other hand, Congress has chosen to remove broadcasting from the dynamics of the free market in favor of a system of nonmarket allocation that preserves government ownership of spectrum space while removing true economic value from frequencies. Under this system the government uses public-interest standards to administer spectrum assignments at no substantial cost to the broadcaster. The broadcaster is then free — so long as he continues to act in the public interest — to reap the monetary rewards of his enterprise and is subject only to the general tax laws of the country.

Laissez-faire vs. Government Licensing

Broadcasting stations are licensed; newspapers and magazines are not. The printed press functions under a laissez-faire assumption that rejects government regulation and oversight in the publishing process.[10] Government restriction is encountered only in such areas of general concern as antitrust and civil rights. On the other hand, the licensing assumption of the regulation tradition permits infiltration of government into most precincts of broadcasting affairs. In this regard Congress, the courts, the White House, and the FCC assume major roles.

Federal licensing of radio stations has been practiced in this country since 1912. Whereas the earliest broadcasting legislation was interpreted as doing little more than mandating the issuance of licenses, later legislation granted the FCC the discretionary power to license using a standard of "public interest, convenience and necessity." On the basis of this power, regulation has extended for more than half a century to such areas as engineering specifications, network arrangements, multiple and cross-media ownership, business practices, commercial advertising, employment practices, procedures for accountability, and – most important from a First Amendment standpoint – program content.

Private Ownership vs. Public-Trustee Principle

The public-trustee principle is the heart of the regulation tradition. It is an ingenious construct that combines public ownership, private use, government licensing, nonmarket allocation of spectrum space, free expression, and public-interest obligations. Publishers, operating in the open-market system, own their enterprise and their resources, and, except for antitrust considerations, are free to use them and to transfer them at will. Such is not the case with broadcasters. On the theory that the public owns the airwaves, the broadcaster is considered a "public trustee," and as such is permitted private gain from use of public property so long as he uses that property in the public interest. The license is nothing more than a franchise to use the assigned portion of the spectrum for a particular period in a particular way. Transfer procedures are rigid and subject to review.

Editorial Autonomy vs. Governmental Management of Information

In the American experience, freedom of the press subsumes two principles: no restraint prior to dissemination, and subsequent

punishment for unprotected speech. While the laissez-faire assumption of the journalism tradition forges a system in which predissemination editorial autonomy is guaranteed, the regulation tradition's public-trustee principle — with its emphasis on public-interest obligations — invites prior governmental intrusion into program content.[11]
Though the Communications Act expressly forbids censorship, proscriptive and prescriptive regulation directed at broadcast programming has in effect supported a policy of information management carefully designed to avoid the appearance of blatant censorship. With punitive sanctions as leverage, "no prior restraint" under regulatory policy has given way to a framework of "prior standards"; "journalistic autonomy" has become "journalistic discretion"; and FCC definitions of obscenity and other types of unprotected speech are more restrictive than the established Supreme Court definitions.[12]

Proscriptive content intrusion has focused on such areas as false and misleading advertising, deceptive program materials, excessive commercial practices, obscenity, indecency, violence, and children's programming. However, it is the prescriptive rulings focusing on programming balance, responsiveness to local needs, and fairness in political and public affairs programming that have generated the most severe First Amendment criticism. Of these, section 315 of the Communications Act, which requires equal opportunity for political candidates; section 312, which requires reasonable access for candidates for federal office; and the Fairness Doctrine — clearly articulated as "the single most important requirement" and as the *"sine qua non"* for license renewal[13] — have received the most vocal attention. Together, as codified by FCC rulings, they require the broadcaster to conform to prescribed standards of content selection, emphasis, orientation, and time and cost considerations; failure to comply has been cause for governmental sanction ranging from a fine to refusal to renew the license.

LIFE IN AN IRON WEB

Because of the structure of broadcast regulatory policy, the government is in a position to affect broadcast organizations in ways that potentially filter down to news programs. This powerful leverage, together with doctrines actually regulating public affairs programming, threatens the integrity of broadcast journalism. Indeed, during the Nixon presidency the White House, by skillfully exercising its available options, did in fact trigger a chilling effect on the vigorousness of television's dissent and controversiality. Newspapers, governed by a public policy grounded in laissez-faire tradition, were not so vulnerable to the White House offensive, and therefore were able to assume positions of independence.

The pervasiveness of the government's regulation of broadcasting affairs subjects broadcasters to heavy burdens. Although license renewal has generally been pro forma,[14] at all times government oversight and the license renewal process hang as a sword of Damocles threatening the security of broadcasters. Consequently, in protection of their economic interests, broadcasters dodge and weave, constructing elaborate organizational policies – formal and informal – to conform broadcast content to their perceptions of the government will. From the highest executive on down, a socialization process that is both spoken and unspoken ensures a brotherhood of sensitivity throughout the organization, so that the news staff, even without specific injunctions from above, understands its role in the giant drama. And if the chilling of dissent in commentary on administration affairs appears crucial for government favor, and ultimately for security and profits, then so be it.

During the Nixon administration the White House, by increasing the volume and intensity of its anti-media efforts, was able to intimidate network television into diminishing the vigorousness of its commentary relating to the White House. That period was a trying one for the American public. The country was wracked with division because of involvement in the unpopular Vietnam war, and a White House scandal threatened the integrity of the 200-year-old Constitution. Event upon event provided more than enough grist for the journalistic mill. It seemed that now, more than ever, political commentary had a function not to be compromised. Nonetheless, whenever the White House anti-media assault reached a critical level of intensity, television commentary, unlike its newspaper counterpart, would take refuge in excessive attention to nonissues, avoidance of discussions of the White House scandal, blandness in comment on government, and reduced vigorousness in discussions of the president – all the while showing exceptional vigor in discussions of the "safer" nongovernmental problems.

The country survived, extricated itself from the scandal, and went on. The full press was credited with having done its job. Indeed, from some perspectives journalists were hailed as heroes. But at least one genre — network television political commentary — succumbed in part to its own vulnerability.

It seems to be of little comfort to broadcasters that the probability of having their licenses renewed is extremely high. Between 1978 and 1981 the FCC approved 97 percent of television license renewals, denying or revoking only four licenses for such reasons as unethical business practices and misrepresentations of fact.[15] Similar numbers had faced broadcasters during the Nixon years, for in the history of television up to 1969, only seven television licenses had been denied or revoked.[16] More imagined than real, it is the threat of losing their licenses that infuses broadcasters with vulnerability. What is real, however, are the FCC's other sanctions — fines, cease-and-desist orders, short-term renewals, and designations to hearings — which it exercises frequently and that often require elaborate and costly burdens of response by broadcasters. These sanctions, together with the limited term of the license, the massive paperwork burdens placed on broadcasters by license renewal and other procedures, and — most important — content guidelines that must be considered in all television program decisions, imbue the government with an authority that is ubiquitous and seemingly omnipotent. Thus, while denial of license is relatively rare, the presence of government in broadcasting affairs is heavy and threatening. For this reason broadcasters believe they are vulnerable; by so believing, of course, they become vulnerable.

In light of the importance of broadcasting to our society, it is unconscionable that government regulation promotes such a posture. A communications/information explosion and the vast audience it has generated have endowed television with enormous power in dissemination of news. Indeed, television has become the dominant news medium in this country, but as a vulnerable press it is a crippled press.

During the Nixon administration broadcast regulatory policy was tested and found wanting. By exercising leverage gained in part through the licensing process, the White House was able to chill dissent in network television news programs. It is not improbable that similar situations occurred in both earlier and later administrations. For so long as television regulatory policy remains essentially unchanged, the ability of the government to manipulate television news is to be expected.

Regulatory policy must not continue to provide the environment in which the White House or any other entity of government can succeed in chilling television's voice in the marketplace. For when people committed to self-government are deprived of the reasoning, doubt, or debate necessary to decide issues, both the political system and the people become bankrupt. The First Amendment stands as a guarantee of an unfettered and vigorous press — television no less than newspapers — in which debate on public issues and criticism of government and public officials are "uninhibited, robust, and wide-open." It still remains for broadcast regulatory policy to rise to that challenge.

NOTES

1. See chapter 6, section "Charting Storms of State." See also chapter 10, section "Old Questions of Who and How Much," and chapter 11, section "In Praise of a Festering Sore."

2. According to A. C. Nielsen Company, *National Audience Demographics Reports, Nielsen Television Index*, network television in February 1970 had a nightly audience of 44,270,000 people and 24,517,000 households. See chapter 9, note 1, for further breakdown. (These statistics were given to author during phone interview with a representative of the A. C. Nielsen Co.)

3. According to Roper surveys, 64 percent of the people polled get most of their news from television; 49 percent named newspapers as their major news source, radio was named as the major source by 19 percent, and magazines by 7 percent. Only 11 percent of the people rely on media other than television and newspapers. (Obviously, multiple responses were permitted.) In addition, television and newspapers led as the most believable media, with 51, 22, 7, and 9 percent of the people citing television, newspapers, radio, and magazines, respectively. See the Roper Organization, "Changing Public Attitudes Toward Television and Other Mass Media 1959-1976" (New York: Television Information Office, 1977), pp. 3-4.

4. For a classic explanation of the libertarian and the social responsibility traditions of the press (in addition to explanation of authoritarian and Soviet Communist traditions), see Fred S. Siebert, Theodore B. Peterson, and Wilbur Schramm, *Four Theories of the Press* (Urbana: University of Illinois Press, 1956).

5. *Fairness Doctrine and Public Interest Standards*, 39 FR 26372.

6. *New York Times Co.* v. *Sullivan*, 376 U.S. 254, 270.

7. R. H. Coase, "The Federal Communications Commission," *Journal of Law and Economics* 2 (October 1959): 5-6.

8. Coase advances this position in "The Federal Communications Commission."

9. In 1981 the total number of daily newspapers (morning and evening) was 1,747. The total number of broadcasting stations in the same year was 9,953 (8,933 radio stations and 1,020 television stations). It must be noted, however, that weekly newspapers numbered 7,238 and semi-, bi-, and triweekly papers numbered 635. *The Ayer Directory of Publications 1981* (Philadelphia: Ayer) and *The Broadcasting Yearbook 1981*.

10. "Oversight" as used here refers to government involvement in journalistic affairs prior to dissemination. The printed press, like the electronic press, is subject to punishment for unprotected speech subsequent to dissemination (such as defamation, invasion of privacy, obscenity).

11. For example, the Fairness Doctrine, political broadcasting equal opportunity requirements, requirements for program balance, and the prime-time access rule. In addition, programming is reviewed in comparative hearings when it has been designated as an issue.

12. Under a definition enunciated in *Roth* v. *United States*, 354 U.S. 476 (1957), and as augmented in subsequent cases, three elements must coalesce to account for the legal definition of obscenity: the dominant theme of the material taken as a whole appeals to a prurient interest in sex; the material is patently offensive because it affronts contemporary community standards relating to the description or representation of sexual matters; and the material is utterly without redeeming social value. In June 1948 the Criminal Code (18 USC 1464) had incorporated the section from the Communications Act that made it a criminal act to broadcast obscene, indecent, or profane language. In the FCC case, *In Re WUHY-FM Eastern Educational Radio*, 24 FCC 2d 408 (1970), the commission, considering the case of a broadcast in which an interviewee interspersed unorthodox expletives into his language, defined the indecency standard as twofold: patently offensive by contemporary community standards and utterly without redeeming social value. It thus removed the immensely protective safeguard implemented by the Supreme Court: dominant theme appealing to prurient interest in sex. In 1978, in *FCC* v. *Pacifica Foundation*, 98 S.Ct. 3026, the U.S. Supreme Court upheld the FCC's right to regulate a broadcast that is indecent although not constitutionally obscene. However, at this time the Court expressly refused to review the FCC's definition of "indecency."

13. *Fairness Doctrine and Public Interest Standards*, 39 FR 26372, 26375.

14. Of the 9,236 radio and television license renewal applications received by the FCC from 1978 through 1980, 8,135 (88 percent) were disposed of favorably; 47 (0.5 percent) were designated for evidentiary hearings. In actions on applications from previous years, 21 licenses (0.2 percent) were denied or deleted. Action on the remaining applications was not reported. Television license renewal applications for this period totaled 937; those disposed of favorably amounted to 910 (97 percent); those designated for hearings amounted to 8 (0.9 percent); there were 3 denials and 1 deletion (together amounting to 0.4 percent). *FCC Annual Reports 1978, 1979, 1980*, and *1981* updates (Washington, D.C.: Government Printing Office).

15. *FCC Annual Reports 1978, 1979, 1980,* and *1981* updates.

16. John D. Abel, Charles Clift III, and Fredric A. Weiss, "Station License Revocations and Denials of Renewal, 1934-1969," *Journal of Broadcasting* 14 (Fall 1970): 411-421.

BACKGROUND

2

THE SEPARATE TRADITIONS
OF
FIRST AMENDMENT THEORY

[The First] Amendment rests on the assumption that the widest
possible dissemination of information from diverse and antagonistic
sources is essential to the welfare of the public, that a free press is a
condition of a free society.

Associated Press v. *United States*[1]

Since 1791, when freedom of speech and press gained constitutional sanction, these guarantees have been revered by Americans
as the indispensable requirements for democratic society. But these
guarantees have not been static; in the course of history the simple
words have been interpreted and reinterpreted, defined and redefined, idealized and compromised — each time in the light of
contemporary social, psychological, political, and economic experience. What we term First Amendment theory is the constellation
of interpretations, definitions, prescriptions, and proscriptions
that articulates the American commitment to freedom of expression.
The original intent of the First Amendment was never really articulated and never universally understood, even at the time of its
enactment. Some viewed the amendment as a rejection of the English
law of seditious libel, while for others it was a rejection of licensing
procedures; for some the protection of speech was perceived as
absolute, while for others it was relative.

That the confusion existed from the very beginning is evidenced
by the enactment of the restrictive Alien and Sedition Acts just
seven years after the ratification of the Bill of Rights. But though

rhetorical precision was absent, what remained to become a tradition for the American people was a shared passion for a vague but instantly recognizable ideal, the heritage of free people everywhere.[2] Except for strict absolutists, most civil libertarians today eschew attempts to reconstruct the original intent of the amendment. Instead, they advocate a type of practical idealism in which ideals, contemporary priorities, and feasibility are balanced to form workable definitions.

THE WARP AND THE WOOF OF
FIRST AMENDMENT THEORY

The First Amendment simply states: "Congress shall make no law . . . abridging the freedom of speech, or of the press. . . ." But the amendment, while guaranteeing freedom of expression, is set forth in language that is at once vague and specific. It specifically names Congress as the addressee of the protection but is vague as to the recipient; it is rigid as to the guarantee but vague as to the substance of the guarantee. This failure to define the major concepts has caused a swell of confusion. Today scholars and others are still asking: Freedom of the press for whom? From whom? Where? When? To what degree? Which press? What speech? Is the right absolute or qualified? Does it guarantee publisher's autonomy or the people's right to know or the people's right of access? Is it oriented toward issues or toward persons? Is its purpose to free the publisher from the government or to free the people from the publisher? Does it confer special privileges on the press that are not conferred on ordinary citizens? Does it differentiate between expression on public and on private property? And, most germaine, does it guarantee different freedoms for broadcasting than it does for the printed press?

As articulated by the United States Supreme Court, First Amendment law dates from shortly after World War I. The introduction of conscription in World War I, American participation in the war, and the anti-radical and anti-Communist hysteria that produced such repressive legislation as the Espionage Statute of 1917 caused a flurry of civil rights protest that ultimately made its way to the courts. Through a variety of cases representing the age-old clash between authority and freedom of expression, the courts freely interchanged precedents from speech and press issues to struggle with the problem of assigning meaning and purpose to the yet undefined constitutional guarantee. In 1925, in a decision referred to as the turning point in the history of personal liberty, the constitutional protection was extended to the states.[3] From that time on, First Amendment law as a constantly evolving body of principles and definitions has assumed an enormous role in all phases of public affairs.

Among the major themes running throughout First Amendment theory, the most frequently cited are the importance of freedom of speech and press in a democratic society, the "marketplace of ideas" theory, the role of the press as critic of the government, the doctrine of no prior restraint, the goal of vigorous debate on issues of public importance, and the dangers of the "chilling effect."

In a variety of ways the Supreme Court has promoted a free press as "indispensable to the discovery and spread of political truth."[4] The protection given speech and press was designed "to assure unfettered interchange of ideas"[5] among the electorate, so that the people could bring about changes in their government by lawful means. According to the Court, an "enlightened citizenry" and an "informed and critical public opinion" are coveted goals "which alone can . . . protect the values of democratic government."[6]

In the belief that truth is more apt to surface in an environment sanctioning "free trade in ideas,"[7] the Court has repeatedly expressed "a profound national commitment to the principle that debate on public issues should be uninhibited, robust, and wide-open."[8] Referring to public discussion as "a political duty,"[9] the Court has interpreted a "broadly defined freedom of press"[10] in ways calculated to avoid censorship, the "chilling effect," manipulation of the marketplace of ideas, and other "perils" to a free society.

The ability of the press to criticize government freely "is at the very center of the constitutionally protected area of free discussion."[11] In the Pentagon Papers case the Court was explicit in describing this most vital of First Amendment Functions:

In the First Amendment the Founding Fathers gave the free press the protection it must have to fulfill its essential role in our democracy. The press was to serve the governed, not the governors. The Government's power to censor the press was abolished so that the press would remain forever free to censure the Government. The press was protected so that it could bare the secrets of government and inform the people. Only a free and unrestrained press can effectively expose deception in government.[12]

To protect the role of the press in discussion of governmental affairs, the Court's traditional interpretation of the First Amendment "erects a virtually insurmountable barrier" between government and the media by precluding "government tampering, in advance of publication, with news and editorial content."[13] Thus, "no prior restraint" has become the hallmark of First Amendment theory. Of course, where journalistic abuses may exist, "subsequent punishment . . . is the appropriate remedy, consistent with constitutional privilege."[14]

WHEN IS A RIGHT A WRONG?

Even in the United States, where the freedoms of speech and press are guaranteed by the Constitution, and where the people regard these protections as the essence of freedom itself, there are other priorities of social living that subtly but certainly work to diminish those freedoms of expression. For years the Supreme Court has engaged in what is known as ad hoc balancing in attempts to weigh equities in issues pitting the First Amendment against other societal pressures. In those cases, while bowing to the importance of a preferred position for the press, the Court has declared that civilized living demands no less than preservation of national security and social order along with protection of reputation, privacy, property, and moral standards. But every decision to balance is a decision against free expression. And to the extent that free speech and a free press are the fundamental requirements of a democratic society, there are those absolutists who hold that, through balancing, our political vitality is being undermined while the quality of our individual lives is being heightened.

Since 1919 the major responsibility for interpreting the First Amendment has fallen to the Supreme Court. Struggling with a wide assortment of freedom-of-speech issues, the Court has vacillated among a variety of theories, definitions, dichotomies, and formulas.

Within the context of such major formulas as the "bad tendency test,"[15] the "clear and present danger doctrine,"[16] the "preferred freedoms theory,"[17] and "ad hoc balancing,"[18] the Court has given definition to such issues as "fighting words," "hostile audience," "speech plus," "symbolic speech," and "speech-action," and to such individuals as "public officials," "public figures," and "private persons."

What has been obvious in the Supreme Court's brief history of addressing First Amendment issues is that, notwithstanding Justices Black and Douglas, who tended toward an absolutist interpretation, the majority has regularly considered relative values. What is equally obvious is the penchant of the Court for proceeding within the context of a dichotomous, "either-or" perspective. When, in 1931, in the landmark case *Near* v. *Minnesota*,[19] the Court defined the parameters of freedom of press as twofold — no prior restraint but subsequent punishment — the Court was identifying the point of dissemination as crucial. It forbade governmental restraint prior to dissemination but condoned punishment for offending words already disseminated. Thus the Court has created a "before-after" framework within which to consider First Amendment issues, and within that framework it has given legal distinction to protected vs. unprotected speech[20] where debate on public issues and criticism of government are protected while such speech as obscenity and defamation are unprotected. Scholars have referred to this dichotomy as "the two-level theory."[21]

Given the Court's tendency to interpret the First Amendment in dichotomous terms, it is easy to comprehend its willingness to embark on a two-tiered interpretation of press freedom once broadcasting became a viable medium. In various references the Court has observed that, although broadcasting functions in a medium different from print, it is nevertheless to be recognized as "press" along with newspapers and magazines. In a concurring opinion Justice Douglas could not have been more explicit when he said:

> . . . TV and radio, as well as the more conventional methods for disseminating news, are all included in the concept of "press" as used in the First Amendment and therefore are entitled to live under the laissez-faire regime which the First Amendment sanctions.[22]

But the fact remains that television and radio do not enjoy the laissez-faire regime of the First Amendment. Since the early days of radio, broadcasting has been a licensed medium with affirmative responsibilities to the public. And as the years have passed, the gulf between the two approaches — the laissez-faire tradition governing the affairs of the printed press and the affirmative tradition governing the affairs of broadcasting — has grown wider and more entrenched.

GLIMMERINGS OF THE REGULATION SNOWBALL

Although the Radio Act of 1912 was the first comprehensive radio legislation in this country, the concept of broadcast regulation stemmed from the late nineteenth century, when national and international efforts were made to regulate telegraphy.[23] But it was not until the federal courts adjudicated challenges to the Radio Act of 1927, and in particular to the authority of the Federal Radio Commission (FRC), that the pattern of broadcast regulation became firmly entrenched in the United States. From that time on, the course was set for broadcasting's departure from the traditional laissez-faire approach to the press. During the seven years of the FRC's existence, the federal courts decided 41 cases that contested the basic power of the commission to regulate broadcasting. Essentially these early decisions supported and defined the immediate role of the regulatory agency. But because the Radio Act of 1927 was for the most part incorporated into the Communications Act of 1934, the legislative basis of our present system, these early judicial decisions also had the effect of determining the direction and shape that regulatory policy would assume in the future.

In two Supreme Court decisions during the FRC era, the basic regulatory assumptions as we know them today were given ultimate approval. In 1931, in *American Bond and Mortgage* v. *United States*,[24] the Court sanctioned congressional authority to regulate broadcasting, and by extension supported the regulatory authority of the FRC; the following year, in *FRC* v. *Nelson Brothers*,[25] the Court affirmed the discretionary standard "public interest, convenience or necessity" and granted the commission wide-ranging power to supervise the "scope, character and quality" of broadcast services. Thus, the stage was set for the pervasive role that regulatory policy was to play in broadcasting affairs.

It is profoundly important to recognize that while these early judicial decisions set the course for governmental regulation of broadcasting, they had not been considered in a First Amendment context. Instead, the issues seem to have been perceived economically, in terms of government priorities vs. private privilege. Without so much as a glance at the issue of free expression, the cases were decided in light of Article 1, section 8 (the commerce clause) of the Constitution.[26]

While broadly affirming the commission's right to consider the quality and character of broadcast services, the Court in these early decisions made no mention of the commission's right to evaluate program content per se. It required two more major decisions and a span of 37 years before such a right was affirmed.

In 1943, just short of a decade after enactment of the Communications Act of 1934 and its establishment of the Federal Communications Commission, the Supreme Court, in *National Broadcasting Company* v. *United States*,[27] considered chain broadcasting and the question of the FCC's authority to regulate business arrangements between networks and their affiliates. On the basis of the public interest standard, the Court interpreted the commission's regulatory powers as clearly extending to matters beyond the engineering and technical arenas. Speaking for the Court, Justice Frankfurter used what was to become a much-quoted metaphor to describe the scope of the commission's mandate:

> . . . we are asked to regard the Commission as a kind of traffic officer, policing the wave lengths to prevent stations from interfering with each other. But the [Communications] Act does not restrict the Commission merely to supervision of the traffic. It puts upon the Commission the burden of determining the composition of that traffic.

In the final words of the decision, the question of First Amendment rights was briefly addressed and summarily dismissed:

> The licensing system established by Congress in the Communications Act of 1934 was a proper exercise of its power over commerce. The standard it provided for the licensing of stations was the "public interest, convenience, or necessity." Denial of a station license on that ground, if valid under the Act, is not a denial of free speech.

The Fairness Doctrine and Red Lion

It was not until 1969, in *Red Lion Broadcasting Co.* v. *FCC*,[28] that the Supreme Court squarely considered the interface of broadcast regulation with First Amendment principles. The issue that presented the opportunity was the Fairness Doctrine and its corollary, the Personal Attack Rules. These policy statements, issued by the FCC to ensure expanded and fairer broadcast debate, imposed on the broadcaster affirmative responsibilities with respect to program content. Originally set forth by the FCC in 1949, the basic premises of the Fairness Doctrine, as they have evolved, are the following:

The licensee has an affirmative obligation to provide coverage of issues of public importance.

It is the responsibility of the licensee to provide reasonable opportunity for opposing viewpoints.

The Personal Attack Rules, articulated in 1967 as corollaries to the Fairness Doctrine, were codified for dealing with attacks made upon the integrity of a person or group. Essentially, under the Fairness Doctrine and its corollaries, the commission has prescribed standards of public affairs programming that the broadcaster may defy only at his own peril. "The single most important requirement" and the "*sine qua non*"[29] for license renewal are the terms the FCC has used to underscore the urgency that it attaches to these doctrines. Reams of rigid definitions and specific procedures have been articulated to clarify the policies and, at the same time, to warn broadcasters of the leverage available to the commission. The sanctions available for Fairness Doctrine violations range from fines[30] to three levels of license manipulation: revocation, refusal to renew, or short-term renewal.

Any discussion of the evolution of the Fairness Doctrine must necessarily begin with the Brinkley and the Shuler cases of the early 1930s, the first known instances in which licenses had been denied on the basis of program content (Brinkley had used his station to promote goat gland rejuvenation operations; Shuler, to attack religious and other groups), and go on to include as milestones: the 1941 *Mayflower* decision, which refused the broadcaster the right to advocate over the air;[31] the 1949 report *In the Matter of Editorializing by Broadcast Licensees*, which revoked the earlier decision and stands today as the foundation of the Fairness Doctrine;[32] the 1959 amendment to Section 315 of the Communications Act, which is considered to have provided the statutory authorization;[33] and the landmark Supreme Court decision, *Red Lion Broadcasting Co.* v. *FCC*, which affirmed the constitutionality of the Personal Attack Rules and the Fairness Doctrine generally. In addition to the major milestones mentioned above, there are countless other rules, judgments, and legal decisions that have further defined and delineated the obligations of broadcasters under the Fairness Doctrine. Detailed descriptions of the evolution of the Fairness Doctrine are readily available elsewhere, and therefore will not be undertaken here.[34]

Because *Red Lion* articulates the judicial justification for broadcast regulatory policy as we know it today, it is valuable to reconsider the facts and opinion. As part of a syndicated "Christian Crusade" series broadcast from, among others, a small radio station in Red Lion, Pennsylvania, Rev. Billy James Hargis unleashed a stinging personal attack on Fred J. Cook, an aggressive prize-winning reporter, for views expressed in his book *Goldwater: Extremist on the Right*. Hargis referred to Cook as "a professional mudslinger" and accused him of dishonesty, falsifications, and Communist associations. Cook, on the basis of the Fairness Doctrine and the Personal Attack Rules, demanded free time to reply. The station (WGCB), owned by Red Lion Broadcasting Company, refused. The FCC held for Cook, finding that the station had failed to meet its Fairness Doctrine obligations. On appeal, the District of Columbia Court upheld the FCC's position. However, in a parallel action the Court of Appeals for the Seventh Circuit, acting on a suit initiated by the Radio-Television News Directors Association, held the Personal Attack Rules to be unconstitutional.

At the Supreme Court level Justice White delivered the unanimous opinion of the court.[35] Identifying the public as the focus of First Amendment protection, he contended that "[I]t is the right of the viewers and listeners, not the right of the broadcasters, which is paramount." He then went on to outline a comprehensive First Amendment theory that justified both the licensing system and the Fairness Doctrine. Referring to government licensing in the context of a limited spectrum and to "public interest" goals in the context of monopoly, the opinion described the need for an affirmative approach to broadcasting. While recognizing that broadcasting is a medium clearly within the pale of First Amendment interests, the Court cited as precedent an earlier holding that differences in the characteristics of the medium justified differences in the First

Amendment standards applied.[36] Following this line, the Court upheld the Fairness Doctrine as an instrument designed to guarantee First Amendment protection in the face of hostile forces. Thus, with an enthusiasm evidenced from a unanimous decision,[37] the Court condoned governmental involvement in program content and solidified standards for broadcasting that differed substantially from those for the printed press. By so doing, the Supreme Court once again underscored its willingness to embrace a two-tiered approach to First Amendment principles.

Red Lion and Tornillo

In *Red Lion* the Supreme Court made it eminently clear that it was not prepared to extend to broadcasting the kind of First Amendment protection that it had consistently accorded the printed press. Its resolve in this regard was reinforced in 1973 — just five years after *Red Lion* — in *Miami Herald* v. *Tornillo*.[38] In his comprehensive book on the Fairness Doctrine, Fred Friendly, former CBS news executive, offers a chapter entitled "Fair vs. Free: Squaring Tornillo and Red Lion."[39] Here Friendly describes *Tornillo* as "the Fairness Doctrine test case for newspapers." The issue in *Tornillo* was virtually identical to that in *Red Lion*: the right of government to dictate news content in the press. Patrick Tornillo, a candidate for the Florida State Legislature, had been criticized in an editorial appearing in the *Miami Herald*. On the basis of a never-tested, 50-year-old Florida statute that provided for the right of free reply for candidates attacked by a newspaper, Tornillo demanded his space to reply. He was refused by the newspaper on First Amendment grounds. At the Supreme Court level the decision was unanimous in favor of the paper. In a comment made during oral arguments, Justice Blackmun articulated the mood of the Court: ". . . for better or worse we have opted in this country for a free press, not fair debate."[40] Writing for the Court, Chief Justice Burger — while recognizing present and potential abuse from "this trend toward concentration of control of outlets to inform the public" — rejected remedies involving governmental enforcement. The use of governmental coercion, he claimed, "at once brings about a confrontation with the express provisions of the First

Amendment and the judicial gloss that the Amendment developed over the years."

While both *Red Lion* and *Tornillo* were unanimous decisions, they seem stunningly contradictory so far as First Amendment considerations are concerned. In *Tornillo* the Court recognized that "the press is not always accurate, or even responsible, and may not present full and fair debate on important public issues." But in deference to First Amendment values, "society must take the risk," and the press must not be burdened with "the heavy hand of government intrusion." In *Red Lion*, however, fairness, along with "suitable access to social, political, esthetic, moral, and other experiences," is identified as a public right not to be abridged. And it is legitimate for government to act to ensure that right. In *Tornillo* the Court stated unequivocally that under government-enforced right of access, "political and electoral coverage would be blunted or reduced"; in *Red Lion,* however, the possibility of self-censorship and reduced or wholly ineffective coverage resulting from government-enforced fairness was regarded as "at best speculative." In *Tornillo* the Court stated: "It has yet to be demonstrated how governmental regulation of this crucial process [editorial selection] can be exercised consistent with First Amendment guarantees of a free press as they have evolved at this time." Yet, in *Red Lion* the Court held "that Congress and the [Federal Communications] Commission do not violate the First Amendment when they require a radio or television station to give reply [time] to answer personal attacks and political editorials."

Recognizing that both decisions addressed essentially the same issue, albeit in different media, what is most striking, in view of the apparent contradictions, is that nowhere in the latter decision was there an attempt to reconcile with the former. In fact, nowhere in the *Tornillo* opinion is there a reference to *Red Lion*. Friendly argues that the Court's "inability to cope with *Red Lion* and *Tornillo* in the same opinion suggests that it recognizes the inherent contradiction of the two cases."[41]

Broadcasters and legal scholars alike are unable to "square" *Tornillo* and *Red Lion*. In tandem the two decisions stand as monuments to a double standard in public policy relative to freedom of the press. The decisions confirm that broadcasting, while being hailed as equal to the printed press in American society, is saddled with governmental requirements that restrict its freedom in ways consistently upheld as unconstitutional when applied to the printed press. As Friendly succinctly puts it, ". . . the government can be the ultimate referee for what Cronkite or Chancellor or their producers believe to be fair, because the stations which carry them are licensed, but it may not intrude on the news judgments of James Reston, *Time* or *Rolling Stone*, because the printed press is not subject to licensing."[42]

THIRD COUSINS, ONCE REMOVED

What, precisely, is the relationship of the First Amendment to First Amendment theory and of public press policy to both? The First Amendment, as an attempt to harness an ideal for all times, was of necessity articulated in broad terms. It was an attempt to translate passion into language and, as such, could only be incomplete. It remained for the courts to interpret the amendment in the context of the American ethic as they saw it. In a speech before the Elmira, New York, Chamber of Commerce, Justice Holmes remarked, "The Constitution is what the Judges say it is."[43] This terse appraisal candidly explains the relationship of First Amendment theory to the First Amendment. Considering the First Amendment as one generation away from the ideal of free expression, First Amendment theory, as the judicial explanation of the First Amendment, is two generations away from the ideal.

Public policy has been defined as a series of directives embodying the values of a society.[44] Its function is to maintain a steady course toward the achievement of long-range goals and to promote behavior sufficient to overcome whatever threats and dangers may occur.

Public press policy is designed to govern the activities of the press. In this country public press policy seeks to reconcile the values articulated in First Amendment theory with such "threats and dangers" as the profit motive, scarce resources, monopoly, and new technology. Since it is based on judicial interpretations of the First Amendment, public press policy is three generations away from the ideal of free expression.

In the United States, inasmuch as the courts have perceived the problems of broadcasting and of the printed press as being separate and unique, there have evolved two separate traditions of First Amendment theory and, consequently, two separate traditions of public press policy.[45] Figure 2.1 presents a model of the First Amendment family tree. Here the two traditions of public press policy are shown in terms of their relationship to each other and to their idealistic and theoretical antecedents. Conceived in tiers, public policy for the printed press is regarded as closer to the ideal of free expression than is public policy for broadcasting, in that the latter represents a more fettered, more contrived construction.

Shakespeare described two persons as being "a little more than kin, and less than kind," a situation in which, describing two members of the same family, one was no more like the other "than I to Hercules."[46] And so it is with the broadcasting press and its cousin the printed press. Though both were born to the family of

FIGURE 2.1
The First Amendment Family Tree: Relationship of the First Amendment to Public Press Policy

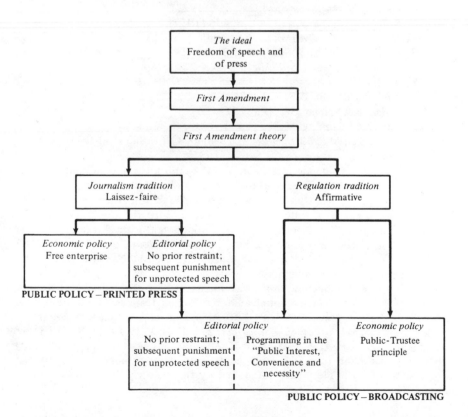

the First Amendment, broadcasting is just a small step removed from the directly lineal position enjoyed by the printed press. However, translated into philosophic terms, that step becomes a leap so vast and pervasive that, at one and the same time, it denies broadcasting its natural legacy, taxes the integrity of our information system, and ultimately threatens the fundamental assumptions of our republic.

NOTES

1. *Associated Press* v. *United States*, 326 U.S. 1 (1945).

2. In 1513 Niccolo Machiavelli, writing in *The Prince*, recognized that people who had once experienced liberty and self-government would cling tenaciously to that memory and would be quick to fight for that liberty again. "They do not and cannot cast aside the memory of their ancient liberty," he warned, which is "forgotten neither by lapse of time nor by benefits received."

3. *Gitlow* v. *New York*, 268 U.S. 652 (1925).

4. *Whitney* v. *California*, 274 U.S. 357 (1927).

5. *Roth* v. *United States*, 354 U.S. 476 (1957).

6. *New York Times* v. *United States*, 403 U.S. 713 (1971).

7. *Abrams* v. *United States*, 250 U.S. 616 (1919).

8. *New York Times* v. *Sullivan*, 376 U.S. 254 (1964).

9. *Whitney* v. *California*, 274 U.S. 357 (1927).

10. *Time* v. *Hill*, 385 U.S. 374 (1967).

11. *Rosenblatt* v. *Baer*, 383 U.S. 75 (1966).

12. *New York Times* v. *United States*, 403 U.S. 713 (1971).

13. *Miami Herald Publishing Co.* v. *Tornillo*, 418 U.S. 241 (1974).

14. *Near* v. *Minnesota*, 283 U.S. 697 (1931).

15. The "bad tendency test," used for the earliest cases, condoned suppression of expression that appeared to have a tendency to lead to substantial evil. Evidence of corruption of public morals, of disturbance of the public peace, or of a crime was not required. According to the Court, the government was entitled to "extinguish the spark without waiting until it has enkindled the flame or blazed into conflagration." *Gitlow* v. *New York*, 268 U.S. 652 (1925). This test has been all but abandoned, except perhaps for the philosophy behind suppression of pornography.

16. The "bad tendency test" was superseded by the "clear and present danger doctrine," originally enunciated by Justice Holmes in his dissent in *Schenck* v. *United States*, 249 U.S. 47 (1919), and refined by Justice Brandeis in his opinion in *Whitney* v. *California*, 274 U.S. 357 (1927). It condones suppression of expression that immediately and clearly threatens valid social objectives. Although used in various cases from 1919 through the 1950s, the doctrine was for the most part abandoned by the majority in *Dennis* v. *United States*, 341 U.S. 494 (1951).

17. The "preferred freedoms theory," sometimes called "definitional balancing," was first described by Justice Stone in a footnote in *United States* v. *Carolene Products Co.,* 304 U.S. 144 (1938). It holds that legislation restricting the political freedoms should be given more precise judicial scrutiny than other legislative challenges. In general the courts have always granted a presumption of constitutionality to challenged legislation, but according to the "preferred freedoms theory," any legislation concerning those freedoms protected by the First Amendment cannot claim the normally recognized presumption of constitutionality. Since the 1964 decision in *New York Times* v. *Sullivan,* 376 U.S. 254, the courts have extended this preference to issues involving other than legislative challenges, particularly in the areas of defamation and privacy, where the "actual malice" test accords a heavy presumption in favor of First Amendment freedoms.

18. "Ad hoc balancing" suggests a formula whereby the court in each case balances the individual and social interest in freedom of expression against the social interests that require restriction of expression. While still very much in vogue with the courts, the test is criticized as evasive of responsibility to articulate legal doctrine. By addressing the issues on a case-by-case basis, the Court is "cast loose in vast space, embracing the broadest possible range of issues to strike a general balance in the light of its own best judgment." Thomas I. Emerson, *Toward a General Theory of the First Amendment* (New York: Random House, 1966), p. 54.

19. *Near* v. *Minnesota,* 283 U.S. 697 (1931).

20. When in *Roth* v. *United States,* 354 U.S. 476 (1957), the landmark case in obscenity, Justice Brennan, speaking for the majority, referred to obscenity as "not within the area of constitutionally protected speech or press," he was underscoring the protected vs. unprotected speech dichotomy.

21. First Amendment scholar Thomas I. Emerson, in *The System of Freedom of Expression* (New York: Random House, 1970), p. 487, criticized this theory as a mistaken approach to First Amendment adjudication:

> Thus the Court uses the two-level approach to cut off consideration of what society is attempting to protect by obscenity laws, what the actual effects of obscenity may be. . . . Furthermore, the two-level theory abandons all First Amendment doctrine in an important area of expression and leaves that expression with only due process protection.

22. *Columbia Broadcasting System, Inc.* v. *Democratic National Committee,* 412 U.S. 94, 161 (1973). For a similar reference see *United States* v. *Paramount Pictures, Inc.,* 334 U.S. 131, 166 (1948), where the Court said: "We have no doubt that moving pictures, like newspapers and radio, are included in the press whose freedom is guaranteed by the First Amendment."

23. In 1849 Germany and Austria entered into what is credited as being the first international treaty regulating telegraphic communications. Other treaties followed: the Austro-German Telegraphic Union in 1857 and the first International Telegraphic Convention in 1865. In the United States the Interstate Commerce Act was amended in 1910 to bring interstate and foreign wireless, as well as wire, communication under federal control. That same year the Wireless Ship Act was passed, which required large passenger ships to carry radio equipment.

24. *American Bond and Mortgage* v. *United States*, 289 F.2d 318 (C.C.A.III) (1931); opinion affirmed 282 U.S. 374.

25. *FRC* v. *Nelson Brothers Bond and Mortgage Co.*, 289 U.S. 266 (1932).

26. Much of the information on these early judicial decisions is in Don R. Le Duc and Thomas A. McCain, "The Federal Radio Commission in Federal Court: Origins of Broadcast Regulatory Doctrines," *Journal of Broadcasting* 14, no. 4 (Fall 1970): 393-410.

27. *National Broadcasting Co.* v. *United States*, 319 U.S. 190 (1943), in Frank J. Kahn, ed., *Documents of American Broadcasting*, 2nd ed. (New York: Appleton-Century-Crofts, 1973), p. 518.

28. *Red Lion Broadcasting Co.* v. *Federal Communications Commission*, 395 U.S. 367 (1969).

29. *Fairness Doctrine and Public Interest Standards*, 39 FR 26372 (1974) at 26375.

30. The 1960 amendment to the Communications Act provided the FCC with authority to impose fines of up to $1,000 per day of violation, with a maximum of $10,000 for repeated violations of FCC rules. In this same amendment the FCC was also given the authority to grant licenses for periods shorter than three years.

31. *In the Matter of the Mayflower Broadcasting Corp. and the Yankee Network*, 8 FCC 333 (1941). With this decision the FCC banned editorializing by broadcast licensees. In 1949, after much public criticism and eight days of hearings, the FCC reversed itself on the basis of the public's right to hear. A new policy statement followed in which editorializing was made an affirmative duty. (See note 32.)

32. *In the Matter of Editorializing by Broadcast Licensees*, 13 FCC 1246 (1949).

33. 47 USC 315 (a). Originally an FCC interpretation of the public interest standard, the Fairness Doctrine is considered to have received legislative sanction in the 1959 amendment to section 315 of the Communications Act. After listing the exemptions from the political broadcasting requirements, Congress included the following words: "Nothing in the foregoing sentence shall be construed as relieving broadcasters . . . from the obligation imposed upon them under this Act to operate in the public interest and to afford reasonable opportunity for the discussion of conflicting views on issues of public importance."

34. See John M. Kittross and Kenneth Harwood, eds., *Free and Fair: Courtroom Access and the Fairness Doctrine* (Philadelphia: Association for Professional Broadcasting Education, 1970), pp. 117-192; Fred W. Friendly, *The Good Guys, the Bad Guys and the First Amendment: Free Speech vs. Fairness in Broadcasting* (New York: Random House, 1976); and Steven J. Simmons, *The Fairness Doctrine and the Media* (Berkeley: University of California Press, 1978).

35. Only seven justices participated in the decision. Not having heard the oral argument, Justice Douglas took no part in the decision.

36. *Joseph Burstyn Inc.* v. *Wilson*, 343 U.S. 495, 503 (1952).

37. While Justice Douglas did not participate in the *Red Lion* decision, he later vented his opposition in a concurring opinion in *Columbia Broadcasting*

System v. *Democratic National Committee*, 412 U.S. 94 (1973) at 154:

> Red Lion . . . , in a carefully written opinion that was built upon predecessor cases, put TV and radio under a different regime. I did not participate in that decision and, with all respect, would not support it. The Fairness Doctrine has no place in our First Amendment regime. It puts the head of the camel inside the tent and enables administration after administration to toy with TV or radio in order to serve its sordid or its benevolent ends.

38. *Miami Herald Publishing Co.* v. *Tornillo*, 418 U.S. 241 (1974).

39. Friendly, *The Good Guys, the Bad Guys, and the First Amendment*, ch. 12.

40. Ibid., p. 194.

41. Ibid., p. 195.

42. Ibid., p. 197.

43. Quoted in Le Duc and McCain, "The Federal Radio Commission in Federal Court," p. 394.

44. Daniel Lerner, "Effective Propaganda: Conditions and Evaluation," in Wilbur Schramm and D. F. Roberts, eds., *The Process and Effects of Mass Communication* (Urbana: University of Illinois Press, 1971), p. 480.

45. See chapter 1, section "Serving Two Masters," for a detailed comparison of the two traditions of public press policy: the journalism tradition, governing the affairs of the printed press and sometimes of broadcasting, and the regulation tradition, governing the affairs only of broadcasting.

46. William Shakespeare, *Hamlet*, act I, scene 2, ll. 65, 153.

3

THE IMPORTANCE OF
OPINION JOURNALISM

Democracy needs not only meat and potatoes of fact and information.
It also needs the vitamins and minerals of argument and debate.

Bill Monroe[1]

The winner of one of broadcasting's highest awards, NBC newsman Bill Monroe decried the present shortage of tough, carefully
wrought broadcast commentaries. Recalling the glory days of the
1940s, when such commentators as Elmer Davis, Raymond Gram
Swing, Boake Carter, and H. V. Kaltenborn graced the country
with their voices of knowledge, conviction, and individuality,
Monroe underscored the importance of commentary to our democratic system. With this observation and with his urgings for a resur-
gence of vigorous commentary in broadcast programming, Monroe
has sided with the logic of classic communication and political
theory. Vigorous and diverse expression of personal "philosophy,
conclusions, opinions, bias and evaluations"[2] on the great issues
of the day has long been held by historians, sociologists, jurists,
and other political analysts to be an indispensable component of
a free press functioning in a free society.

THREE FACES OF THE PRESS

In what has become a model analysis, sociologist Harold Lasswell has suggested that the communication process in society

performs three functions: surveillance of the environment, correlation of the parts of society in responding to the environment, and transmission of the social heritage from one generation to the next.[3] The surveillance function serves to tell things as they are, to disclose threats and opportunities affecting the community, and to keep the members apprised of the events as they happen. It encompasses the information component; it transmits news of what has been and what is; and, in press jargon, it deals in hard news or spot news. The correlation function supplies the context that members can use for understanding and for making judgments about the various events. It refers to the ideas component; it explains what should, would, or could be; and it deals in background, causality, discussion, interpretation, criticism, opinion, prescription, and advocacy. In practice, it corresponds to interpretive journalism — with what we know as editorials, commentary, letters to the editor, and, possibly, feature stories. In broadcasting it can also be found in introductions to or wrap-ups of otherwise factual reportage, in documentaries, and in talk shows and forums. The transmission function serves to maintain the social and political values of the community and to perpetuate those values to future generations. It translates into the more esoteric aspects of mass communication, those symbolic meanings hidden between the lines that, through suggestion and example, serve to reinforce societal values, hopes, and goals.

It is Lasswell's transmission function that in great part explains the rationale of the First Amendment. Political scientists and political leaders alike have long recognized the importance of a government's communication system for the perpetuation of that government's values and for the accomplishment of its desired ends. History is replete with attempts by political leaders to transform communication channels into instruments for their own gain. As far back as imperial Athens, Themistocles had propaganda messages about his armies engraved on stones at watering places sure to be visited by the opposing Ionian fleet; Alexander the Great dispatched runners from Persia to Macedonia to spread news of his victories; and Frederick II, a Holy Roman emperor of the thirteenth century, used bards and troubadours to strengthen his position with the pope.

The press as a political instrument is no less important in a democracy, where, as a mechanism for enlightening the electorate, it becomes central to both the operations and the shape of the system itself. In the 1949 British *Report of the Royal Commission on the Press*, the interface of the press with democratic society was addressed:

> The democratic form of society demands of its members an active and intelligent participation in the affairs of their community, whether local or national. It assumes that they are sufficiently well informed about the issues of the day to be able to form the broad judgments required by an election, and to maintain between elections the vigilance necessary in those whose governors are their servants and not their masters. More and more it demands also an alert and informed participation not only in purely political processes but also in the efforts of the community to adjust its social and economic life to increasingly complex circumstances. *Democratic society, therefore, needs a clear and truthful account of events, of their background and their causes; a means whereby individuals and groups can express a point of view or advocate a cause.*
>
> *The responsibility for fulfilling these needs unavoidably rests in large measure upon the Press . . . the main source from which information, discussion, and advocacy reach the public.*[4]

Two years earlier, in a similar analysis of responsibilities of the press in a democracy, the Commission on Freedom of the Press, an American nongovernmental panel, had identified five requirements of our society and, by inference, the five services required of the press: a truthful, comprehensive, and intelligent account of the day's events in a context that gives them meaning; a forum for the exchange of comment and criticism; a means of projecting the opinions and attitudes of the groups in the society to one another; a method of presenting and clarifying the goals and values of the society; and a way of reaching every member of the society by the currents of information, thought, and feeling that the press supplies.[5]

Both the British and the American commissions saw the press as a vehicle for "information, discussion, and advocacy" — or, as described by the latter group, as a supplier of "information, thought, and feeling." The combination of fact with opinion advocated as essential to a press functioning in a democratic society corresponds neatly with Lasswell's category scheme of "surveillance, correlation, and transmission." Table 3.1 shows the correspondence of Lasswell's categories with those of the two commissions — or, to state it otherwise, it shows which functions of the press respond to which needs of democratic society.

Obviously it would be a mistake — as some would have it — to define good journalism within the limits of factuality and objectivity. For while factuality, objectivity, and the absence of obvious personal bias are the sine qua non for surveillance of the environment, press responsibility must also respond to the correlation function, which requires subjectivity, interpretation, and advocacy in addition to factuality and objectivity. This is not to say, of course, that the information or "hard news" component of journalism functions wholly apart from subjective criteria. For without doubt, presentation of hard news certainly requires selectivity and is subject to bias as a hidden standard. Edith Efron, in her controversial study *The News Twisters*, stressed that "selectivity — the decision to include, or exclude information — is the essence of a news operation." The events selected for coverage, the issues discussed, the

TABLE 3.1
Three Matched Views: Requirements of
the Press in a Democratic Society

Requirements Stated by Royal Commission on the Press	*Requirements Stated by Commission on Freedom of the Press*	*Lasswell's Function of Communication*
1. Clear and truthful account of events	Truthful, comprehensive and intelligent account of the day's events	Surveillance
2. Background and causes	Context and meaning	Correlation
3. Forum for discussion and informed criticism	Forum for exchange of comment and criticism	Correlation
4. Means for individuals and groups to express a point of view	Means of projecting the opinions and attitudes of groups	Correlation
5. Means to advocate a cause	- -	Correlation
6. - - - - - - - - - - - - - - -	Method of presenting and clarifying goals and values of the society	Transmission
7. - - - - - - - - - - - - - - -	Way of reaching every member of the society	Transmission

facts included, the perspectives unveiled, the words, the connotations, the inferences, judgments, and solutions – are all a matter of choice.[6]

But while selectivity is inherent in the news process, and while a certain amount of bias may be inevitable, most responsible journalists, working within the context of canons of professional ethics, seek to curb such tendencies. Therefore, though opinion may infuse so-called objective news, this covert dimension cannot be relied on for dependable service of the republic in fulfillment of the correlation requirement. For this reason most codes of journalistic ethics, while eschewing bias in news reports, recognize the press's "obligations as teacher and interpreter"[7] and support interpretive journalism, when clearly identified as such and when separated from news reports, as a legitimate and vital component of the American press.

A MATTER OF TERMS

Interpretive journalism comes in many shapes with real or arbitrary distinctions. Journalists have attempted to distinguish its various levels and to assign labels to differing combinations of fact and opinion. But while accepted practice defines "editorial" as the unsigned opinion of management,[8] attempts to articulate firm boundaries and conditions for the rest of the genre have been regarded as arbitrary. Before leaving NBC, newsman Chet Huntley recommended avoidance of "all those confusing words which are frequently applied to our trade: editorializing, slanting, analyzing, commenting, observing, opinionating, and so on and so on." Instead, he favored universal use of the term "judgment."[9] Some have attempted to cast such terms as "analysis," "interpretation," "background," and "perspective" in a neutral light where the emphasis is on objectivity, inference, and context. They would reserve the term "commentary" for expressions of opinion and judgment. But Efron refers to this distinction as "the most important myth" and goes on to claim:

> In fact, there is no difference in any of these forms from the point of view of freedom from editorializing. These supposedly neutral forms are frequently indistinguishable from each other. Political opinion by reporters is to be found in all of them and there is absolutely

no distinction between the *kind* of political opinion that shows up
in all of them.[10]

In the present study "political commentary" is the term of
choice. It is defined as "formal, considered, media-disseminated
discourse on news and public affairs in which analysis, interpretation,
and/or opinion are identified as such, developed and completed
within a single segment of space or time separated from the regular
news coverage, and presented as the editorial responsibility of a
single, named professional journalist." By this definition political
commentary is distinguished from speech on private or purely
personal matters, from extemporaneous or casual speech such as
that found in conversations or interviews, from speeches delivered
by persons who are not professional journalists, and from the
editorial that is presented as the view of management rather than
of an identified journalist. By requiring that political commentary
be identified as such and separated from the regular news, the
definition distinguishes political commentary from comments
embedded in the news or included in introductions or conclusions
to documentaries, feature articles, and other types of journalism.
Referring to both print and broadcasting, the term "political commentary" is used interchangeably with "news analysis," the short-
ened term "commentary," and most of the rest of Chet Huntley's
"confusing words."

COMMENTARY AS TRUMP

The columnist is the autocrat of the most prodigious breakfast table
ever known. He is the voice beside the cracker barrel amplified to
transcontinental dimensions. He is the only non-political figure of
record who can clear his throat each day and say, "Now, here's what
I think . . ." with the assurance that millions will listen.

The Columnists
by Charles Fisher[11]

Rather than merely to report on events, tradition holds that the
primary responsibilities of political commentary are to proffer new
ideas, to spot trends, to provide background and context, to analyze
and probe, and to stimulate debate and discussion of important

public issues. Scholarship would add other roles. In a functional analysis of mass media activities, sociologist Charles R. Wright suggests that commentary functions on four levels: societal, individual, specific subgroup, and cultural. On the societal level commentary serves to warn of threats and dangers, to promote calm in the face of panic, to prepare the public for emergencies, and to tell the people what's important to think about; on the individual level, to provide efficiency in understanding the news, to prevent overreaction, anxiety, or apathy, and to tell what issues are important; on the level of specific subgroups (such as government officials), to legitimize their position of power and to help preserve their power; and on the cultural level, to provide cultural growth and to protect against invasion by foreign or undesirable values, ideologies, or behaviors.[12]

In a lighter vein, newspaper columnist Nicholas von Hoffman, writing on TV commentary, suggests there are other possible functions of commentators:

One of the unstated functions of the network TV commentators may be to tell us it's okay to think what we're thinking, that certain judgments are within the acceptable spectrum of opinion and that if we articulate them at the office we're still within safe limits. . . .

Except when we pay our income taxes, it is probably through television that most of us experience the reality of the national political union; it may be that what is important for us is that our commentators appear at their scheduled times to burble at us. The precise nature of their burbling is less important than our seeing them do it, provided they say nothing too terribly alarming.

. . . perhaps [another] one of the functions of commentators is to give the illusion that free speech and debate is taking place without running the risks of having any. The network can look responsible and responsive while keeping Congress and the Federal Communications Commission tranquilized.[13]

Von Hoffman's cynical comments notwithstanding, political commentary has been hailed by the a U.S. district court as representing "the highest level of First Amendment rights,"[14] and its impact on American affairs is well-documented. The effects of printed commentary at the dawn of our nation's history in such writings as Thomas Paine's *Common Sense*, the columns of John Fenno and of Philip Freneau, and *The Federalist* papers are well known. Recent examples of influential columnists are many. Walter Winchell, an enormously popular newspaper columnist and radio commentator, is credited with "inventing" Broadway and with developing popular sentiment for Franklin D. Roosevelt. Indeed, Roosevelt is said privately to have credited Winchell with his election to a third term.[15] In the 1960 presidential campaign, Walter Lippmann (who, David Halberstam claims, "more than any other man determined critical Washington's taste buds")[16] is said to have led the popular swing toward John F. Kennedy. In a different vein, James Reston's reports from China were said almost single-handedly to have kindled American interest in acupuncture.[17]

But, according to media critic Ben Bagdikian, the primary impact of a public affairs columnist is not on the public at large "but rather on a few hundred key people, mostly political leaders in Washington." From a 1966 study Bagdikian drew the following conclusions: that columnists not published in Washington have little impact on political affairs; that columnists published in morning papers are more influential than those published in afternoon papers; and that a columnist's friendship with a president multiplies his influence "beyond the intrinsic power of his words."[18] Richard Weiner, author of a directory of syndicated columnists, further notes that in the United Nations and in Congress, the most quoted columnists appear in newspapers having morning distribution.[19]

One explanation for the importance of top columnists is their influence on the editorial writers around the country. David Halberstam referred to this business of editorial leapfrog in explaining the ground swell for John F. Kennedy: "Lippmann influenced Reston, and Reston influenced the writing press and the television commentators, who influenced the television reporters."[20] In turn, the top columnists influence the several hundred foreign press correspondents stationed in New York and Washington. Most foreign newspapers rotate their correspondents every few years. Struggling with English and unfamiliar with American customs, these newcomers to the United States are often overwhelmed with the sophistication of American politics and with the responsibility of covering so vast a country. Consequently, they look to a few Washington columnists for guidance. Relying on the grapevine for direction, they may follow one columnist for vigorousness, one for balance, one for trend spotting, and another for astuteness, diligence in

research, or his sympathies for the people back home. Whatever the reason, the views of such columnists as Tom Wicker, James Reston, Rowland Evans and Robert Novak, and Joseph Kraft often find their way to foreign newspapers — a practice that ultimately influences foreign attitudes toward Americans and toward the United States generally.

While hyperbole abounds in many discussions of the impact of columnists, they are not without their detractors. Harold Ickes called them "calumnists" and, identifying their stock in trade as "falsification and vilification," he argued that the columnist "is journalism's Public Enemy No. 1, and if the American press is to improve itself, it must get rid of him."[21] Westbrook Pegler, a columnist himself, expressed his equally critical view:

> Of all the fantastic fog-shapes that have risen off the bay of confusion since the big war, the most futile, and, at the same time, the most pretentious, is the deep-thinking, hair trigger columnist or commentator who knows all the answers just offhand and can settle great affairs with absolute finality three days, or even six days, a week.[22]

More recently, Vice-President Spiro Agnew, in the first of his infamous media critiques, questioned the power over public opinion of "a small group of men, numbering perhaps no more than a dozen anchormen, commentators and executive producers . . . who not only enjoy a right of instant rebuttal to every Presidential address, but, more importantly, wield a free hand in selecting, presenting, and interpreting the great issues in our nation."[23]

Scholarly research has also questioned the possible dysfunctions of commentary. Thomas A. Bailey, in cataloging the myth-makers of American history, has lumped commentators with all journalists and has identified the press, along with poets, playwrights, pedagogues, "patrioteers," politicians, and historians "as muddiers . . . of historical waters."[24] Along the same lines Herbert J. Altschull, critical of what he calls the "jackal syndrone" in explaining the rippling influence of commentary, has asked, Do the comments of the commentators become embedded in contemporary history? Does instant analysis become instant history? Too often, he concludes, the inaccuracies of news analysts become the "facts" of future historians and scholars.[25] From another perspective Wright has identified the possible dysfunctions of commentary as weakening

an individual's abilities to judge for himself; increasing social conformity, thereby impeding social change or cultural growth; contradicting a carefully structured image of a particular person or group; and promoting foreign or undesirable values, ideologies, or behaviors.[26]

IN THE BEGINNING

The first syndicated newspaper columns in America date from the Revolutionary War, when Boston patriots discoursed on the impact of the war. But until the Civil War the use of syndicated columns was sporadic, amounting to isolated experiments. In the 1850s, however, Ansel Nash Kellogg, now know as the father of the newspaper syndicate, developed the concept into a major business. Today several hundred syndicated columnists are recognized as a major component of the American press, adding "a spice, personality, diversity of opinion, and style to a local newspaper . . . and serving as an exciting, invaluable supplement to the blandness of some wire service reportage and the trivia of much local data."[27]

H. V. Kaltenborn is credited with delivering the first radio news commentary in 1922. In the 1930s and 1940s, when radio moved with the nation through the Depression, the New Deal, and World War II, Kaltenborn, along with others such as Floyd Gibbons, Father Coughlin, Dorothy Thompson, Elmer Davis, Drew Pearson, and Walter Winchell, exerted an incalculable influence on American public opinion.

Indeed, as the nation has grown in size and sophistication, political commentary has come to assume an exalted position in societal affairs. In 1967 the Federal Communications Commission conceded the special nature of commentary as a critical tool for the vitality of the republic by exempting that genre — referred to as "commentary or analysis" — from the requirements of its Personal Attack Rules when such commentary is contained within newscasts, interviews, or on-the-spot coverage of news events.[28] Editorials of the licensees were granted no such exemption. In 1973, in a labor dispute involving William F. Buckley, Jr., and M. Stanton Evans in their capacity as broadcast commentators, a U.S. District Court decision dealt with the uniqueness of commentary per se. Defining

the commentator as one paid to discuss "news, current events, politics, social, economic, religious, moral and ethical problems — all of the great issues which divide us," the District Court went on to exclude from the definition "those who merely read news or comments prepared by others or for which they have no substantial editorial responsibility . . . and those who comment only on such uncontroversial subjects as the weather, and with respect to whom no personal First Amendment rights could be asserted." Describing the importance of commentary and the special nature of commentators, this court asserted:

> There are a limited number of persons in the country . . . qualified by education and dogma to be hired to discharge this public duty of fair and balanced presentation of competing viewpoints . . . to assert for themselves, and for the general public, the rights assured by Congress to hear broadcasts of commentary, analysis and political opinion from diverse philosophic viewpoints.[29]

Criticism notwithstanding, commentary looms as a precious commodity in American affairs. Angering some, frightening others, there are nevertheless few persons who would not recognize its value to our republic when responsibly prepared and delivered. Political scientists have identified its functions and have underscored its role in maintaining our political structure; historians have documented its impact on the course of our affairs; the courts have recognized it as unique among types of journalism; and in a way not accorded other types of interpretive journalism, the FCC has protected the integrity of commentary by exempting it from one of its most rigid obligations.

Given such testimony to the uniqueness and indispensability of political commentary in American society, it is essential to evaluate the quality of the commentary delivered to the American public through its primary media, television and newspapers. Therefore this study, which focuses on television and newspaper political commentary, is addressing a problem of major significance.

NOTES

1. Bill Monroe, executive producer and moderator of NBC's "Meet the Press," was the 1978 recipient of the Radio-Television News Directors

Association's top honor, the Paul White Memorial Award. These lines are quoted from his acceptance speech.

2. *Evans* v. *American Federation of Television and Radio Artists*, 354 F.Supp. 823 (S.D.N.Y. 1973), in Donald M. Gillmor and Jerome A. Barron, *Mass Communication Law*, 2nd ed. (St. Paul, Minn.: West Publishing, 1974), pp. 674-676.

3. Harold D. Lasswell, "The Structure and Function of Communication in Society," in Bernard Berelson and Morris Janovitz, eds., *Reader in Public Opinion and Communication*, 2nd ed. (New York: The Free Press, 1966), p. 189.

4. "The Standard by Which the Press Should Be Judged," in *Report of the Royal Commission on the Press* (1947-1949), pp. 100-106, repr. in Berelson and Janovitz, *Reader in Public Opinion . . .*, p. 535. Emphasis added. In this report "press" was defined to refer to newspapers and periodicals. Radio was dismissed as unessential and ineffectual, in spite of the BBC record of service in World War II.

5. *A Free and Responsible Press: Report of the Commission on Freedom of the Press* (Chicago: University of Chicago Press, 1947), pp. 20-29. Excerpted in Berelson and Janovitz, eds., *Reader in Public Opinion . . .*, p. 529.

6. Edith Efron, *The News Twisters* (Los Angeles: Nash Publishing, 1971), pp. 8-9.

7. American Society of Newspaper Editors, "Canons of Journalism," adopted by Sigma Delta Chi (1972).

8. The FCC has defined "editorialization" as the use of radio facilities by licensees thereof for the expression of the opinions and ideas of the licensee on the various controversial and significant issues of interest to the members of the general public afforded radio service by the particular station. *Editorializing by Broadcast Licensees*, 13 FCC 1246 (1949).

9. Efron, *The News Twisters*, p. 104 (footnote) as reported from *Variety*, March 25, 1970.

10. Ibid., p. 103.

11. Charles Fisher, *The Columnists* (New York: Howell, Soskin, 1944), quoted in Richard Weiner, *Syndicated Columnists* (New York: Richard Weiner, 1977), p. 20.

12. Charles R. Wright, *Mass Communication: A Sociological Perspective*, 2nd ed. (New York: Random House, 1975), pp. 12-13. In this analysis Wright includes "commentary" with editorials and other types of journalism equated with Lasswell's "correlation function."

13. Nicholas von Hoffman, "TV Commentators: Burbles from Olympus," *Columbia Journalism Review*, January/February 1976, pp. 9-13. Quotations used here found on pp. 9, 11, and 13 respectively.

14. *Evans* v. *AFTRA*, p. 845.

15. Weiner, *Syndicated Columnists*, p. 9.

16. David Halberstam, *The Best and the Brightest* (New York: Random House, 1972), p. 26.

17. Weiner, *Syndicated Columnists*, p. 49.

18. Ibid., describing Bagdikian, pp. 53-54.

19. Ibid., p. 23.

20. Halberstam, *The Best and the Brightest*, p. 26.

21. Weiner, *Syndicated Columnists*, quoting Ickes, p. 11.

22. Ibid., quoting Pegler, p. 11.

23. Speech delivered on November 13, 1969, by Vice-President Spiro T. Agnew in Des Moines, Iowa. Transcript in William E. Porter, *Assault on the Media: The Nixon Years* (Ann Arbor: University of Michigan Press, 1976), pp. 255-262, at 257. Excerpted passages in this quotation are reversed to conform to present context.

24. Thomas A. Bailey, *Journal of American History* 55, no. 1 (June 1968): 5-21, repr. in Herbert J. Altschull, "The Journalist and Instant History: An Example of Jackal Syndrome," *Journalism Quarterly* 53, no. 3 (Autumn 1973): 489-496, at 489.

25. Altschull, "The Journalist and Instant History," pp. 489-490.

26. Wright, *Mass Communication*, pp. 12-13.

27. Weiner, *Syndicated Columnists*, pp. 20-21.

28. 47 CFR 73.123; 73.300; 73.598; 73.679. Note that while Personal Attack Rules exempt categories of commentary, the Fairness Doctrine is applicable to those situations.

29. *Evans* v. *AFTRA*; *Buckley* v. *AFTRA*, in Gillmor and Barron, *Mass Communication Law*, p. 675.

4

MORE THAN ADVERSARIES: NIXON AND THE PRESS

By the simple logic of question and answer the relationship between press and government is necessarily an adversary one on every level of government. For that reason, press-government tension is inherent in our system and the tensions naturally increase as the complexities and dimensions of the role of government increase, thus raising more and more questions about its performance.

Press Freedoms Under Pressure:
Report of the Twentieth Century Fund
Task Force on the Government and the Press[1]

Edmund Burke, speaking of the three estates in Parliament, noted that "in the Reporters' Gallery yonder, there sat a Fourth Estate more important [by] far than they all."[2] In the United States the Fourth Estate has historically served our democracy by functioning in an adversary relationship with the government. With a fervor born of self-interest romanticized by a sense of mission and patriotism, each party — both the press and the government — plays its role. Flexing its muscle, each acts to survey, stimulate, inspire, influence, or perhaps outwit or checkmate the other. And, as tradition would have it, the true winners to emerge from this vast effort are our democratic system and the public. It is the press-government adversary relationship that reinforces the promise of integrity in government and that promises to actualize the people's right to know. Television news executive William J. Small has written that "Government, like any of us, cannot be counted on to announce errors that it has made. Government won't expose thievery or fraud or ineptitude. The rogue is always the first to protest his innocence." Only the press and the political opposition, he continues, see useful purpose in exposing government's imperfections.[3] Fueled by the tension of the adversary relationship, the mission of the press is to search for reality that may be other than the proclaimed official version, to render an honest measuring of government effectiveness, and, within this context, to stimulate both the government and the governed to reflection, action, or resistance.

The need for separate antagonistic parts functioning in the context of self-governance was envisioned very early by the founding fathers. Writing in *The Federalist*, James Madison conceived a structure of government in which "its several constituent parts may, by their mutual relations, be the means of keeping each other in their proper places."[4] Madison understood the importance of vigilance to the well-being of a republic, the importance "not only to guard the society against the oppression of its rulers, but to guard one part of the society against the injustice of the other part."[5] And, as a principal architect of the First Amendment, he understood the role that a free and independent press would play in that vigilance.

In discharging its basic responsibility as watchdog of government, the press is subject to several obstacles and conflicts of interest. The government, as the source of much news, has in effect the power to manipulate the news. It has the power to initiate news, to make public what it will, and to try to keep its affairs — or any part of its affairs — secret. While the president seeks publicity to enhance his ability to govern or to get reelected, he also seeks — for good reasons and for questionable ones — to minimize, suppress, or magnify information or to control its timing, mode of presentation, and, if possible, its bias. The press, for its part, has a professional and an economic interest in maintaining its editorial independence while presenting the news in its most complete, most objective, and most salable form, in which the affects of timing, style, and impact are maximized. Efforts to negotiate these obstacles are continual and, as summarized in the report of the Twentieth Century Fund task force, "put reciprocal pressures on press and government which in effect put the First Amendment right continually to the test as the government tries to limit and the press seeks to advance it."[6]

PRESIDENTS AND THE PRESS

From George Washington on, American presidents have understood the dynamics of the adversary press-government relationship and have tended to accept the inevitable tension as an indispensable counterbalance to their vast power. In fact, over our history there has evolved a genuine symbiosis between the president and the working journalist covering him in which each takes part of his or her identity from the other while relying on that other as a means of advancing personal or professional ends. Between the two there have become established elaborate conventions, expectations, and unarticulated ground rules. Journalists for instance, generally committed to their role in the welfare of the American system, have often ignored reports or rumors of personal scandal, incompetence, or the like that they have perceived as irrelevant to the public cause. And journalists have regularly cooperated in mutually advantageous private "background" meetings in which the government is permitted to advance its positions under a cloak of anonymity.

Thus, over the years the press has been a willing accomplice to image making, politicking, government secrecy, official trial balloons, and justifications for policy mistakes. The president, for his part, has appeared to pamper the press by giving reporters comfortable accommodations, feeding them frequent news releases, entertaining them, and encouraging social relationships with Washington officialdom. And, traditionally, the president has confined his anger to tongue-lashings, petty revenge, or reprisals directed at particular reporters for particular stories. Angered over media treatment, Herbert Hoover limited his press conferences and converted the few he still held to arrogant monologues after which he would refuse to answer questions. During World War II, Franklin Roosevelt "awarded" a German Iron Cross to a particularly troublesome reporter. And it is Roosevelt who is credited with initiating the "backgrounder," which denies reporters the right to report news briefings with any attribution more specific than "informed sources," "high government officials," or "an administration source." In the middle of his term, Harry Truman announced that he was "saving up four or five good, hard punches on the nose, and when I'm out of this job, I'm going to run around and deliver them personally." John Kennedy canceled all White House subscriptions to the *New York Herald Tribune* and (unsuccessfully) asked the *New York Times* to remove from Vietnam assignment reporter David Halberstam, who was perceived as opposed to the administration's Mideast policy. Lyndon Johnson made telephone calls to harangue columnists and editors and, in a style typical of the crassness that the press took great delight in exposing, he would grab newsmen by the lapels, spill drinks on them in his private plane, and call them to his office late at night to denounce them with a few choice words.

William Porter, in his richly detailed book *Assault on the Media*, has delineated a classic pattern of falling-out between modern presidents and the press. From early optimism and friendliness the relationship moves first to quarrels centering on salience and timing. Then, triggered by the inevitable decline of popularity in public opinion surveys and by what he considers the press's unreasonable insistence on agenda setting, the president moves to pique, anger, and a sense of persecution; to closer attention to the media; to attempts to circumvent the media by appealing directly to the people; and ultimately to invective, petty revenge, and a posture of unrelieved but guarded bickering.[7]

THE PRESIDENT WHO WOULD RULE THUNDER

That there has always been a struggle between the president and the press is fact. That, in their own way, presidents have always tried to manipulate, use, anticipate, intimidate, bully, cajole, or bribe the press is also fact; and that the struggle has always veered between poles of apparent camaraderie and open conflict is fact again. But the use of ground rules and restraint that for years had guided the business of reporting government suddenly gave way in the Nixon administration. With Richard Nixon, who "conceived and nursed one of the monumental grudges of the century,"[8] hostility toward the press became acute, and the traditional bickering and petty revenge escalated to all-out offensive. Apparently scarred from what he perceived as hostile media coverage of his political milestones — his 1946 congressional victory, his coauthorship of the Mundt-Nixon Bill, his involvement in the Chambers-Hiss case and other security hearings, his vice-presidential experience, and his presidential and gubernatorial defeats of the early 1960s — Nixon approached the media warily. Even before his first presidential term officially got under way, an elaborate apparatus was constructed for media relations. Indeed, from the very first days an anti-media campaign was launched — an orchestrated set of anti-press maneuvers that grew to exhibit unprecedented zeal and intensity.

Numerous people have attested to this phenomenon. Perceiving Nixon's feelings for the press as "a loathing so raw, ugly and obvious," newsman Timothy Crouse noted that "no other president had ever worked so lovingly or painstakingly to emasculate reporters."[9] "I've lived with White House anger before but I've never seen anything that achieved this kind of fury and heat," remarked *Washington Post* publisher Katharine Graham.[10] "Undisguised hostility," wrote the *New York Times*;[11] "unwilling to accept the traditional role of an independent press in a free society," concluded a report prepared for the National Press Club;[12] "a massive federal-level attempt to subvert the letter and the spirit of the First Amendment," charged a report of the American Civil Liberties Union.[13] In his book *Fear in the Air*, Harry Ashmore noted that "Washington correspondents could recall no instance in which presidential dealing with the media had ever descended to such a level and attained such a concert."[14]

Departing from the traditional pattern of presidential-press gamesmanship, Richard Nixon and company moved on to what his legal counsel John Dean described in a White House memo as "the use of the available machinery of government to screw our enemies." The scope of this government offensive was enormously extensive and pervasive. The usual "machinery of government" — CIA, FBI, IRS, and the Justice Department — was combined with myriad legal, extralegal, and outright illegal mechanisms designed to apply unprecedented levels of overt or subtle pressures at every point where the media were vulnerable. As a result the public was either misinformed or denied the flow of legitimate information necessary to the conduct of its affairs. By widening the scope of claimed executive privilege, by flouting the spirit and intent of the Freedom of Information Act through increasing remoteness of high-echelon officials, by downgrading the importance of in-depth questioning about policy, by diminishing the number of scheduled press conferences to an unprecedented low, and by attempts to bypass the sophisticated White House press corps in favor of local editors, information channels were tightly controlled, and a rigid wall of secrecy and falsehood came to surround sensitive government affairs.

Even before Inauguration Day announcement was made that a new position, director of communications for the executive branch, was to be created for centralized control and coordination of media releases of all executive departments. Shortly thereafter the Office of Telecommunications Policy was established to formulate major policy guidelines for commercial and public television, cable television, satellite communications, and common carriers. Seen by many as a threat to the existing Federal Communications Commission, the new agency became a powerful voice in policy decisions concerning the role and appropriate content of broadcasting. With the appointment of Ronald Zeigler – a man with a background in corporate advertising – as press secretary, White House press affairs came to be dominated by public relations criteria rather than by journalistic ones. Emphasis was placed on aggressive use of television and radio in controlled settings, and with increasing frequency television programs on all networks were simultaneously preempted for presidential addresses. Consequently, the delicate balance of the three branches of government was threatened as broadcasters succumbed to the unprecedented demand for time, thereby permitting disproportionate exposure, and thus power, to the presidency.[15]

Newly renovated press quarters were strategically placed so as to deny reporters sight of and access to White House visitors. And to an extent never before experienced, press coverage was carefully and systematically monitored, and newsmen and executives were made keenly aware of presidential pleasure or displeasure and of their own professional and economic vulnerability. Evincing outright hostility to the notion of the reporter's right to practice his profession, police masqueraded as journalists, and other existing agencies of government were mobilized to gather intelligence or to initiate lawsuits, tax audits, and other forms of harassment.

Various other tactics were geared toward undermining the media's ethics, independence, aggressiveness, profits, and morale. Through a system of rewards and punishments, promises and threats, harangues and tirades, attempts were made to pit reporter against reporter and broadcasting affiliates against the networks, and to undermine the credibility of the media generally. Delay and favoritism became standard in the issuing of White House press passes and distribution of information; television interests of aggressive newspapers were challenged; antitrust suits were initiated against media combinations; and telephone calls and records of reporters and their organizations were monitored. There were critical and threatening speeches by the vice-president and other officials assaulting the integrity of network news and selected metropolitan newspapers. There was a dramatic increase in subpoenas and contempt citations as the government demanded documents, outtakes, and reporters' testimony.[16] There was a presidential veto of public broadcasting's appropriations and the systematic dismantling of public broadcasting's structure, which had been designed to insulate against government control. And for the first time in more than 150 years — in the affair of the Pentagon Papers — there was a federal challenge to the right of the press to be free from prior restraint.[17]

Appendix A presents a chronological listing of the anti-media efforts initiated by the Nixon White House. Spanning the period from Nixon's inauguration to his resignation — January 20, 1969, through August 9, 1974 — there are, in all, 256 events listed. Each event listed in the chronology was validated by a panel of media executives, active at the time of the Nixon tenure, as representing "an effort — directly or indirectly emanating from the Nixon White House — to discredit, harass, intimidate, manipulate, or otherwise influence the news media."[18] Reflecting the executives' perceptions as to severity of anti-media intent, a rating of "mild," "moderate," "strong," or "very strong" is assigned to each event in the chronology.

SIESTA AT WATERGATE

There was abundant evidence that the "Watergate Affair" was an extraordinary and ominous story of major proportions. Serious men, including conservatives such as William F. Buckley, Jr., and U.S. Senator Strom Thurmond, saw it as a dangerous corrosion of the American political system. There was little excuse for its not attracting massive press investigative and display attention.

Ben H. Bagdikian[19]

While not directly related to the press, the "Watergate Affair" —
a term that has become shorthand for pervasive and blatant White
House immorality and criminality, the cover-up, related court
and congressional proceedings, and, finally, the president's resignation — has raised serious questions concerning the press. For Watergate represented a scandal of monumental importance, "a constitutional crisis," as it was aptly called by one observer. Where was
the press during this momentous course of events? Where were the
broadcast commentators? the newspaper columnists? How early
did they perceive the staggering implications for our republic?
How vigorously did they pursue the developments? Were the commentators different from the columnists in these respects? To what
extent did each fulfill its historic responsibility as government
watchdog and critic?

Researching "a guide for the people of the United States of
America," William A. Dobrovir and his associates listed 28 violations
of law "committed or caused either by the President personally
or by persons answerable to him."[20] The crimes charged span three
general categories: crimes against persons and constitutional rights;
crimes committed in financing President Nixon's reelection; and
crimes committed for the personal enrichment of the president.
Together they involve violations of the U.S. Constitution, the
Criminal Code of the United States, the Internal Revenue Code,
the Criminal Code of the District of Columbia, and the California
Penal Code. Specifically, the crimes charged refer to such incidents
as illegal wiretaps of government officials and newsmen; use of
the IRS for tax audits to intimidate leading Democratic political
figures, Americans opposed to the Vietnam war, and journalists
viewed as unsympathetic to White House policies; domestic intelligence plans that authorized burglary, wiretapping, bugging, opening
of the mail, and other illegal acts to gather intelligence on American
citizens; burglary of the office of Daniel Ellsberg's psychiatrist for
the purpose of obtaining information to use in the Pentagon Papers
trial; obstruction of justice by approaching Judge W. Matthew Byrne
while he was sitting judge in the Ellsberg trial to inform him that
he was being considered for the FBI directorship; political espionage
to undermine the opposition party; breaking and entering the offices
of the Democratic National Committee in the Watergate office building; obstruction of justice and perjury in the Watergate cover-up;
conspiracy to defraud the United States by obtaining and using

illegal campaign contributions from corporations and foreign nationals; bribery and fraud in the ITT, Dairy, Hughes, Vesco, and other cases in which legislation or court proceedings were pending or contemplated; embezzlement and fraud by expending public funds to improve the private residences of the president; and tax evasion by improperly backdating and claiming presidential papers as a tax-deductible gift that was never validly made.

Given the mounting clues to governmental fraud and criminality, one would assume that the press — in its grand tradition of imagination, skepticism, tenacity, and professionalism — would have recognized early that "someting is rotten in the state of Denmark."[21] Yet, as the press has amply admitted, it missed the real story of 1972. Reporter Timothy Crouse, describing the "boys in the bus" covering the presidential election of 1972, and John Osborne and Dan Rather of the White House press corps, have agonized over their failure to stand up against the "mesmerizing power of the presidency."[22] Indeed, Crouse reports that "even the best of the White House correspondents despaired of making the President account for the actions of his Administration." While Rather cites logistics of movement and monetary expense as among the prime reasons for television's failure to "get out in front," Bagdikian, commenting on the media generally, has suggested a combination of pro-Nixon bias, laziness, and intimidation:

> Nixon's strategy was standard for an incumbent sure of victory. The failure was that of a news system which did not systematically remind the public of the fact that it was electing a President for four years without knowing how he responded to issues in the campaign — of a news system that was biased in favor of the President or lazy or fearful of the operatives at 1600 Pennsylvania Avenue, or of the Federal Communications Commission, the Attorney General's Anti-Trust Division, the FBI, the Internal Revenue Service, the Securities and Exchange Commission, or the effect of governmental denunciation on a newspaper's standing in the stock market.[23]

While the press as a group slept, two neophyte, enterprising general assignment reporters — Carl Bernstein and Bob Woodward — along with the management of the *Washington Post*, who supported them — emerged as genuine heroes. Though other news institutions, including *Newsday*, the *New York Times*, the *Los Angeles Times*, and *Time* magazine, had contributed to the unfolding developments of the Watergate story, for the most part the revealing exposés that catalyzed governmental bodies into action emerged in seven watershed articles by Bernstein and Woodward.[24] Benjamin C. Bradlee, executive editor of the *Washington Post*, has recalled the loneliness of the early days when the *Post* doggedly championed the story almost single-handedly. Bagdikian has calculated that of the 433 Washington reporters available for assignment to Watergate coverage, only 15 actually were so assigned.[25] Robert C. Maynard, the *Post* ombudsman-critic, found that in a survey of 500 political columns written between June and November 1972, there were fewer than 24 Watergate pieces.[26] Indeed, in the sample used in the case study presented in this book, the newspaper columnists ignored Watergate for 6 of the 26 months of the Watergate period (from break-in to resignation) — approximately 23 percent of the time. Television commentators, however, ignored Watergate for 15 of the 26 months — approximately 58 percent of the time.

But by and by, television commentary notwithstanding, the press began to pay attention, and in the end it did its job of exposing the government to the people, becoming, like so many others involved in the Watergate drama, a most reluctant hero. But nagging questions still remain. Would the Watergate affair have surfaced were it not for the heroics of a few dynamic print journalists? How can the press strengthen its psychological defenses in order to better field threats to its independence? And by what legal means can the press, particularly broadcasting, be better insulated from government manipulation?

NOTES

1. Twentieth Century Fund, *Press Freedoms Under Pressure* (New York: The Twentieth Century Fund, 1972), p. 109.

2. Edmund Burke, *Heroes and Hero-Worship* (1841), quotation in John Bartlett, *Familiar Quotations*, 13th ed. (Boston: Little, Brown, 1955), p. 473.

3. William J. Small, *Political Power and the Press* (New York: W. W. Norton, 1972), pp. 23-24.

4. *The Federalist (1787-1788). Selections* (Chicago: The Great Books Foundation, 1955), p. 24.

5. *The Federalist*, p. 29.

6. Twentieth Century Fund, *Press Freedoms Under Pressure*, p. 110.

7. William E. Porter, *Assault on the Media: The Nixon Years* (Ann Arbor: University of Michigan Press, 1976), pp. 3-5. For additional discussions of

presidential relations with the press, see James Keogh, *President Nixon and the Press* (New York: Funk and Wagnalls, 1972), pp. 16-37; Small, *Political Power and the Press*, pp. 43-63; and Newton N. Minow, John Bartlow Martin, and Lee M. Mitchell, *Presidential Television* (New York: Basic Books, 1973), pp. 25-47.

8. Timothy Crouse, *The Boys on the Bus* (New York: Random House, 1972), p. 180.

9. Ibid.

10. Quoted in Aaron Latham, "How 'The Washington Post' Gave Nixon Hell," in Michael C. Emery and Ted Curtis Smythe, eds., *Readings in Mass Communication: Concepts and Issues in the Mass Media*, 2nd ed. (Dubuque, Iowa: Wm. C. Brown, 1974), p. 387.

11. *New York Times*, editorial, Summer 1972, quoted in Marvin Barrett, ed., *The Alfred I. duPont-Columbia University Survey of Broadcast Journalism 1971-1972: The Politics of Broadcasting* (New York: Thomas Y. Crowell, 1973), p. 65.

12. *The Press Covers Government: The Nixon Years from 1969 to Watergate* (Washington, D.C.: Department of Communication, the American University, 1973), p. 34.

13. Fred Powledge, *The Engineering of Restraint: The Nixon Administration and the Press* (Washington, D.C.: Public Affairs Press, 1971), p. 6.

14. Harry S. Ashmore, *Fear in the Air* (New York: W. W. Norton, 1973), p. 113.

15. Premise held by Minow, Martin, and Mitchell, *Presidential Television*, pp. 10-11.

16. While many subpoenas and contempt citations were issued at the federal level, many also were issued at the state level. Porter, *Assault on the Media*, p. vii, suggests that such lower-level tactics derived "in part from a spirit generated through those top level attacks."

17. The Pentagon Papers case represents the first time since the expiration of the Alien and Sedition Acts in 1803 that the government entered legal suit for prior restraint of the press. See *New York Times* v. *United States*, 403 U.S. 713 (1971). For extended discussions of the anti-media abuses of the Nixon administration, see Ashmore, *Fear in the Air*; Powledge, *The Engineering of Restraint*; Porter, *Assault on the Media*; Twentieth Century Fund, *Press Freedoms Under Pressure*; *The Press Covers Government*; and Marvin Barrett, ed., *The Alfred I. duPont-Columbia University Survey of Broadcast Journalism*, (New York: Grosset and Dunlap, 1969, 1970, 1971; Thomas Y. Crowell, 1973, 1975).

18. A panel of 19 men who were media executives during the Nixon presidency rated 359 events of a chronology of media and media-related events during the Nixon administration. Each event listed was initiated by the federal government during the years 1969-1974. The chronology had been compiled by this researcher from careful examination of the media trade press, eye-witness accounts, and a variety of other publications. The panel was asked to rate each event on a scale of 0 through 8, where 0 indicated belief that the event was free of any direct or indirect anti-media effort emanating from the White

House, or that the event was grounded in normal public interest concerns, conventional morality, contemporary First Amendment theory and/or normal market affairs; and where the rating of 1 through 8 indicated belief that the event represented some degree of an effort — directly or indirectly emanating from the Nixon White House — to discredit, harass, intimidate, manipulate, or otherwise influence the news media. For an event to be included in the revised chronology, newly labeled Chronology of the White House Anti-Media Assault during the Nixon administration, one criterion was that it had to be rated as an anti-media effort by 10 (53 percent) of the executives on the panel. Of 359 events originally listed, 256 were rated to fit the category "anti-media." For further discussion see chs. 5 and 6.

19. Ben H. Bagdikian, "Election Coverage '72: The Fruits of Agnewism," *Columbia Journalism Review*, January/February 1973: 9-23, at 12.

20. William A. Dobrovir, Joseph D. Gebhardt, Samuel J. Buffone, and Andra N. Oakes, *The Offenses of Richard M. Nixon: A Guide for the People of the United States of America* (New York: Quadrangle/The New York Times Book Co., 1974), p. 3.

21. William Shakespeare, *Hamlet*, act I, scene 4, l. 90.

22. See Crouse, *The Boys on the Bus*, p. 236; and Dan Rather, *The Camera Never Blinks* (New York: William Morrow, 1977), pp. 234-237.

23. Bagdikian, "Election Coverage '72," p. 11.

24. Articles described in Crouse, *The Boys in the Bus*, pp. 293-295: (1) August 1 — Report that a check for $25,000 given to Maurice Stans (finance chairman of the Nixon campaign) by Kenneth Dahlberg (campaign finance chairman for the Midwest) had ended up in the Florida bank account of Bernard L. Barker (one of the Watergate burglars). This study, researched mainly by Carl Bernstein, was the first article to show a definite financial link between CREEP (Committee to Re-elect the President) and the Watergate break-in. (2) September 16 — Report that the money paid for the Watergate bugging had come from a secret fund of more than $300,000. The fund had been kept in the safe of Maurice Stans and was controlled by aides of John Mitchell (Nixon's former campaign manager). (3) September 17 — Report that two officials of CREEP, Jeb Magruder and Herbert Porter, had each withdrawn $50,000 from the secret fund. (4) September 29 — Report that John Mitchell had personally controlled the secret fund. (5) October 10 — Report that the Watergate bugging attempt was only one part of a massive Republican spying and sabotage campaign that had been operating since 1971. It identified Donald Segretti and White House aide Ken Clauson as saboteurs and revealed details of the "Canuck letter," a forged letter printed in a New Hampshire newspaper and considered to have hurt Senator Edmund Muskie's chances in the Democratic presidential primary election. (6) October 15 — Report that Dwight Chapin (Nixon's appointments secretary) had been Donald Segretti's White House contact. (7) October 25 — Report that H. R. Haldeman (Nixon's closest aide) was one of five presidential associates authorized to make payments from the secret fund. See also Carl Bernstein and Bob Woodward, *All the President's Men* (New York: Warner, 1974).

25. Bagdikian, "Election Coverage '72," p. 12.

26. Edwin Diamond, "TV and Watergate: What Was, What Might Have Been," in Emery and Smythe, *Readings in Mass Communication*, pp. 393-396, at p. 393.

THE CASE STUDY

5

RESEARCH DESIGN

GETTING IN FOCUS

All research begins with a question. Steeped in the facts of present knowledge, the research question propels the mind into the world of new insights, theory building, and prediction. How did it happen? What is it like? Could it ever? What if? Why? When? The hunch, a vague and intuitive surmise, is an early attempt to answer this question. It is the hunch — refined and augmented to become the hypothesis — that is the germ of the research design.

In this case the overwhelming fact is the presence of the First Amendment and its constitutional guarantee of freedom of the press. As the Supreme Court has interpreted the amendment, several major assumptions have emerged:

1. That a primary goal of the First Amendment is "uninhibited, robust, and wide-open" debate on public issues

2. That a major function of the press is criticism of government and public officials

3. That the responsibilities of the broadcasting press to the republic are essentially the same as those of the printed press

4. That public policy in the United States accords different treatment to the printed and the broadcasting press.

The Supreme Court has identified the two major interests of the First Amendment guarantee as vigorous debate on public issues and unfettered, vigorous criticism of government and public officials.[1] The paradox of this constitutional mandate as it locks horns with actual public policy is at once obvious. For Congress has chosen to regulate broadcasting with wide-ranging policy that stretches from engineering concerns to certain aspects of program content. The printed press, on the other hand, functions under a laissez-faire regime. The question is clear: While broadcasting is charged with the same responsibilities to the republic as the printed press, can broadcasting as a governmentally regulated medium be expected to exercise its duties of vigorous debate and vigorous criticism of government with the same integrity as the printed press, the unregulated medium?

The case study that follows was undertaken to address this question. On the basis of surveys showing television and newspapers to be the dominant sources of news and public affairs information in this country,[2] and in the belief that political commentary is the journalistic genre most directly capable of demonstrating the values articulated by the Supreme Court as the purpose of the First Amendment,[3] the study focused on political commentary of television and of newspapers. The early hunch was that television was both timid and intimidated; that of the two media, television was the less vigorous; and that as a medium made vulnerable through government regulation, television was less likely than newspapers to criticize government and more likely than newspapers to be intimidated by government pressure. Focusing on the White House with its particular interest in manipulating the news, the research held out the promise of identifying and measuring the "chilling effect," a task heretofore considered difficult if not impossible. Elaborating on the early hunch, six hypotheses subsumed within two general categories structured the research:

Hypotheses of Television's Timidity
1. That television political commentary is less vigorous generally than newspaper political commentary
2. That television commentary is less vigorous in its criticism of the federal government than newspaper commentary

3. That, in the face of a scandal involving the White House, television commentary is later and less vigorous in exposing the affair than newspaper commentary.

Hypotheses of Television's Intimidation by Government Pressure
4. That White House pressure to manipulate the press causes a chilling effect on television commentary
5. That as the intensity of White House pressure increases, the vigorousness of television commentary decreases
6. That as the intensity of White House pressure increases, the vigorousness of newspaper commentary increases or remains relatively stable.

While a cross-media study of the impact of White House pressure on journalism would be valuable regardless of the time period examined, the years of the Nixon presidency were chosen for two reasons. First, even though a press-government adversary relationship is traditional in a democracy, these years have been generally and widely described as unique in terms of the intensity of the administration's anti-media activity. Second, there occurred during these years the Watergate affair, a government scandal that was made obvious by firm evidence; by judicial indictments, convictions, and sentences; by a president's resignation; and by a presidential pardon. How the press responded to this crisis − or, more specifically, the differences between newspaper and television political commentary in this regard − was considered to be highly predictive of press performance in any period.

METHODS AND PROCEDURES

The research was performed in three distinct steps.[4] The first involved a questionnaire survey designed to describe and quantify the "White House Anti-Media Assault," otherwise referred to as WHAMA. The second involved content analysis procedures designed to describe and measure the "comparative vigorousness of newspaper and television commentary." The third step involved data analysis: computations, testing for significant differences between the two media, and correlation analysis to ascertain the relationship between

WHAMA and the vigorousness of television and newspaper commentary. At every stage the research was designed to generate measures of WHAMA's chilling effect on the media, if in fact such had existed. To afford greater precision in analysis, the period of the Nixon administration (January 20, 1969, through August 9, 1974) was divided into 23 quarters. All analysis was performed in the context of these three-month intervals.

The Survey/WHAMA

To quantify the White House Anti-Media Assault, a chronology of 359 media and media-related events occurring during the Nixon years was circulated to a panel of media executives who rated each event in terms of White House anti-media intent as they saw it. Culled from a careful examination of the media trade press during the Nixon presidency, from eye-witness accounts by journalists and other observers, and from a variety of other publications,[5] each event listed in the chronology had been perceived by the researcher as a potential anti-media effort directly or indirectly emanating from the Nixon White House. Selected for inclusion in the chronology was any event appearing as a potential threat to such media concerns as news gathering and news production, editorial and economic autonomy, profits, growth, network/affiliate relationships, and, not least, media credibility with the public. On the assumption that White House anti-media pressure could have been exerted indirectly through a variety of governmental and nongovernmental entities, the events selected were not limited to those where the White House was the initiator but also included those initiated by such bodies as Congress, the FCC, and the federal judiciary.

Entitled "Chronology of Governmental Media and Media-related Events During the Nixon Administration" the list included such items as the FBI investigation of reporter Daniel Schorr; an antitrust suit against NBC, CBS, and ABC; use of wiretaps against newsmen; congressional hearings on a CBS documentary critical of the Pentagon; and the arrest of Les Whitten, the news assistant to investigative columnist Jack Anderson. Also included were all of the period's Supreme Court decisions regarding the media, all presidential press conferences (which were conspicuously few), and all presidential TV addresses (which were conspicuously abundant).

In the interests of scientific "double check," the chronology was circulated to an advisory committee for approval as to objectivity, exhaustiveness, discreteness, significance, relevance, and readability. Since the chronology was to serve as a questionnaire in which each event was to be rated, four persons pretested the rating procedures and reported that a block of two hours was required for completion of the operation.

With the intention of having the ratings reflect media perceptions of the extent and intensity of the anti-media assault, requests to serve on the panel were sent to 41 media executives who had had top-level responsibilities during the Nixon presidency and who were therefore in a position to be sensitive to the currents of press-government relationships at that time. Requests were sent to persons who had been executives at all newspapers appearing on three different lists of "best American dailies,"[6] and to executives at all networks, public broadcasting agencies, broadcasting group combinations, and major broadcast associations. The executive positions of those solicited included chairman of the board, publisher, president, vice-president, and editor (managing, executive, or editor in chief). Of those solicited, 19 agreed to participate on the panel or designated an acceptable substitute. Those participating included 4 newspaper and 15 broadcasting executives.[7]

Listed alphabetically, with the positions they held during the Nixon administration, are those media executives who served on the panel:[8]

James E. Allen – vice-president, Post-Newsweek Stations

Barry Bingham, Jr. – publisher, *Louisville Courier-Journal*

Otis Chandler – publisher, *Los Angeles Times*

Wallace Dunlap – vice-president, Group W, Westinghouse Broadcasting Company

Paul Duke – president, Radio-TV Correspondents Association

Reuven Frank – president, NBC News

Daniel E. Gold – vice-president, Post-Newsweek Stations

Herbert W. Hobler – president, Nassau Broadcasting Company

Robert D. Ingle – assistant managing editor, *Miami Herald*

Lewis Klein — executive vice-president, Gateway Communications

Richard H. Leonard — editor, *Milwaukee Journal*

Elmer W. Lower — president, ABC News

John W. Macy, Jr. — president, Corporation for Public Broadcasting

Richard S. Salant — president, CBS News

William Sheehan — senior vice-president, ABC News

Arthur R. Taylor — president, CBS, Inc.

Franklin A. Tooke — vice-president, Group W, Westinghouse Broadcasting Company

Gerald E. Udwin — national news editor, Group W, Westinghouse Broadcasting Company

Vincent T. Wasilewski — president, National Association of Broadcasters

Blue ribbon panel assembled, the chronology was circulated to the executives, who were asked to rate each event along a nine-point scale from "no White House anti-media effort" to "very strong White House anti-media effort." Instructions to the raters asked, "To what extent do you consider each of the following events to represent an effort — directly or indirectly emanating from the Nixon White House — to discredit, harass, intimidate, manipulate or otherwise influence the news media?" A rating of "0" indicated that the rater believed the event to be free of any direct or indirect anti-media effort emanating from the White House; that he believed the event to be grounded in normal public interest concerns, conventional morality, contemporary First Amendment theory, and/or normal market affairs. A rating of "1" through "8" indicated that the rater believed the event to represent some degree of an effort — directly or indirectly emanating from the Nixon White House — to discredit, harass, intimidate, manipulate, or otherwise influence the news media. There were two gradations for every level of anti-media effort: mild (1,2), moderate (3,4), strong (5,6), and very strong (7,8).

Raters were cautioned that even though they considered an event to represent an unfortunate, improper, or repressive action, they should still award the rating of "0" if they believed that the event did not directly or indirectly emanate from the Nixon White House, or if they believed that the event was grounded in normal affairs independent of any direct or indirect White House anti-media effort. Raters were also advised that the documentation for any event listed in the chronology would be furnished upon request, but should they take exception to the wording of any listing, disagree with the factuality of the event as represented, or otherwise believe the listing to be in error, they should rate the item with "NA" (not applicable). This instruction was designed to account for content validity. By assigning a rating other than "NA," the panel of executives in effect was assigning validity to the chronology.[9]

The data obtained from the questionnaire were used to generate three kinds of information: media executive profiles (how newspaper executives differed in their perceptions from broadcast executives, network broadcasters from nonnetwork broadcasters, and top-top brass broadcasters from broadcasters generally); event profiles (the average scores for each event and identification of those events perceived as harassment as opposed to those events perceived as "business as usual"); and an index of White House anti-media assault (an array of scores combining all ratings for all events in each of the period's 23 quarters).

On the basis of the scores obtained, the original chronology was revised to include only those events perceived by a majority of the executives on the panel to represent anti-media efforts emanating from the White House. In this way the original chronology of "governmental media and media-related events during the Nixon Administration" was validly honed into the newly labeled "Chronology of Anti-Media Efforts by the Nixon White House." Eliminated from the original chronology were those events that had been perceived by a majority of executives to represent "business as usual" (events that had been awarded "0" by a majority of the raters). The Supreme Court decisions, along with presidential news conferences and TV addresses, were among the events that were eliminated. Whereas the original chronology had listed 359 events, the revised version listed only 256 events. The revised chronology, annotated to reflect the averaged ratings by the panel, is Appendix A.

Determining the Sample

During the Nixon administration the three television networks regularly stepped aside from the flow of objective news stories to feature commentary on their evening news programs. Identifying that special segment as "Commentary" by introduction and a superimposed video tag, ABC nightly rotated Howard K. Smith, Harry Reasoner, and Frank Reynolds for discourse on their views of the world. About three times weekly, CBS introduced "Analysis," delivered in most cases by Eric Sevareid. And, beginning in 1971, NBC, also about three times weekly, featured David Brinkley's "Journal." These labeled television discourses, which were nationally broadcast and formally separated from the objective news segments, corresponded neatly with by-lined nationally syndicated columns in newspapers. Jointly referred to as "political commentary," the two genres – television commentary and nationally syndicated newspaper columns – constituted the population from which the research sample was selected.

For the purposes of this study, "political commentary" (sometimes referred to more informally as "commentary") was defined as "formal, considered, media-disseminated discourse on news and public affairs in which analysis, interpretation, and/or opinion are identified as such, developed and completed within a single segment of space or time separated from the regular news coverage, and presented as the editorial responsibility of a single, named, nationally recognized professional journalist." The definition was formulated so as to control for comparability between the two media in national outlook and other areas, and to separate political commentary from other types of newspaper interpretive journalism: editorials, documentaries, feature stories, letters to the editor, conversations, interviews, debates, columns, and speeches by non-journalists, or even bias hidden in hard news.[10]

The parameters of the television sample were determined first, and the newspaper sample was selected to correspond with them. The sample was limited to weekday evening news programs because labeled television commentary during the Nixon period was most prominently and regularly displayed there. To match the sample size required for achieving the .05 level of confidence (the level of probability conventionally accepted in the social sciences for identifying significant findings), a total of 204 television commentaries

— one randomly selected commentary per month per network —
was to constitute the television sample.[11] Primarily to control for
comparability with newspapers, and on the assumption that the text
itself is the most significant data base for measures of vigorousness
in information and ideas, only the audio portion of the commentary
was studied. Support for this choice was lent by a previous study of
network news coverage that found no significant difference in results
from coding audio only and those from coding audio and video
combined.[12] The commentaries were available from the Television
News Archives of Vanderbilt University, where videotapes of network news programs have been collected and indexed since 1968.

In the interests of comparability (historical and other), the number of syndicated newspaper columns selected for the sample was
equivalent to the number calculated to be satisfactory for the television sample. Thus, a random sample of 204 nationally syndicated
political columns[13] was selected for dates corresponding to those
used for the television sample. The columns were selected on a
system of rotation from newspapers identified by *Time* magazine
in 1974 as "the ten best American dailies." The papers used in the
sample were the *Boston Globe, Chicago Tribune, Los Angeles Times,
Louisville Courier-Journal, Miami Herald, Milwaukee Journal, Newsday, New York Times*, and *Washington Post*.[14] Three of these
papers identified themselves as having been committed to McGovern
in the 1972 presidential election, three as committed to Nixon, and
the others as independent or uncommitted.[15] Except for the afternoon dailies *Newsday* and the *Milwaukee Journal*, all of the papers
were published in the morning; the *Boston Globe* published in both
time slots.

Content Analysis

The procedures used for this part of the research were designed
to measure and compare the vigorousness of television and newspaper political commentary. "Vigorousness" was defined in terms
of the standard articulated by the Supreme Court as the purpose of
the First Amendment: "uninhibited, robust and wide-open" debate
on public issues.[16] On the assumption that the Court intended its
standard to represent an exhaustive summary of the qualitative and
quantitative potential of verbal discourse, each of the five concepts

contained within that standard ("uninhibited," "robust," "wide-open," "debate" and "public issues") was further defined and operationalized into a system of measurement designed to account for that universe of potential values. The system used was based on "evaluative assertion analysis," a content analysis technique developed by Osgood, Saporta, and Nunnally in 1956.[17] Evaluative assertion analysis stems from a long history of theoretical research on the measurement of meaning to individuals. Essentially the technique rests on the principle that there are three dimensions embodied in language that correspond to factors found "to be primary in cognition irrespective of culture."[18]

These three dimensions, each of which represents a continuum of values from one pole to its opposite, are evaluative (positive . . . negative), potency (strong . . . weak), and activity (active . . . passive). Through techniques of evaluative assertion analysis these dimensions of language are accessible for measurement. These measurements as applied to political commentary in the present sample, in combination with a subject matter category scheme devised for this study, were considered to be a measure of those qualitative and quantitative values addressed by the Supreme Court. Table 5.1 presents the conceptual and operational definitions of "vigorousness" and traces the evolution of the concepts from the language of the Supreme Court to the operational constructs used in this study.

Reduction to Thesis Statement

Evaluative assertion analysis involves intricate coding procedures. It requires analysis of all significant words in the multiple themes that may be contained within every sentence. It begins with the "raw" message as received and translates that message into all possible evaluative assertions; by assigning scores to the significant words in every assertion, it ends with a statistical summary of the frequency, directions, and intensity (along three dimensions) of the attitudes expressed in the original message. In the interest of feasibility it was necessary to design a procedure that — without sacrificing original context — would be capable of reducing the approximately 11,016 sentences of the 408 commentaries (a number with the potential of yielding 165,240 assertions, 330,480 significant words, and 991,440 actual scores)[19] to a size manageable by manual

TABLE 5.1
Vigorousness Defined and Redefined

Conceptual definition	That quality of interpretive journalism that approximates "uninhibited, robust and wide-open debate on public issues," where "uninhibited" means free from constraints; "robust," strong and powerful; "wide-open," of sufficient quantity; "debate," discourse defending or attacking a given proposition; and "public issues," controversial matters of public importance.
Operational definition	That quality of commentary on network television weekday evening news programs and in nationally syndicated newspaper political columns that approximates "uninhibited, robust and wide-open" debate on public issues, where "uninhibited" is measured in terms of the active-passive dimension of evaluative assertion analysis (EAA); "robust," in terms of the strong-weak dimension of EAA; "wide-open," in terms of proportion of attention to various subject matter categories; "debate," in terms of the positive-negative dimension of EAA; and "public issues," by a subject matter category scheme delineating major issues, minor issues, and nonissues.

Supreme Court Language →	*Conceptual Definition* →	*Operational Definition*
Uninhibited	free from constraints	active-passive dimension of EAA
Robust	strong and powerful	strong-weak dimension of EAA
Wide-open	of sufficient quantity	proportion of attention to various subject matter categories
Debate	discourse defending or attacking a given position	positive-negative dimension of EAA
Public issues	controversial matters of public importance	subject matter category scheme: major issues/minor issues/nonissues

analysis. To this end a procedure of "thesis statement reduction" was developed. By this procedure the thesis statement was excerpted from every commentary, and all subsequent analysis was conducted on the basis of the thesis statement as the recording unit.

The thesis statement is a single sentence that expresses the dominant idea of the discourse. It is the sentence that provides direction and cohesion to the total work, and it is an integral component of all expository types, spoken or written. Rhetoric professors Crosby and Estey suggest the following:

> Most of the writing in serious magazines, in military, professional, political, scientific, and literary reports . . . and in all other forms of nonfiction prose is composed of a mixture of definitive and generative sentences. Each composition has at its core a generative sentence that is the broadest or most complex idea in the work. It is this sentence that gives unity and purpose to the total effort.[20]

Aristotle recognized this universal component of exposition when he said, "A speech has two parts. You must state your thesis, and you must prove it."[21] Commentary, as formal expository discourse, was expected to have its central idea explicitly stated in a generative or thesis statement. In actuality such was the case; trained coders found little difficulty in identifying that sentence.

Covering a variety of contingencies, the *Coding Manual*, developed for training and guiding the coders, presented explicit rules for excerpting the thesis statement. Three coders were carefully trained, and when the composite intercoder reliability correlation reached .87 in the practice sessions, the coders proceeded to the actual data. Working on the actual data, the three achieved a composite intercoder reliability correlation of .81. Returning to code a sample of commentaries two months later, the coders exhibited a composite intracoder reliability correlation of .93.

But Aristotle, other rhetoricians, and reliability coefficients notwithstanding, it was necessary to test the validity of this "thesis statement reduction" procedure. Is the thesis statement a true representation of the range of attitudes expressed in the whole commentary? To address this question, six randomly selected commentaries — three from newspapers and one from each network — were subjected to correlation analysis. The thesis statement was extracted from each and then coded according to the procedures described later in this chapter. Every sentence in each of the six commentaries was similarly coded. The summary scores from the thesis statements were then compared with the summary scores from their corresponding commentaries. When subjected to Pearson's product-moment analysis, the correlation coefficients for the six sets were .98, .94, .99, .98, .99, and .93, with probabilities ranging from .01 to less than .001 (see Table 5.2). The consistency and obvious strength of these correlations were considered to provide ample support for the wisdom of Aristotle's observation and, of course, for the validity of thesis statement reduction as the study's crucial procedures.[22]

Nuts and Bolts

The focus of evaluative assertion analysis is on "attitude objects" that represent the topics being discussed in the commentary. By limiting the number of attitude objects under investigation to a small group, the analysis thus becomes systematized. The attitude objects in this study were based on a category scheme of "major issues," "minor issues," and "nonissues"[23]; definitions of these centered on a 1972 Gallup survey in which the public was asked to identify the major issues of the day. Building on those public responses, "major issues" in this present study referred to those topics identified as representing issues of the highest importance: the Vietnam war, White House and congressional affairs, inflation, crime, drug abuse, poverty, busing, and politics. "Minor issues" referred to topics identified as less important than those considered at the time to be most pressing or to represent acute crises: pollution, local government, church affairs, women's liberation, activities of former officials, and the internal affairs of foreign countries. "Nonissues" referred to topics representing areas of limited interest, of little or no controversiality, or of value to only a small segment of the public: leisure and amusement, travel, art, education, science, invention, and the private lives of celebrities. To allow for finer distinctions in analysis, major issues were subdivided into four categories: federal government, Nixon administration per se, major domestic problems, and Watergate. Table 5.3 presents the attitude object/ subject matter category scheme used in the content analysis, along with the arbitrary symbol used to designate each category.

TABLE 5.2
Six Thesis Statement/Commentary Comparisons
(by vigorousness quotients)

Subject Matter Category	I		II		III		IV		V		VI	
	TS	C	TS	C	TS	C	TS	C	TS	C	TS	C
Federal government	—	—	.585	.262	.128	.151	—	—	.109	.178	.158	.317
Nixon administration	—	—	.036	.105	—	—	—	—	.109	−.001	—	−.088
Domestic problems	.604	.463	.087	.139	—	—	—	—	—	—	—	—
Watergate	—	—	—	—	—	—	—	—	—	—	—	—
Minor issues	.033	.027	.303	.180	.369	.526	.420	.599	.806	1.342	.064	.049
Nonissues	−.385	−.150	−.212	−.0004	.070	.027	.240	.202	—	.023	.064	.038
Correlation*	.98		.94		.99		.98		.99		.93	
Probability	≤.001		≤.01		≤.001		≤.001		≤.001		≤.01	

Key:

I = Tom Wicker, "The Other Prisoners," *New York Times*, September 28, 1971.

II = D. J. R. Bruckner, "Difficult World Monetary Issues Pose Equally Difficult Answers," *Los Angeles Times*, June 12, 1972.

III = William Raspberry, "S. Africa: U.S. Dilemma," *Washington Post*, January 28, 1972.

IV = Harry Reasoner, on Christmas, ABC Evening News, December 21, 1972.

V = David Brinkley, on U.S. and war, NBC Evening News, October 21, 1971.

VI = Eric Sevareid, on Vietnam policy, CBS Evening News, May 25, 1970.

TS = Thesis statement scores.

C = commentary-as-a-whole scores.

vigorousness quotient = Sum of evaluative, potency, and activity mean scores in a subject matter category as weighted by that category's proportionate distribution.

*Pearson's product-moment correlation.

Note: Basic to this analysis was the formation of six subject matter categories. All coding and computations were made in terms of these subject categories. The range of possible scores is −9 to +9. See this chapter, subsection "Nuts and Bolts," for details of procedures used.

83

TABLE 5.3
Attitude Object — Subject Matter Category Scheme

Attitude Object Designation	Class	Definitions and Subtopics
	Major Issues	Topics representing issues of highest importance
		Subcategories
FG		*Federal government entities, policy, acts, and affairs (other than the Nixon administration per se and Watergate)
		including:
		Congressional, judicial and some executive affairs; war and rebellion; defense; diplomacy and foreign relations; domestic initiatives; style and principles; other
FGP		*Nixon administration per se
FD		*Major domestic entities, problems, and affairs
		including:
		Crime/drug abuse; busing/race relations; inflation/unemployment/economics; poverty/welfare; politics; other
FW		*Watergate
BB	*Minor Issues	Topics not representing the acuteness of crises reflected in major issues
		including:
		Pollution/ecology; minorities; state or local government; civil liberties; political personalities; internal affairs of foreign countries; women's liberation; other

CC   *Nonissues   Topics of limited interest, of little or no controversiality, or of value to only a small segment including:

Natural history; travel; social behavior; education; art; medicine, science, and invention; leisure and amusement; personalities; other

*Attitude object categories used in evaluative assertion analysis.

Once the thesis statement was excerpted from every commentary, a trained coder set about the business of transcribing that sentence into an exhaustive set of evaluative assertions. (See Appendix B for a step-by-step example of the coding procedures described in this section.) As used here, the assertion was a simple linguistic construction — subject/verb/complement — where the subject was always relevant to one of the six attitude object categories and the complement was either another attitude object or an evaluative term (noun, adjective, or adverb). Examples of such assertions are the following:

The BOSTON GLOBE/supported/SENATOR McGOVERN.
HENRY KISSINGER/seeks/peace.
The WHITE HOUSE/is/harried.
The FBI/works/diligently.

Where the assertion was not evaluative, as in NIXON/ate/lunch, it would be excluded from analysis. The coder was instructed to search for the multiple themes within every sentence and to pay close attention to using the original words when creating assertions. Where a pronoun or other referent (stated or implied) was used in the thesis statement, coders were to substitute the antecedent for which the referent stood. Where a figure of speech was involved, such as "pot of gold," coding instructions were to substitute a synonym such as "prize" if that would be appropriate to the context. Similarly, if satire, symbolism, or other such modes were involved (as in the columns of Art Buchwald and Russell Baker), and analysis of the original words might be misleading as to the author's intent, the coder was instructed to review the entire commentary and substitute words matching the intent of the message as it was perceived. The *Coding Manual* was very explicit in this matter of assertion formation, offering many examples of the various possibilities that might be encountered.

Next, the literal subject of each assertion was masked — that is, it was assigned to membership in one of the six attitude object categories, and the appropriate symbolic designation was substituted in the assertion. Thus, "NIXON/was/uncertain" became "FGP/was/uncertain." The masking of the attitude objects served two functions. First, it organized the analysis according to the parameters of the study; and second, it permitted the coder to concentrate on the evaluative content of the message itself without being swayed by "outside" information.

The next task was the assignment of quantitative values to the verbs and the complements in the assertions. The critical tool in this procedure was the *Stanford Political Dictionary*. As unique as it is ingenious, this dictionary was developed in 1966 by Professors Robert C. North and Ole R. Holsti for use in a political science study[24] that was designed as a computer-based analogue to evaluation assertion analysis.[25] The dictionary lists nearly 4,000 words perceived as relevant to political documents, each word tagged with three values corresponding to the three dimensions in evaluative assertion analysis: evaluative, potency, activity. The range of options available for tagging in each dimension is from −3 to +3. Picture the terrain as shown below:[26]

Evaluative:	Negative	−3	−2	−1	0	1	2	3	Positive
Potency:	Weak	−3	−2	−1	0	1	2	3	Strong
Activity:	Passive	−3	−2	−1	0	1	2	3	Active

◄─────────── Increasing Intensity ───────────►

Thus the dictionary listing "anarchistic: −1, −3, 2" would give value to the word as "negative 1, weak 3, active 2."

According to North and Holsti, the *Stanford Political Dictionary* was compiled in good scientific order by combining the most frequently used words in the English language (as drawn from the Thorndike-Lorge dictionary) with words culled from treaties and other political documents relating to various international episodes to which the United States had been a party. Assignment of dimensions and intensities to the selected words was reportedly undertaken by a panel of three or more judges whose decisions, made according to rigid procedures, were averaged.[27]

Though the dictionary had been compiled from political texts of an earlier period, experience in this present study showed that it was capable of analyzing nearly 96 percent of the significant words in the political commentary sampled from the media of the Nixon period. For this present study, in those few instances where a word appearing in the commentary was not found in the dictionary, an appropriate synonym was substituted (for instance, "appears" for "seems," "salvage" for "save," "tools" for "implements," "despotic" for "tyrannical"). Where no satisfactory synonym could be substituted or where the word had developed a special connotation during the Nixon era (such as "machismo," "sexist," "desegregation," "chauvinist," "impeach"), the word was placed on a "leftover" list that was circulated to an advisory committee whose members rated each word in terms of the three dimensions. The median scores were selected as the "official" values for the words in question. The advisory committee was also asked to review and approve the synonym substitutions.

In the original version of evaluative assertion analysis, values had been assigned to the significant words by the coders themselves, working according to a prescribed scheme. By eschewing that somewhat intuitive procedure for reliance on the *Stanford Political Dictionary*, this researcher believed that the potential for bias was greatly reduced and the level of reliability was inevitably heightened.[28]

One further procedure requires explanation. It is common in language for the mode of expression to color the intensity of the message. For instance, a statement of aspiration (such as "I hope that the president's bill provides economic relief") is less intense than a statement of probability (such as "It is probable that the president's bill will provide economic relief"), which in turn is less intense than a simple indicative statement (such as "The president's bill provides economic relief"). Thus, a mode-of-expression correction feature was incorporated into the study.[29] For this correction detail seven of the most commonly used modes of expression were listed: aspiration, normative, probability, interrogative, indicative, comparative, and imperative. The list was submitted to the advisory committee for intensity scoring on the basis of 1 to 10. By averaging the committee's responses, weights were assigned to the various modes. Once the dictionary values were assigned to the words, the verb scores in each assertion were weighted in terms of the mode of expression used. By so reducing the score of certain types of expression, hedging, qualifying terms, and "wordsmanship" were presumably measured and accounted for. Table 5.4 presents the modes of expression identified in this study together with their weights and indicators.

Finally the scores were computed, analyzed, and tested. By averaging across the scores in each dimension separately, summary scores were computed for each medium, each attitude object, and each quarter of the period studied. By means of specially designed

TABLE 5.4
Modes of Expression: Weights and Indicators

Code	Weight	Mode of Expression	Conditions	Hypothetical Rhetoric	Verb Indicators	Adverb Indicators
X	0.3	aspiration	desire, hope, goals	It is hoped that . . .	hope to, plan to, desire to, try to, seek to, want to, to be going to, aim to	hopefully
N	0.5	normative	normalcy	It should be that. . .	ought to, should (normalcy only), tends to	usually, typically, often, naturally, ordinarily, inevitably
P	0.6	probability	probability, possibility, expectations	It is probable that . . .	may, might, could, seems to, appears to	probably, possibly, perhaps, likely
T	0.8	interrogative	question, reversed verb	Is it so that . . .		
D	1.0	indicative	unqualified statement, simple, perfect, or pluperfect tenses	It is . . .		
M	1.0	comparative	comparison of similars, contrast of dissimilars	It compares with . . .	be like, favor lean toward, use methods of	similarly, likewise, on the other hand
V	1.0	imperative	command, advice, obligation, subject "you" (understood)	Do it . . . . It must be done . . . . It ought to be done . . .	must ought should	

formulas, various critical indexes were computed: blandness quotient, language intensity, vigorousness quotient, and index of vigorousness. (See the Glossary of Terms for definitions of these indexes.)

EXPECTATIONS REVISITED

> Probably every new and eagerly expected garment ever put on since clothes came in, fell a trifle short of the wearer's expectation.
>
> Charles Dickens, *Great Expectations*

Charles Dickens speaks for us all. No matter how we toil to argue logically; to design for reliability, comparability, significance, and validity; to avoid bias and error; or to build on the best of all possible precedents — feasibility, inaccessible data, limited resources, and, of course, personal inadequacy combine to undermine our best intentions.

The research design just described, as all research designs must be, was constructed on the framework of several underlying assumptions. Without integrity at this basic level, there is only a house of cards. The findings and theories of that large body of previous research on evaluation, potency, and activity as the three dimensions of cognitive meaning represent the most basic assumption of this present design. That evaluative assertion analysis is a valid tool for purposes of this study is a second major assumption. Other assumptions are that the *Stanford Political Dictionary* is a valid instrument for measuring attitudinal dimensions, and that the values assigned to the words culled from the texts of international political documents are valid for this present study dealing with domestic political commentary. Assumptions all, but accepted by this researcher on the weight of logic and the well-received, previous research, which in each instance appeared to demonstrate more than amply the requisite validity, reliability, and utility.

But in the absence of so wide and varied a research history, the following are suggested as methodological limitations, those garments falling a trifle short of the wearer's expectations:

1. There may not be strict comparability between network television commentary and nationally syndicated political columns for reasons that include the following:

a. Television has the ability to make last-minute changes before dissemination; newspapers, because of the technological demands of the medium, do not have such fluidity.
b. Syndicated columnists write their columns with an eye to their commercial value on the market; television commentators are salaried employees for whom writing commentary is part of a multidimensioned job.
c. The rhetoric appropriate for television delivery is not necessarily appropriate for newspaper delivery; television, which is prepared for auditory reception in addition to visual, may use shorter sentences, simpler words, express less complex ideas, and contain more redundancy than newspapers.
d. There are many other differences in history, tradition, economic structure, communication context, and audience characteristics that separate newspapers from television; the news products of the two media may differ to the extent that each defers to those separate influences.

2. In light of examples of cross-media ownership, it might be fallacious to consider newspaper vigorousness as an independent standard, for a newspaper might lessen its vigorousness in an effort to protect its television interests.

3. It may be questionable that media executives' perceptions of the White House anti-media assault, as recalled four or more years after the experience, do in fact represent a reliable measure of their attitudes at the time of the actual assault.

4. The findings in the Watergate analysis may be suspect because the sample, which had been determined on the basis of a long-term general analysis, might have been inadequate for so specific a focus as Watergate.

5. While analysis based on the authors' own words was considered the best way to tap the attitudes expressed, it is quite possible that this method was not sufficiently sensitive to measure the true intent of satire, sarcasm, irony, ridicule, or other types of symbolic or oblique expression, even though special procedures were designed to deal with this type of discourse.

6. While the use of the audio-only portion of television commentary was considered to be the most significant data base for measuring vigorousness of information and ideas, there is recognition that the video component may add untapped dimensions of vigorousness.

NOTES

1. In *Rosenblatt* v. *Baer*, 393 U.S. 75 (1966), the Supreme Court referred to its landmark decision in defamation, *New York Times* v. *Sullivan*, 376 U.S. 254 (1964), and identified the two major interests of the First Amendment guarantee:

> The motivating force for the decision in *New York Times* was twofold. We expressed a "profound national commitment to the principle that debate on public issues should be uninhibited, robust, and wide-open, *and* that [such debate] may well include vehement, caustic, and sometimes unpleasantly sharp attacks on government and public officials." There is first, a strong interest in debate on public issues, and second, a strong interest in debate about those persons who are in a position significantly to influence the resolution of those issues. Criticism of government is at the very center of the constitutionally protected area of free discussion. Criticism of those responsible for government operations must be free, lest criticism of government itself be penalized. (Emphasis and bracketed portions in original)

2. The Roper Organization, "Changing Public Attitudes Toward Television and Other Mass Media 1959-1976" (New York: National Association of Broadcasters, 1977), pp. 3-4. Note that this report was prepared by the NAB's Television Information Office.

3. The requirements of this study focused on narrowing the field of interpretive journalism to a sampling frame that would lend itself to significant and valid analysis in view of the hypotheses under study. Seven basic requirements directed the determination:

a. Directness. That the selected population could most directly demonstrate the qualities of vigorous debate mandated by the First Amendment

b. Ethics. That, without violating canons of ethical and professional journalism, the selected population could accommodate criticism, advocacy, and other varieties of subjective opinion

c. Fluidity. That the selected population have the ability to be relatively current and fluid in presenting ideas — unencumbered by extended budgetary and scheduling consideration

d. Regularity. That the selected population would appear with a reasonably precise regularity

e. National scope. That the selected population deal in national issues

f. Editorial independence. That the selected population be presented as free from overt editorial control by the publisher or broadcaster

g. Comparability. That the selected population be comparable across the selected printed and electronic media.

Eight major interpretive journalism types (bias hidden in hard news, editorials, documentaries/feature articles, public rebuttal to editorials/letters to the editor, labeled network commentary/nationally syndicated by-lined columns) were evaluated in light of the seven basic requirements. Only labeled network commentary and syndicated by-lined newspaper columns met all the requirements.

4. For more detailed description of the methods and procedures of this study, see Marilyn A. Lashner, "The Chilling Effect of a White House Anti-Media Assault on Political Commentary in Network Television News Programs: Comparison of Newspaper and Television Vigorousness During the Nixon Administration" (unpublished Ph.D. dissertation, Temple University, 1979).

5. Search included *Weekly Compilation of Presidential Documents* from 1969 through 1974; such trade publications as *Broadcasting, Television/Radio Age, TV Guide, Variety,* and *Editor and Publisher*; historical and scholarly studies such as William E. Porter, *Assault on the Media: The Nixon Years* (Ann Arbor: University of Michigan Press, 1976), Edward Knappmann, ed., *Government and the Media in Conflict/1970-74* (New York: Facts on File, 1974), Fred Powledge, *The Engineering of Restraint: The Nixon Administration and the Press* (Washington, D.C.: Public Affairs Press, 1971), and Harry S. Ashmore, *Fear in the Air* (New York: W. W. Norton, 1973); publications of groups devoted to preservation of First Amendment values, such as *Freedom of Information Center Digest, Press-Censorship Newsletter,* and *The Quill*; and eyewitness accounts such as Timothy Crouse, *The Boys on the Bus* (New York: Random House, 1973), Dan Rather, *The Camera Never Blinks* (New York: William Morrow, 1977), and Daniel Schorr, *Clearing the Air* (Boston: Houghton Mifflin, 1977).

6. "The Ten Best American Dailies," *Time*, January 21, 1974, pp. 58-61; "Miami Herald, Wall Street Journal Join 'Top 10' in Bernays Quality Poll," *Editor and Publisher*, May 2, 1970, p. 41; and David S. Myers, "Editorials and Foreign Affairs in the 1972 Presidential Campaign," *Journalism Quarterly* 51 (Summer 1974): 251-257, 296.

7. The executives solicited were very kind and supportive for the most part. All answered promptly, and many expressed interest in and praise for the project. Originally 20 executives had agreed to participate, but only 19 completed questionnaires reached the researcher. One top-top brass network executive reported that he had mailed the completed document from abroad, but apparently it got lost en route. Most of the executives refusing to participate explained that they did so because they had since retired, "simply do not have enough time to do this intelligently," or got too many similar requests. One stated that all his present efforts and energies were devoted to "turbulent times" and "rather sweeping changes in his organization." Another wrote that he/she had "neither the time nor the wisdom to contribute to a doctoral dissertation."

8. The role of these media executives was limited to rating the events in the chronology. They bear no responsibility for the analysis of the data, interpretation, or any other facet of this book.

9. Of the 6,821 opportunities for ratings (359 events multiplied by 19 panel members), there were only 20 NA's (0.3 percent) used by only 6 raters. In 28 other cases, the event was left blank (in some cases, a whole page). In these instances it could be assumed that the items had been overlooked, particularly where whole pages were blank. Nevertheless, all events not receiving a numerical rating were considered to be NA, and of these, there were 48 (0.7 percent).

10. See the discussion of the definition of "political commentary" in ch. 3, section "A Matter of Terms."

11. One problem was encountered with regard to the television sample. During the time under investigation, ABC had regular identified commentary, labeled "Commentary," and CBS had regular identified commentary, called "Analysis." But NBC's regular identified commentary, called "Journal," did not begin until August 16, 1971. Before that time there was no specially identified segment to fit our definition. Indeed, a few instances were noted during earlier programs when isolated and sporadic stories were prefaced by the journalist with such comments as "I am now giving opinion," but such "informal" commentary – while possibly fitting our definition – was not identified in the Vanderbilt indexes as anything other than a regular news story and, therefore, could not be retrieved systematically from the data bank. Thus, if the same criteria were used with NBC as with the other two networks, there could be no sample from NBC for the first 31 months. To control for possible bias resulting from a diminished television sample, an alternative means of sample selection was devised: 31 additional CBS and ABC units were alternately chosen from new dates randomly selected within the missing months. All subsequent analysis was performed on two television samples: the primary sample, composed of 68 commentaries each from ABC and CBS and only 37 from NBC (total 173 commentaries); and the alternative sample, composed of 68 plus 16 commentaries from ABC, 68 plus 15 from CBS, and 37 from NBC (total 204 commentaries). The researcher considered – and rejected – other possible schemes for an alternative sample. The options considered were to examine the abstracts or audio tapes of NBC programs for the key dates and select those items that appeared to fit the definition; and to select the last item delivered by an anchorperson for all key dates for which NBC commentary was missing.

12. Richard A. Pride and Gary L. Wamsley, "Symbol Analysis of Network Coverage of Laos Incursion," *Journalism Quarterly* 49 (Winter 1972): 635-640, 647.

13. To distinguish nationally syndicated political columnists from other kinds of private and professional writers featured in newspapers, the requirement was made that columnists selected for the sample be listed as political columnists in either of the two editions of Richard Weiner's directory, *Syndicated Columnists* (New York: Richard Weiner, 1975, 1977).

14. The *Wall Street Journal*, one of those papers listed in the *Time* list of "the ten best American dailies," had a policy of limiting its commentaries to

those that had been written by its own staff members, none of whom were listed in Weiner's *Syndicated Columnists*. Since, according to the parameters of this study, only nine columns per quarter were to compose the sample, no attempt was made to substitute for the *Wall Street Journal*, and the nine newspapers remaining on the *Time* list were accepted as the sampling frame.

15. Those newspapers identified as supporting Nixon were *Chicago Tribune, Los Angeles Times, Miami Herald*; those identified as supporting McGovern were *Boston Globe, Louisville Courier-Journal, New York Times*; the others were independent or uncommitted, though the *Washington Post* did support McGovern on certain issues. The source of these data on 1972 political positions was primarily *Editor and Publisher*, November 4, 1972, pp. 9-14. Information on the positions of the *Boston Globe, Los Angeles Times, Milwaukee Journal*, and *Washington Post* was obtained by this researcher through phone and mail inquiry directly to the newspapers, since they had not participated in the *Editor and Publisher* poll.

16. *New York Times Co.* v. *Sullivan*, 376 U.S. 254, 170 (1964).

17. Charles E. Osgood, Sol Saporta, and Jum C. Nunnally, "Evaluative Assertion Analysis," *Litera* 3 (1956): 47-102. Also described in Charles E. Osgood, "The Representation Model and Relevant Research Methods," in Ithiel de Sola Pool, ed., *Trends in Content Analysis* (Urbana: University of Illinois Press, 1959), pp. 33-88, at 41-54; Robert C. North, Ole R. Holsti, M. George Zaninowich, and Dina A. Zinnes, *Content Analysis: A Handbook with Applications for the Study of International Crisis* (Evanston, Ill.: Northwestern University Press, 1963), pp. 91-102; Ole R. Holsti, "Content Analysis," in Gardner Lindzey and Elliot Aronson, eds., *The Handbook of Social Psychology*, vol. II, *Research Methods* (Reading, Mass.: Addison-Wesley, 1969), pp. 596-692, at 651-653; and Ole R. Holsti, *Content Analysis for the Social Sciences and Humanities* (Reading, Mass.: Addison-Wesley, 1969), pp. 124-126.

18. Ole R. Holsti, "A Computer Content-Analysis Program for Analysing Attitudes: The Measurement of Qualities and Performance," in George Gerbner, Ole R. Holsti, Klaus Krippendorff, William J. Paisley, and Philip J. Stone, eds., *The Analysis of Communication Content: Development in Scientific Theories and Computer Techniques* (New York: John Wiley, 1969), pp. 355-380, at 359. Additionally, the body of research on the measurement of meaning included Fritz Heider, "Attitudes and Cognitive Organization," *Journal of Psychology* 21 (1946): 107-112; Charles E. Osgood and Percy H. Tannenbaum, "The Principle of Congruity in the Prediction of Attitude Change," *Psychological Review* 62 (1955): 42-55; Leon Festinger, *A Theory of Cognitive Dissonance* (Stanford, Calif.: Stanford University Press, 1966); and Charles E. Osgood, G. J. Suci, and Percy H. Tannenbaum, *The Measurement of Meaning* (Urbana: University of Illinois Press, 1957). See also Charles E. Osgood, "The Nature and Measurement of Meaning," *Psychological Bulletin* 69 (May 1952): 197-237.

19. Based on an estimate of 27 sentences per commentary, 15 assertions per thesis statement.

20. Harry H. Crosby and George F. Estey, *College Writing: The Rhetorical Imperative* (New York: Harper and Row, 1968), p. 26.

21. Ibid.

22. It could be argued that even if the thesis statement were to represent the main thrust of the commentary, it might not reflect tangential or casual remarks made in reference to secondary subjects. The figures deny this argument. In no instance did either the thesis statement or the commentary focus on only one subject matter category. The Reasoner piece, the most narrow of all, involved two categories, while Bruckner's involved five. Of the six sets, four had perfect matches in subject matter presence. ("Perfect matches in subject matter presence" refers only to presence of commentary in this area rather than absence of commentary. It does not refer to the amount of commentary in any area. Thus, in the four sets to which reference is made, both the thesis statement and the commentary dealt to some degree with the same categories, even if the degrees differed.) There were only two — Brinkley and Sevareid — where the thesis statement failed to deal with a subject handled by the commentary. But the number of tangential references made in these commentaries was so small in each case that the "aberration" failed to make a significant difference in the overall correlations. See Table 5.2 for identification of commentaries referred to here.

23. Essentially the category scheme used for the present study was based on the typology used in Patrick D. Maines and John C. Ottinger, "Network Documentaries: How Many, How Relevant?" *Columbia Journalism Review*, March/April 1973, pp. 36-42. Following the example of Maines and Ottinger, the category scheme for this present study was based on the 1972 Gallup survey; however, minor adjustments in the typology were made on the basis of other category systems in order to better conform to the particular research question of this study. The category systems providing additional input are found in Chilton R. Bush, "A System of Categories for General News Content," *Journalism Quarterly* 37 (Spring 1960): 206-210; Guido H. Stempel III, "Content Patterns of Small and Metropolitan Dailies," *Journalism Quarterly* 39 (Winter 1962): 88-90 at 89; and Paul J. Deutschmann, *News-page Content of Twelve Metropolitan Dailies* (New York: E. W. Scripps, 1959), pp. 58-62.

24. North et al., *Content Analysis*. Holsti and others used the dictionary in an accumulation of later studies that contributed to the expansion of the vocabulary listings, other refinements, and more research data. See Holsti, "A Computer Content-Analysis Program for Analysing Attitudes"; and Philip J. Stone, Dexter D. Dumphy, Marshall S. Smith, and Daniel M. Ogilvie, *The General Inquirer: A Computer Approach to Content Analysis* (Cambridge, Mass.: M.I.T. Press, 1966), pp. 186-191; and Holsti, *Content Analysis for the Social Sciences and Humanities*, pp. 156-194.

25. While the present study did not make use of that computer program per se — because in many ways its focus was not relevant to this study — much of its conceptual framework, as well as the dictionary, was incorporated into the manual analysis used here.

26. Holsti, *Content Analysis for the Social Sciences and Humanities*, pp. 156-194.

27. Stone et al., *The General Inquirer*, pp. 188-189; and Holsti, "Content Analysis," in Lindzey and Aronson, *The Handbook of Social Psychology*, vol. II, p. 666.

28. This is not to deny the high level of reliability reached by Osgood et al., "Evaluative Assertion Analysis," in the techniques they originally developed and reported.

29. The mode of expression correction feature as here described is based in good measure on the principles and procedures set forth in Holsti, *Content Analysis for the Social Sciences and Humanities*, pp. 179-182. Holsti's list of commonly used modes of expression was accepted by this researcher. The weighting scheme, however — along with the conditions, hypothetical rhetoric, and linguistic indicators — was developed by this researcher for this study.

6

NIXON'S "WHAMA": INDEX OF WHITE HOUSE ANTI-MEDIA ASSAULT

WHAMA is a statistic. An acronym for "Index of White House Anti-media Assault," it is an array of quantified data reflecting the ebb and flow of White House anti-media maneuvers during the 23 quarters of the Nixon administration (January 20, 1969, through August 9, 1974). It was generated by a procedure whereby media executives contemporary with the Nixon administration used a nine-point scale ranging from "No White House anti-media effort" to "Very strong White House anti-media effort" to rate events in a chronology of governmentally initiated media efforts during the Nixon period.[1] By summing the means of the scores for each event in each quarter, an index was computed that was presumed to represent both the frequency and the intensity of the White House anti-media assault over the entire Nixon presidency. Derived from perceptions of newspaper and television executives of varying status, WHAMA was computed generally for all executives combined, and then for the various executive subgroups represented: newspaper, broadcast, nonnetwork, network, top-top brass all, top-top brass newspaper, and top-top brass broadcast.

Representing the combined perceptions of media executives regarding Nixon's anti-media intent, WHAMA became the lens through which to view the Nixon strategy. By yielding to graphing, charting, and various types of statistical analysis, WHAMA imposed shape, size, and flow on what was otherwise a multitude of separate events. But most important was its role in the analysis of the chilling effect. The definition of chilling effect — "a significant reduction in measures over time, and in light of influence by an outside factor, of the vigorousness of journalistic coverage of public issues" — implies a span of time, the presence of a causal factor, and diminished vigorousness of the target communication. As one of its goals this study set out to demonstrate that Nixon's anti-media assault was a causal factor in the diminished vigorousness of television commentary. WHAMA represented the quantification over time of that hypothetical causal factor. As such it was the independent variable in all tests relating to the chilling effect and media vulnerability.

FINDING THE FACE IN WHAMA

The White House anti-media assault was Richard Nixon's legacy to ill will, rancor, and arrogance. Add to this disdain for the First Amendment, contempt for the collective intelligence, and misguided use of power in an attempt to stifle dissent. By unleashing a steady barrage of mild to oppressive anti-media initiatives, Nixon sought positional advantage over what he perceived to be his enemy. Though White House/press tension — even intrigue and machination — has been common to all administrations, observers everywhere have charged the assault on the press by this administration with being unique in its fury and fire.[2]

WHAMA, as the collective summary of separate events, represented government anti-media initiatives that in and of themselves had face and character. While some initiatives were innocent and benign, others baited, disturbed, hounded, or drew blood. Some gave little more than cause for hesitation, while others inflicted tribulations ranging from annoyance to torment. And while some were sufficiently explicit to leave no room for doubt, others were vague and ambiguous in meaning or implication.

On the basis of the executives' ratings, descriptive statistics for each event were calculated; and the secrets buried deep in the frequency counts, means, medians, modes, and standard deviations were unearthed and interpreted. Thus, in addition to WHAMA, which was an index of summary statistics, the data were able to shed light on the faces and characters of the separate events generating WHAMA.

Of the 359 events in the chronology, only 94 (26 percent) were met with unanimous reaction. So forthright were these initiatives in their hostility that they were awarded anti-media ratings by all 19 executives. However, there was no event so benign as to be passed off by all raters as free of White House machinations. Twenty events, however, were rated free of anti-media intent by as many as 14 (74 percent) of the executives. These events were primarily Supreme Court decisions, seemingly routine operations of the FCC and other governmental agencies, and events initiatied by such "white hats" as Elliot Richardson, who replaced John Mitchell as attorney general. Presumably the few executives who perceived White House intrigue in these events were taking into account the mood of the Court or agency as a result of Nixon's judicial and other appointments.

Among those other events judged to be benign by most executives were presidential news conferences and televised presidential addresses. These events had been included in the chronology in the belief that in combination they represented potential anti-media efforts. Throughout the Nixon years there had been much criticism by media observers of the long intervals between press conferences, the exclusion of broadcasters from many that were held, and the frequent presidential addresses preempting programs on all three television networks. As much information as possible was included in the language of the chronology so as to provide a clue to the offending dimensions. But since most executives awarded a "not anti-media" rating to these events, it is entirely possible that the chronology as presented was not a sufficiently sensitive instrument to measure the anti-media intent possibly inspiring those events.[3]

On the basis of mean scores, 27 events (11 percent of those rated anti-media) were judged "very strong" and thus were considered to represent the harshest kind of anti-media effort; 101 (40 percent) were perceived as strong efforts; 76 (30 percent) as moderate efforts; and 52 (20 percent) as mild efforts.

Included among those efforts considered by most executives to represent the utmost in harshness were President Nixon's use of wiretaps against newsmen; FCC Chairman Dean Burch's telephoning heads of networks to request transcripts of commentaries critical of a presidential speech; White House memos outlining efforts to curtail media criticism; Vice-President Agnew's speeches critical of the press; White House aide John Ehrlichman's suggestion to the president of CBS News that correspondent Dan Rather be removed from the White House press corps; the Pentagon Papers affair; White House orders implementing an FBI investigation of CBS correspondent

Daniel Schorr in reprisal for critical news articles; and the secret IRS subpoena of the *New York Times* Washington Bureau's telephone records.

Still representing harassment of high order for most executives, but also reflecting doubt on the part of some as to White House involvement or anti-media intent, were those events whose combined scores placed them on the second highest level of hostility: the challenge by associates of President Nixon of the broadcast licenses owned by the Post-Newsweek Corporation; the President's veto of a two-year funding package for the Corporation for Public Broadcasting; a Justice Department antitrust suit against ABC, CBS, and NBC; government-issued subpoenas to news organizations demanding reporters' unedited files, photographs, film, and notebooks; White House aide Charles Colson's series of meetings with network chief executives to "split the networks in a way very much to our advantage"; intervention by the White House in the congressional probe of the CBS documentary "The Selling of the Pentagon"; and pressure by the White House to change the formats of an ABC program dealing with the supersonic transport plane and a CBS program dealing with Watergate.

Those events considered to be moderate anti-media efforts (or that reflect either moderate disunity among executives as to White House involvement or moderate agreement that the event represents the proper behavior of government) include the Republican National Committee's complaint to the FCC regarding a CBS program giving voice to "the loyal opposition"; the masquerade of an army agent as a reporter; the display of administration favoritism to certain media organizations; announcement of the White House intention to take a central role in the formulation of cable regulation; and caustic public comments by the president about the media.

Those events considered to be mild anti-media efforts (representing either the lowest level of petty annoyance, the lowest level of executive agreement as to White House involvement, or the greatest display of recognition of government's appropriate business) included a proposal for a 142 percent second-class postal rate increase; President Nixon's series of invitations to selected journalists of a "conservative or moderate inclination" for news briefings; FCC rhetoric regarding the banning of cross-media ownerships; and White House insistence on putting comments on "background."

RAINING DAGGERS: A FREQUENCY COUNT

According to the perceptions of the media executives rating the events of the chronology, there was not a quarter when the administration failed at least to jostle — if not to pound — the press.[4] (See Table 6.1.) The lowest number of anti-media incidents perceived in any quarter was 5; the highest was 34; the average was 16. Judging from frequency alone (and using the metaphor of a rainstorm to demarcate the arbitrarily determined gradations), there were 6 quarters of restrained showers (5-9 incidents); 10 quarters of rain as usual (10-19 incidents); 4 quarters of gusting downpour (20-24 incidents); and 3 quarters of deluge (25-34 incidents). "Gusting downpour" occurred in quarters 5, 11, 17, and 18 (January-March 1970, July-September 1971, January-March 1973, and April-June 1973); "deluge" occurred in quarters 10, 14, and 20 (April-June 1971, April-June 1972, and October-December 1973). These data, which describe periods of heightened activity spread rather evenly throughout the Nixon era, contradict a scholar who diminished the extent of Nixon's anti-media offensive by reporting, "Much goes on during 1971 and 1972, but there is almost no activity after Nixon's public recognition of a Watergate scandal."[5] While the precise nature of the White House activity may have been different in the last year or so — less vindictive, more rhetorical than actual — the WHAMA indexes show that the anti-media assault, at least as perceived by the media, continued in full measure until almost the bitter end.

CHARTING STORMS OF STATE

WHAMA, as computed, reflected not only the frequency but also the intensity of the anti-media assault. Thus a quarter with a heavy precipitation of mild or moderate attacks could generate an index comparable with that of a quarter with a few very strong attacks. As a rule, however, the quarters with the greatest number of actions yielded a higher WHAMA.

Except for the last two quarters, when the anti-media assault diminished to little more than an echo, WHAMA showed fluctuating bursts of pace and strength. For instance, a quarter dominated by such events as requests for transcripts of television commentaries

TABLE 6.1
**WHAMA: Sum of Means per Event of Media Executives'
Perceptions of White House Anti-Media Efforts**

Quarter	Number of Efforts	All Media (N = 19)	Newspaper (N = 4)	Broadcast (N = 15)	Broadcast Nonnetwork (N = 10)	Broadcast Network (N = 5)	Top-Top Brass*		
							Newspaper & Broadcast (N = 5)	Newspaper (N = 2)	Broadcast (N = 3)
1	14	21	21	22	21	22	34	23	42
2	8	18	21	17	20	16	27	19	32
3	5	14	13	14	16	13	19	12	23
4	17	72	79	70	78	66	82	81	83
5	24	66	63	67	61	70	89	61	108
6	19	42	50	40	37	41	64	50	73
7	15	38	40	38	34	40	53	46	58
8	9	29	33	28	27	28	37	37	37
9	8	30	31	30	29	31	37	33	40
10	29	113	120	112	114	110	143	127	154
11	22	85	90	84	86	82	106	103	108
12	12	42	54	39	38	39	58	57	59
13	19	52	66	49	49	48	74	76	73
14	25	80	93	77	71	80	107	97	113
15	12	42	44	42	41	42	60	55	63
16	16	74	77	73	71	74	84	82	85
17	20	71	82	68	71	66	89	91	89

18	20	86	96	84	77	87	104	103	105
19	10	28	37	26	24	28	46	48	45
20	34	133	146	130	132	129	171	172	170
21	11	34	42	31	28	33	48	50	47
22	5	13	16	12	11	13	19	17	20
23	5	9	15	7	7	7	20	20	20

Total efforts = 359.
Total executives = 19.
N = number of executives in a particular category.
*Criteria: Executive with highest level of operating responsibility (board chairman, publisher, corporate president, station manager).

Responsible for all facets of operation.
Responsible for profit/loss.

critical of the president, two speeches by Vice-President Agnew attacking and discrediting newspapers and television, and subpoenas to four newspapers, three magazines, and one television network was followed by a period that included little more than warnings against songs glorifying drugs, talk of increasing FCC fees, presidential news briefings limited to friendly journalists, and removal of the White House press corps to less advantageous quarters. That, in turn, was followed by the Pentagon Papers affair, in which the government, for the first time in more than 150 years, sought to establish the legality of censorship.

One point needs to be made here. The events are listed in the chronology according to the dates when they purportedly happened. In most cases the date when the event actually happened and the date when the information about the event was made public were very close — certainly within the same quarter. In some cases, however, the report of the event was substantially later than the date on which the event had actually occurred. The White House anti-media memos represented such a case. According to the dates on the memos, they were issued from October 1969 through November 1972. But it was not until October 1973, during the congressional hearings, that their existence was made public. To account for this discrepancy, two versions of WHAMA were computed: "WHAMA as ordered" and "WHAMA as reported." In the former the events were listed according to the dates of their occurrence. In the latter such events as the White House memos were removed from the original order and reinserted in the quarter when they were made public. The "WHAMA as ordered" indexes were believed to reflect most accurately the actual activity of the White House, whereas the "WHAMA as reported" indexes were believed most likely to reflect the media's awareness of government activity. Since the premises of this study focus on media attitudes, the analysis and findings described here are based on the second set of indexes, referred to simply as "WHAMA."

As perceived by all executives combined, WHAMA ranged from 9 to 133, the mean being 52. There was a definite difference in indexes over the various subgroups. For newspaper executives the mean was 58, whereas it was 50 for broadcasters — presumably reflecting the higher tolerance that broadcasters had for government intrusion.[6] By far the biggest difference was between top-top brass and the lower-level executives, particularly in the case of broadcasters. The difference between perceptions of top-top brass newspaper executives, with a mean of 68, and those of lower-level newspaper executives was significant, but less so than that between the different levels of broadcasters. For with a mean of 72, the perceptions of top-top brass broadcast executives in some quarters exceeded those of lower-level broadcasters by more than 75 percent. Thus the data suggest that top-top brass executives were sui generis in their suspicion of government, but that top-top brass broadcasters, to an even greater degree than their newspaper counterparts, were exceptional for their low tolerance and ready anger so far as government and media were concerned.[7] While nonnetwork broadcast executives appeared to be slightly higher in their judgments than network broadcasters, this difference was neither consistent nor substantial.

According to the WHAMA indexes for all media executives combined, there were five peaks in the White House assault — five quarters of feverish frequency and intensity sandwiched between valleys of lesser activity. (See Figure 8.1.) The highest peak appeared in quarter 20 (October-December 1973), which, other than experiencing the release of 10 White House anti-media memos, seemed to reflect no major incident — just a steady barrage of 20 mild-to-strong efforts that seemed more to threaten than to implement action. Among the efforts included in this quarter were President Nixon's explosion at a news conference, during which he accused the press of the most "outrageous, vicious, distorted reporting" he had seen in 27 years of public life; White House aide Patrick Buchanan's statements on a television talk show in which he proposed antitrust actions as a means of breaking up network dominance over broadcast journalism; and an FCC ruling that NBC had violated the Fairness Doctrine in its documentary "Pensions: The Broken Promise."

The second highest peak occurred in quarter 10 (April-June 1971). The Pentagon Papers affair dominated this quarter, but included in the 29 efforts were the White House's suggestion to CBS that Dan Rather be transferred, an address by Vice-President Agnew in which he argued that media counterattacks would "backfire," and the initiation of a congressional probe of the CBS documentary "The Selling of the Pentagon."

The other peaks occurred in quarters 4, 14, and 18 (October-December 1969, April-June 1972, and April-June 1973). Included were such hostilities as the veto of Public Broadcasting funding, Agnew speeches berating the press, antitrust suits against the networks, subpoenas to news organizations, confiscation of reporters' credentials and materials at the Wounded Knee Indian uprising, and more Agnew speeches.

Except for the peak at quarter 4, all peaks occurred during quarters when the WHAMA index exceeded 80, the arbitrarily determined critical level of the White House anti-media assault, earlier described as television's breaking point, which always appeared to precipitate diminished vigorousness in television commentary.[8] More than gusting downpour or deluge, we have in these quarters four raging cyclones — threatening storms that travel widely, bringing driving rain, unbridled wind, and often heavy damage.

NOTES

1. See chapter 5, section "The Survey/WHAMA."

2. See chapter 4.

3. Ibid. Note especially discussion of procedures for revising the chronology.

4. The figures in this section are based on the actual count of the executives' ratings. Though the validated chronology that constitutes Appendix A (a version that was revised from the original chronology on which the ratings were made) does not include any anti-media events for quarter 22, there were a few executives — not a majority — who had perceived anti-media intent during that quarter in the presidential press conferences and televised addresses. As an effort to take into account the perceptions of all the executives participating in the study, the report here is based on the actual WHAMA indexes that include ratings on all events in the original chronology. For the most part, however, the data reported match the majority perceptions that are reflected in the revised chronology as printed.

5. William E. Porter, *Assault on the Media: The Nixon Years* (Ann Arbor: University of Michigan Press, 1976), p. viii.

6. For expanded discussion of this point, see chapter 10, section "Profiles of High Places."

7. Ibid.

8. See chapter 1, introductory comments.

7

THE NEWSPAPER/TELEVISION DIFFERENCE

Newspapers began as a medium of information and ideas. In time, advances in technology, competition in the marketplace, and the desire for increased readership and profits stimulated attention to entertainment values.

*Newspapers as "the press" have traditionally assumed the role of the fourth estate, for the most part seriously going about their daily business of enlightening the citizens of our republic.

Newspapers essentially have an anonymous, heterogeneous, relatively small local readership numbering in the many thousands. And because of locally managed organizational structure,

Television began as an entertainment medium. In a very short time advances in technology, competition in the marketplace, government oversight, and the desire for respectability stimulated attention to the values of information and ideas.

*Television as "the press" has been thrust into the role of the fourth estate by dint of its enormous popularity, and for just a fraction of its daily programming, it seriously goes about the business of enlightening the citizens of our republic.

Television essentially has an anonymous, heterogeneous, relatively large national audience numbering in the many millions. And because of the structure of the broadcast industry, in which

even in the case of chain ownerships, newspapers are generally
able to tailor their news coverage
for mass appeal to a somewhat
specialized public.

networks depend heavily on the
affiliates for program clearance,
news and other programs are
generally tailored for mass appeal
to a wide spectrum of separate
factions.

Most newspapers are financed
by a combination of advertising
revenue and circulation revenue.

Television, except for public
television, is financed exclusively
by advertising revenue.

Because newspapers allocate
most of their nonadvertising
space to news and public affairs,
reports and columns can be
many and in-depth.

Because television allocates
only a small portion of its nonadvertising time to news and
public affairs, news programs and
reports must be severely limited
in number and length.

Because newspapers are a linear medium appealing to the eye,
which actively and selectively
scans at the reader's pace, complex linguistic constructions can
be featured without jeopardizing
comprehension.

Because television is a multidimensioned medium bombard-
ing the senses with transient
sound, sight, and motion, visuals
are accompanied by simpler linguistic constructions in order to
heighten comprehension.

On and on goes the contrast. Not to forget, of course, such other
differences as speed, effects, social utility, and − possibly the most
important from our point of view − the fact that television is a regulated industry and newspaper publishing is not.

Any one of these differences in structure, style, or other factors
could provoke bias in the final news product − differences in the
content of television and newspaper political commentary. Because
television is essentially an entertainment medium without a tradition
of journalistic expertise, does television commentary fail to reflect
the responsibility that newspaper columns usually display? Because
television speaks in less complex language, does television commentary reside in the world of trivia and less complex ideas? Because
broadcast economics depend exclusively on the advertising dollar,
does television commentary somehow reflect biases toward the
commercial sector to an extent not found in newspaper columns?

And, most relevant to this study, because television is a regulated medium and newspapers are not, does television commentary tend to tread more lightly than newspapers where government is concerned?

Digging for bias in communication content requires a sensitive hand. It cannot be accomplished as broad-based random exploration. It must be, instead, the product of meticulous design and sharp focus. But focus on one area necessarily precludes sharp insights in another, and many avenues are thus left unexplored — avenues that in fact may suggest alternative explanations for whatever findings the research has revealed.

So it was here. This study set out to identify and measure differences between newspaper and television political commentary. The focus of the study was narrowed to government regulation — its presence in television and its absence in newspapers — just one of the many factors with the potential to influence differences in the news product. Content analysis procedures were designed accordingly. Thus, other differences and biases that might have come to light, had other perspectives guided the research, were left unexplored. At the same time, of course, the research itself and its findings were made vulnerable to a variety of alternative explanations that, in the absence of further study, only logic and plausibility can refute.

HOW, IN A NUTSHELL

As described in an earlier chapter,[1] content analysis was the method of choice for measuring the comparative vigorousness of newspaper and television political commentary; "vigorousness" was defined in terms of "uninhibited, robust, and wide-open" debate on public issues, the standard articulated by the Supreme Court as the purpose of the First Amendment. Using a random sample of commentary from network television evening news programs aired during the 23 quarters of the Nixon administration (January 20, 1969-August 9, 1974)[2] and a similarly selected sample of nationally syndicated political columns in newspapers, the procedures involved formation of subject matter categories based on a scheme of major issues, minor issues, and nonissues, with major issues further subdivided into "federal government," "Nixon administration per se," "domestic issues," and "Watergate." As a means of operationalizing each of the five concepts in the Supreme Court's standard, measures of relative attention to each subject category were combined with measures of evaluation (positive . . . negative), potency (strong . . . weak), and activity (active . . . passive) as used in evaluative assertion analysis, a classic technique developed in 1956. Means, proportions, and various summary statistics generated from specially designed formulas were calculated for each medium, columnist/commentator, and network, and became the bases for the analysis. Listed below are the dimensions of vigorousness expressed in the Court's standard and the corresponding statistics used for measurement and comparison.

Dimension of Vigorousness	*Statistic Used for Measurement*
Uninhibited	Activity means
Robust	Potency means
Wide-open	Proportionate attention to issues of public importance (major issues, minor issues, nonissues)
Debate	
Tendency to take a point of view	Evaluative means (with signs)
Tendency to emphasize either positive or negative views	Evaluative absolute means (without signs)

INDEX OF VIGOROUSNESS

The index of vigorousness was a single statistic representing the total performance for each medium in each of the 23 quarters. It combined the scores for all subject matter categories arbitrarily weighted by 300, 200, or 100, according to the respective major issue, minor issue, or nonissue designation. A gross measure obliterating fine distinctions, the index of vigorousness nevertheless was able to present an overall view of newspaper/television performance.

According to the index of vigorousness, political commentary in network television news programs was generally less vigorous than in nationally syndicated newspaper columns. But while this was the picture overall, there were quarters when television commentary

TABLE 7.1
Index of Vigorousness: Nationally Syndicated Political Columns in Newspapers vs. Political Commentary in Network Television News Programs

Quarter	Newspapers	Television
1-23	501	405
1	278	294
2	604	577
3	380	246
4	501	691
5	503	613
6	459	333
7	449	433
8	513	362
9	497	749
10	450	264
11	564	226
12	365	491
13	473	576
14	280	487
15	691	381
16	319	204
17	540	618
18	541	354
19	304	403
20	596	172
21	669	177
22	546	455
23	747	235

equaled or surpassed the vigorousness of newspaper columns. Indeed, this phenomenon was seen in nine of the quarters studied. What this observation suggests is that television commentary always had the potential of matching the vigorousness of newspaper columns. The evidence contradicts observers who would claim that television commentators are not as capable as newspaper columnists; that television, being an entertainment medium, is not conducive to vigorous news analysis; that television journalism, bereft of the long-standing traditions of the printed press, is not capable of a full measure of professionalism; that television journalists, aware of the enormous and unique power of the medium, tend to dampen their vigorousness in the interests of responsibility; or that the exigencies of television do not permit time to develop vigorous commentary. The evidence suggests otherwise: that, during the Nixon period, television commentators had the capability of being as critical, tenacious, and professional as their newspaper counterparts. Why, then, were they not consistently so?

DIMENSION BY DIMENSION

While the index of vigorousness presented a bird's-eye view of newspaper/television performance, it was less discriminating, and therefore less useful, than statistics calculated for each subject matter category. For this reason the evaluative, potency, and activity means for each subject category, in addition to the vigorousness and blandness quotients (summary statistics computed for each category),[3] became central to the comparisons. (Tables C.1 through C.5 report the results of the newspaper/television comparisons in light of significance testing by the Mann-Whitney U.) As is conventional in the social sciences, significant findings were based on demonstration of a probability level of .05. Unless otherwise noted, all findings cited in the discussion are at that level or below. One special note: In an effort to tease out more information from the data, two new variables were formed by rearranging certain of the subgroups in the major issues category: "government" (composed of federal government, Nixon administration, and Watergate) and "President" (composed of Nixon administration and Watergate). These new variables appear in all the tables as major issues subgroups.

Examination of the vigorousness and blandness quotients (see Table 7.2) shows that over the whole period, for all issues combined, television commentary was significantly less vigorous ($p = .02$) and more bland ($p = .002$) than newspaper columns. While this timidity existed generally, it was identified by the vigorousness quotient as having occurred especially in discussions of domestic problems, Watergate, the president, and major issues generally. (For graphic representations of these phenomena, see Figure 7.1 and 7.2.) The blandness quotient was able to ferret out, additionally, television's timidity in discussions of the federal government, the Nixon administration, and minor issues. What follows is a discussion of the separate dimensions that contributed to the vigorousness and blandness summaries.

"Uninhibited?"

Not television. Not when it really counted.

It was as if in television commentary, the crises of the day were reported in the language of acquiescence, compliance, and acceptance. No words of remonstration, expostulation, or protest here. For, according to the data, television commentary was significantly more inhibited than newspaper columns in discussions of major issues, particularly Watergate. Measurement in this dimension was based on the tendency to use passive rather than active rhetoric — words like "imagine," "receive," "linger," or "wait" rather than such words as "hurry," "strike," "lobby," or "campaign." (See Table C.1.)

"Robust?"

Rarely.

Comment on major issues, particularly domestic problems and the president, and nonissues as well, provided the grist for television's undoing here; for while newspapers appeared to shout and flex muscle when discussing these topics, their television brothers were tiptoeing and speaking in hushed tones. Measurements in this dimension were based on television's tendency to use weak rather than strong rhetoric. While the newspaper columnists used such words

TABLE 7.2
Television Timidity, by Subject Matter Categories:
Vigorousness Quotient and Blandness Quotient Analysis,
Newspaper Columns vs. Television Commentary

Hypotheses: Television was less vigorous than newspapers
Television was more bland than newspapers

Subject Matter Category	Vigorousness			Blandness		
	Z Score	Probability (1-tailed)	Significance	Z Score	Probability (1-tailed)	Significance
Major issues subgroups						
Federal government	.80	.21		-1.70	.04	*
Nixon administration	1.43	.08		-1.98	.02	*
Domestic problems	1.64	.05	*	-1.39	.08	
Watergate	1.86	.03	*	-1.82	.04	*
Government (fed/admin/Wtrgt)	1.51	.07		-2.53	.006	**
President (admin/Wtrgt)	1.81	.04	*	-1.88	.03	*
Major issues	1.86	.03	*	-2.24	.01	**
Minor issues	-.36	.36		-2.15	.02	*
Nonissues	-.34	.37		-.51	.31	

All issues combined (unweighted)	2.04	.02	*
All issues combined (weighted)	2.05	.02	*
index of vigorousness	−2.98	.002	**

Notes: Negative Z score (vigorousness) indicates Television was more vigorous than newspapers. Positive Z score (blandness) indicates Television was less bland than newspapers.

Legend: Mann-Whitney *U* test
*p ≤ .05, hypothesis demonstrated.
**p ≤ .01, hypothesis demonstrated.

117

FIGURE 7.1
Criticism of the President: Comparison of Vigorousness Quotients, Newspaper Columns vs. Television Commentary

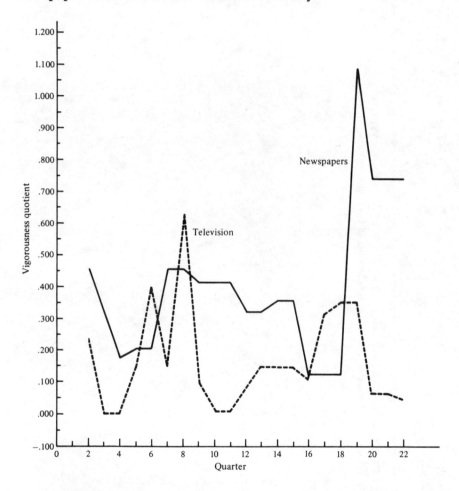

Notes: Represents combined scores of Nixon administration and Watergate. Smoothed curves: medians by three.
Legend: ——————— Newspapers   - - - - - - - - - Television

FIGURE 7.2
Watergate Commentary: Comparison of Vigorousness Quotients, Newspaper Columns vs. Television Commentary

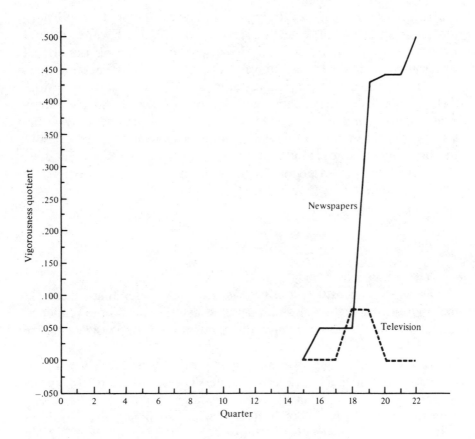

Note: Smoothed curves: medians by three.

Legend: —————— Newspapers - - - - - - - - - - Television

as "limitless," "rugged," "dominant," or "strategic," the television commentators were using the likes of "minimum," "infancy," "tentative," and "somewhat." (See Table C.2.)

"Wide-Open?"

Often, but not enough.

In terms of all issues discussed, television devoted proportionately less attention than newspapers to discussions of Watergate and proportionately more attention to discussions of nonissues. In all other areas — major issues, minor issues, and major issues subgroups — there appeared to be no real difference in the amount of attention. Television's disproportionate emphasis on nonissues and its corresponding avoidance of Watergate went far in supporting the hypothesis that television was more likely than newspapers to behave timidly in the event of a government scandal. This is not to say, of course, that attention to Watergate by newspaper columnists was itself a harvest of abundance. (See Table C.3.)

"Debate?"

Yes, sometimes.

Debate, conceptually defined as discourse defending or attacking a given proposition, was interpreted as referring to the tendency to take a point of view, and the tendency to emphasize positive or negative views.

In most cases there was no significant difference between television and newspapers in their willingness (or lack thereof) to express a point of view. Balance, counterbalance, and fence-straddling appeared generously in both media, while such negative words as "contemptible," "perilous," "traitor," and "terrorize" were juggled with such positives as "enthusiastic," "honorable," "friend," and "extol." But in commentary on the president, when either the administration or Watergate was at issue, television consistently lagged behind newspapers by showing a reluctance to express opinion ($p = .02$). However, on those occasions when television was willing to take a stand on the administration, that view was generally negative — significantly more so than newspapers.

The achievement of this convoluted posture — significantly little opinion with significantly more negativism — reflected consummate skill in wordsmithing and acrobatics. For coupled with television's persistent emphasis on the negative when discussing the administration, there was what appeared to be resolute avoidance of positive words and reliance on such neutral words as "discuss," "event," "additional," or "provision." Thus, while newspapers tended to extreme balance in talk of the administration, carefully mixing praise with censure, television's negativism toward the administration was unrelieved because of its refusal to find positive things to say and its careful use of neutral terms.

But even though television would strike an "if you can't find anything bad to say, don't say it at all" posture in commentary on the Nixon administration, it appeared to back down on other fronts. For in discussions of the federal government (p = .07) and of minor issues (p = .06), television showed a greater (though not significant) tendency than newspapers to emphasize positive views. Thus the emphasis on the negative in commentary on the Nixon administration appeared to have been balanced by an emphasis on the positive in commentary on the federal government. This balance of negative Nixon talk with positive federal talk and of negative nonissues talk with positive minor issues talk could be interpreted as television's attempts to "make amends" and to present fairness. It is just possible that in addition to good politics, the Fairness Doctrine was at work here; for after nearly a quarter century spent in walking a tightrope, skillful and adroit maneuvering are bound to be ingrained as habit. (See Tables C.4 and C.5.)

THE SHAPE OF TIMIDITY

Television's timidity was everything the term implies — a shrinking from dangerous circumstances rather than a thoroughgoing abdication. Timidity here and not there. Timidity there and not here. Hesitancy. Reluctance. Finesse. Or, to put it figuratively, fudging on taxes rather than outright civil disobedience.

Specifically, timidity in television commentary where newspaper columns were used as the standard took the shape of diminished vigorousness across the board, particularly in comment on the president and other major issues; excessive blandness over all categories except nonissues; inhibition in discussions of major issues, particularly Watergate; lack of robustness in discussions of the president and other major issues, particularly domestic problems; more attention to nonissues and less to Watergate; reluctance to express opinion on the president; exceptional precision in positive/negative balance across the various categories of government; and exceptional "fairness" almost everywhere. All this was relieved by doggedly persistent negativism in those few instances when the commentators would deign to speak in judgment of the president.

NOTES

1. See chapter 5, section "Content Analysis."
2. Before August 16, 1971, NBC had aired no formal commentary (as defined in this study) on its nightly news programs. Therefore, for quarters 1 through a portion of 11, the television sample was composed only of commentaries from ABC and CBS. To control for possible bias as a result of this omission, an alternative television sample was selected in which additional ABC and CBS commentary was used to make up the deficit. All analysis was performed on both samples. A comparison of the two sets of data revealed that there were slight differences in significance levels among the various major issues subgroups. In that the primary sample (without the extra ABC and CBS commentaries) yielded the more conservative results, all discussion refers to that sample. See also chapter 5, section "Determining the Sample."
3. See glossary for definitions and formulas.

8

CHILLING EFFECT

Once we narrow the ambit of the First Amendment, creative writing is imperiled and the "chilling effect" on free expression . . . is almost sure to take place.

Time v. *Hill*[1]

For purposes of this study, "chilling effect" was defined as "a significant reduction, in measures over time, and in light of influence by an outside factor, of the vigorousness of journalistic coverage of public issues — where a target population is measured against a comparable alternative population used as a standard." Translated into operational terms, the chilling effect would be demonstrated when fluctuations in measures of an outside factor correlate negatively with measures of vigorousness that represent the difference between measures of a target population and those of another population used as a standard. The term, as here defined, implies a span of time, the presence of a causal factor, a target population, and another population used as a standard. The span of time selected for this study was the 23 quarters of the Nixon administration; the factor singled out as a potential cause was the White House anti-media assault; and the standard against which television commentary (the target population) was compared was nationally syndicated political columns in newspapers. Television and newspapers had been selected for study because the latter function under public policy that forbids government oversight of journalistic content, while the former functions under public policy that in many ways requires such government oversight.

COLLISION COURSE

To test the comparative impact of Nixon's anti-media assault on newspaper and television commentary, the index of White House anti-media assault (WHAMA)[2] was correlated with the vigorousness measures of each medium (the index of vigorousness, the vigorousness quotient, and the blandness quotient). In this way it was possible to assess the vulnerability of newspapers and television to White House pressure and to determine whether the fluctuations in vigorousness or blandness in each medium operated in concert with, or independently of, the White House assault. Data here allowed inference into newspaper and television trends over the period, the susceptibility of each medium to intimidation by government, and media heroics — which medium exhibited them and which did not.

But a prime objective of this study was to identify and measure the chilling effect of WHAMA on television. Recall that "chilling effect" was defined in terms of the difference between a target population and a comparable population used as a standard. Since television commentary was considered to be the target population in this study, while newspaper columns functioned as the standard, "difference scores" were obtained by subtracting newspaper vigorousness scores from television vigorousness scores. These television/newspaper difference scores (more simply called difference scores) were computed for the blandness and vigorousness quotients of each quarter and each subject matter category. Because difference scores represented television's relationship to newspapers at every point in the distribution under consideration, they were considered to be the most accurate measure of comparative television/newspaper vigorousness. The difference scores were also subjected to correlation analysis. While the correlations of WHAMA with the scores of each medium separately would give insight into the relationship of each medium to the anti-media assault, the correlation of WHAMA with television/newspaper difference scores was considered the superior measure for identifying and measuring the chilling effect.

The correlation coefficient derived from Pearson's bivariate correlational analysis was the statistic of choice for these measurements.[3] If the correlation coefficient (hereafter referred to as r) was close to zero, the assumption was made that there was no linear relationship between the two variables; as the value of r got closer to +1 or −1, the assumption became stronger that there was a linear relationship. A correlation coefficient of less than .20 was considered to indicate a slight but negligible relationship; a coefficient between .20 and .40 was considered to indicate a definite but small relationship; a coefficient between .40 and .70, a moderate relationship; and anything higher, a strong or very strong relationship.[4]

The probability levels were of importance only to the extent that they referred to the relationship described. A low correlation coefficient with a high probability score would mean only that there was a high probability that a low relationship existed between the variables. A more meaningful relationship would be expressed as a high coefficient correlation with a low level of probability ($p \leqslant .05$). Where appropriate in this discussion, reference will be made to relationships showing substantial correlation coefficients but unacceptable levels of probability. These relationships, of course, must be considered in the light that there was a strong probability that they could have happened by chance.

Two Media Under Siege

Correlation analysis between WHAMA and the index of vigorousness of each medium proved fruitless, the correlation coefficients being too low and the probability levels too high to allow for any meaningful inference. The index of vigorousness was used here for gross measurement of the press-government relationship over the period. But apparently this all-inclusive index harbored competing distributions that in combination masked significant differences that were subsequently shown to have existed.

The more valuable insights were suggested by correlation of WHAMA with the blandness and vigorousness quotients for each medium. Here newspaper and television performance in each subject matter category was put to the test separately. Did television and newspapers, either or both, react to White House pressure by varying their bite in commentary on sensitive topics? Would they react one way in commentary on major issues and another way in commentary on minor issues or nonissues? One way in government talk and another in nongovernment talk? One way in federal government talk and another when the focus was on the president himself?

Definitely, say the data. From examination of the relationship of WHAMA to the vigorousness quotients of each subject matter category, it appeared that WHAMA had a "slight but negligible" negative effect on both newspapers and television, in commentary on major issues. Even though these findings were not statistically significant, they do suggest that neither medium went unscathed by the White House offensive; that increased pressure by the administration took its toll on newspapers and television alike, each at the very least growing more cautious, politic, and defensive. But television alone went beyond caution when the focus was on government ($r = -.32$; $p = .03$) or on the president himself ($r = -.33$; $p = .03$). Revealing a timidity that was "definite but small" and more than minimally significant, television succumbed to White House intimidation by soft-pedaling its commentary on the administration and government generally. Newspapers, on the other hand, grew more bold in this arena. For as WHAMA escalated in intensity, newspapers grew vigorous in its discourse on the administration ($r = .35$; $p = .03$). Retaliating with their own brand of shell and mortar, newspaper columnists translated White House aggression into a boomerang turned on itself. Not so the television commentators, who, in the words of T. S. Eliot, "curled once about the house, and fell asleep," never finding "the strength to force the moment to its crisis."[5] (See Figure 8.1 and Table C.6.)

Correlation of WHAMA with the blandness quotients of each medium showed a variation of the same theme. Newspaper blandness — sometimes more, sometimes less — seemed to operate in all categories independently of the White House assault. But television, which generally reacted to increased WHAMA by cutting down on blandness ($r = -.36$; $p = .03$), reversed postures and reacted with significantly increased blandness in commentary on major issues ($r = .44$; $p = .009$), particularly where government ($r = .31$; $p = .04$) was concerned. So once again television was revealed as the intimidated medium backing off from the brandished fist; for as the White House increased the frequency and intensity of its anti-media assault, television retreated to neutral, weak, and passive language

FIGURE 8.1
Press Reaction to White House Pressure: WHAMA vs. Commentary on the Nixon Administration, by Vigorousness Quotient

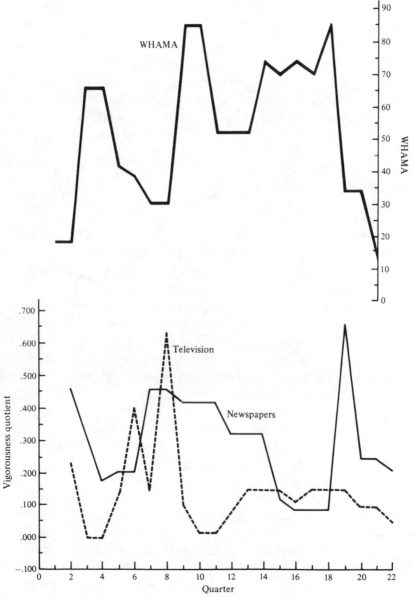

Note: Smoothed curves: medians by three.

Legend: ━━WHAMA━━Newspaper columns. ▪▪Television commentary.

when commenting on that White House — a clear departure from the more forthright rhetoric it used almost everywhere else. (See Table C.7.)

Chilling Effect Analysis

To be sure, there were hints of the chilling effect in the pair of correlations showing newspapers and television with diametrically opposed postures in commentary on the administration. But, as was explained above, chilling effect analysis was considered best served by correlation of WHAMA with difference scores (television scores minus newspaper scores), a procedure that focused on the target population not as an entity in itself but in terms of the standard with which it was being compared.

Chilling Effect in Evidence

Penetrating the psychological drama played out in the remote reaches of will and emotion, correlation of WHAMA with vigorousness quotient difference scores produced the object of long and tedious endeavor: television caught in the act of being itself. For with a highly significant and solid negative correlation ($r = -.46$; $p = .007$),[6] the analysis revealed a direct link between WHAMA and timidity in television commentary pertaining to that White House. (See Table C.8.) As the assault became more severe, television — separating itself from newspapers — significantly reduced its vigorousness in all discussion of White House affairs, while in commentary on other less sensitive topics, it remained unaffected. Here was more than commanding evidence of a chilling effect — a chilling effect directly inspired by White House show of force. Intimidation. Government anti-media leverage that worked. Figure 8.2 is a graphic representation of this phenomenon; the upper display represents WHAMA and the lower represents television's vigorousness vis-a-vis newspapers. In the lower display the bar at .000 represents equivalence of television/newspaper vigorousness; the scores above the bar represent TV performance that is more vigorous than that of newspapers, while scores below the bar represent TV performance that is less vigorous than that of newspapers. Within this context one can readily see television's tendency to

FIGURE 8.2
Chilling Effect: WHAMA vs. Commentary on the Nixon Admin-
istration, by Vigorousness Quotient, by Television/Newspaper
Difference Scores (television scores minus newspaper scores)

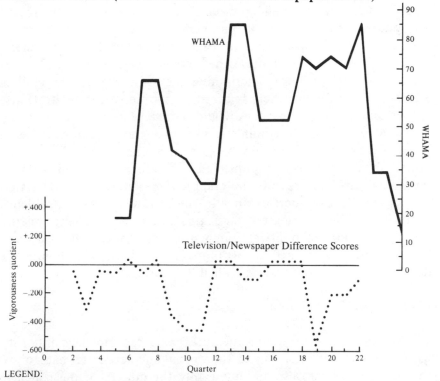

LEGEND:
.000: Television vigorousness = Newspaper vigorousness
 +: Television vigorousness > Newspaper vigorousness
 −: Television vigorousness < Newspaper vigorousness

Note: Smoothed curves: medians by three.

operate consistently in the negative, or timid, area in commentary
on the Nixon administration. By examining the ups and downs of
the vigorousness curve in light of fluctuations in the WHAMA curve,
one can capture a visualization of the chilling effect at work.

Reverse Chilling Effect

There was one other observation of note: a significant and
substantial positive correlation ($r = .33$; $p = .03$) between WHAMA
and television's discussion of domestic issues. As the White House

offensive grew stronger, television, unlike newspapers, grew more vigorous in comment on domestic problems. (The data reveal that newspapers actually showed a downward trend in this category during this period.) These findings suggest a phenomenon that was tagged the "reverse chilling effect," defined here as "increased vigorousness in discussions of one or more subject matter categories when, over the same period of time and under the same general circumstances, one or more other subject matter categories met the criteria set forth for determining the existence of the 'chilling effect.'" The inference here is that in response to the White House anti-media assault, television would compensate for its timidity in commentary on the administration by increased vigorousness in such areas as domestic problems where it might consider itself to be "safe" from White House pique, and therefore from White House reprisal. Figure 8.3 presents the graphic representation of WHAMA's impact on television performance in the area of domestic problems. It shows television, at least so far as this kind of government pressure and this category of political commentary are concerned, as a timid but not intimidated medium. (Compare this figure with Figure 8.2 for a picture of chilled vs. non-chilled journalism.)

Blandness by Intimidation

Whereas the vigorousness measures weighted language intensity with frequency of attention to the various subject matter categories, the blandness measures considered only the quality of the language used. Thus, a chilling effect on vigorousness would in part suggest avoidance of that particular category; a chilling effect in terms of blandness, however, would suggest only that there was a change in the quality of the language used – a tendency to increased quali-fication of terms and increased use of neutral, weak, and passive rhetoric.

Blandness correlational analysis on the difference scores showed several highly significant, substantial relationships. In discussion of major issues generally ($r = .52$; $p = .01$) and specifically in discus-sions of government ($r = .44$; $p = .01$), television's blandness ap-peared to increase as the severity of the government assault increased. Here again, the evidence suggested a chilling effect.

But in all issues combined ($r = -.41$; $p = .01$), including discus-sions of nonissues ($r = -.28$; $p = .05$), the correlations were suggestive

FIGURE 8.3

Reverse Chilling Effect: WHAMA vs. Commentary on Domestic Problems, by Vigorousness Quotient, by Television/Newspaper Difference Scores (television scores minus newspaper scores)

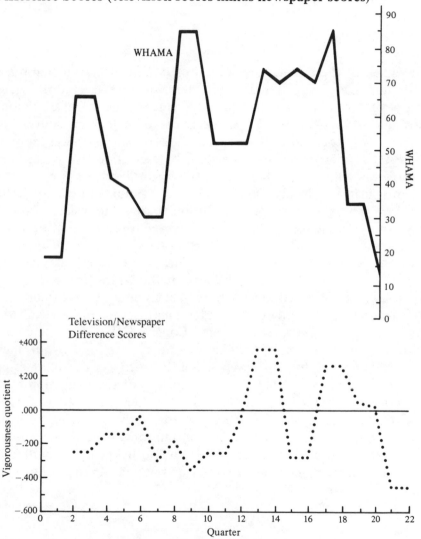

Note: Smoothed curves: medians by three.

LEGEND:

.000: Television vigorousness = Newspaper vigorousness

+: Television vigorousness > Newspaper vigorousness

−: Television vigorousness < Newspaper vigorousness

131

of a moderate tendency on the part of television to reduce bland-ness in the face of increased severity of the anti-media assault. Here again, it is possible that a "reverse chilling effect" was operative. (See Table C.9.)

THE FACT OF THE MATTER

When all the calculations were done and the data on Nixon and the press had been squeezed dry, television's biggest open secret was teased out into the light of day. The chilling effect of Nixon's strong-arm tactics on the vigorousness of television journalism, heretofore little more than speculation or surmise, was now an observable, measurable phenomenon. By escalating and intensifying the force of its anti-media assault, the Nixon White House was able to intimidate an already timid medium. It was able to manipulate the nation's most popular press, and by provoking diminished vigorous-ness in the commentary of eminently revered journalists, the White House was able subtly to restrain criticism of the Nixon administra-tion that was aired to more than 44 million Americans nightly.

This study focused on the ability of the White House to trigger a chilling effect in commentary on television news programs. But the White House is only one of several participants in the regulatory policy-making process, others being Congress, the FCC, the courts, citizen groups, and the broadcast industry itself.[7] Any of these other entities might also have the ability to trigger a chilling effect in television news, as might the assumptions of the regulation tradi-tion itself, ownership patterns, and advertiser pressure. And while the chilling effect was identified by this study as having occurred in television commentary, it is not improbable that the chilling effect could have occurred as well in such other genres as hard news coverage, documentaries, or interviews. Such findings, however, are left to other studies.

NOTES

1. *Time* v. *Hill*, 385 U.S. 374 (1967).
2. In these analyses the vigorousness measures were correlated separately with "WHAMA as ordered" (where events in the chronology were ordered

according to the dates they happened) and "WHAMA as reported" (where events were ordered according to the dates they were reported to the public). For fuller explanation, see chapter 6, section "Charting Storms of State." Furthermore, the vigorousness measures were correlated with WHAMA as calculated for all media executives combined and for each executive subgroup (newspaper, broadcast, nonnetwork, network, top-top brass all, top-top brass newspaper, top-top brass broadcast). (See chapter 10, section "Profiles of High Places.") The data reported here refer to correlations where the independent variable was "WHAMA as reported," all media executives combined. Whatever important differences appeared in the analyses among the various WHAMA subindexes are reported when those differences suggest unique inferences. For one such discussion see chapter 10, section "Old Questions of Who and How Much."

3. It is recognized that, strictly speaking, causality cannot be inferred from correlation analysis, that strong correlations describe strong relationships and nothing more. But while causality as an absolute truth is not accepted in the social sciences, its proxy — which is a construct of the mind, often a consequence of statistics — fills in as a logical compromise. As no more than a proxy for truth, causality in the social sciences is an insight that convention has come to accept when supporting evidence is based on plausibility, apparent validity and reliability, and certain arbitrary levels of probability. The logic of the evidence produced in this study lends strong support — even if not absolute proof — for assertions of causality regarding press-government relationships during the Nixon era. Bear in mind that while correlation of WHAMA with TV vigorousness would indicate "relationship," the additional step of comparing television as the target population with newspapers, a comparable population, was undertaken as a means of getting beyond mere "relationship" and into the area of causality.

4. Based on J. P. Guilford, *Fundamental Statistics in Psychology and Education* (New York: McGraw-Hill, 1950), p. 165.

5. Thomas Stearns Eliot, "The Love Song of J. Alfred Prufrock," ll. 22, 80.

6. All analysis of television was performed on two separate samples. (See chapter 5, note 12, for explanation.) While all data reported are in terms of the primary sample, it is interesting to note that the alternative television sample showed the same chilled relationship but to a stronger degree ($r = -.50; p = .004$).

7. Based on the analysis described in Erwin G. Krasnow and Lawrence D. Longley, *The Politics of Broadcast Regulation*, 2nd ed. (New York: St. Martin's Press, 1978), pp. 47-50.

OTHER ANALYSIS

9

RANKING THE NEWS ANALYSTS

In the early 1970s, when America was staggering under the weight of a government gone sour, the people needed heroes. They needed to learn the truth behind the tangle of government-issued lies and confusion. They needed help in piecing together the parts of the complex drama. They needed stability and continuity. But most of all they needed assurance that the white hats were coming to save the day and that life as they knew it would go on.

About three times weekly Eric Sevareid told America what it was all about. With language of pious eloquence, he held nervous hands and soothed jangled nerves. Silver-haired, kindly, the quintessential sage, he was soothsayer, oracle, and the most knowing of persons to 19 million who tuned in nightly to the CBS evening news. But Sevareid was not the only wise man to dwell on the mountain. At NBC, 18 million listeners tuned in David Brinkley; and at ABC, 8 million listened for the words of Howard K. Smith, Harry Reasoner, and sometimes Frank Reynolds.[1]

The nationally syndicated newspaper columnists, traditionally the voices beside the cracker barrel, were also in the business of dispensing insight and collecting publics. Usually unable to command the sheer numbers of their television brothers, the newspaper columnists — more elite but no less habit-forming — inspired cultlike devotion as they explained and expounded in a wide variety of newspapers from coast to coast. Analyzing, synthesizing, chiding, criticizing, or confirming, finding symbolic imperatives in the most obscure events, architects of political swings, diplomatic maneuvers, and public morale — here were statesmen in the best sense. Remembered for their triumphs in the past, they were read, respected, and even feared by leaders at home and abroad. When much later, during the Watergate hearings, former Presidential Counsel John Dean disclosed that columnists Jack Anderson, Rowland Evans, Clayton Fitchey, Joseph Kraft, James Reston, and Tom Wicker were included on President Nixon's "Enemies List," the people could applaud and take pride. It was as they had always believed.

The political analysts, from their separate pulpits in both newspapers and television, were tycoons in the business of veneration and visibility. No other persons or institutions commanded such a public gathering so often, so regularly, and for so long a period. Not the president, not the pope, not Johnny Carson; not movies, soap operas, or baseball.

What measure of journalism was in all this influence, power, and hoopla? Stripped of the charisma, color, and hype, what is the barebones reality of what the commentators and columnists actually said? The power of words, "so nimble and so full of subtle flame,"[2] has been known to topple governments, to move nations to arm and men to weep. Words aptly spoken can light up the dark; they can persuade, goad, inspire, wound, and heal. How so the words of the media analysts? What passion boiled in their poetry? What thunder? What clamor? How relevant were they? How early did they perceive that "something is rotten in the state of Denmark"?[3] And how did the television commentators stack up against the syndicated columnists?

For answers to these and other questions, basic and summary statistics were computed for the various columnists and commentators represented in the sample. Each was studied for his place in the "uninhibited/robust/wide-open/debate" schemata and then ranked from the most to the least according to the index of vigorousness. The sample, originally prepared for the larger project on newspaper/television differences during the Nixon administration, involved random selection within the two media limited only to specific dates, networks, and newspapers. No attempt was made in that sampling process to gather a sizable body of work from any one journalist; thus, the sample came to include the work of 9 television commentators and 35 newspaper columnists, each represented from 1 to 61 commentaries.[4]

Because meaningful analysis of an individual's journalistic performance would require a sizable body of his output, five was arbitrarily chosen as the minimum number of commentaries for a data base.[5] Thus, any journalist who was not represented in the sample by five or more commentaries was eliminated from individual analysis. In all, 23 journalists were analyzed for their individual performance during this period. Those journalists whose commentaries appeared in the sample for the larger study but who, because they were represented by too small a data base, were eliminated from analysis at this level were newspaper journalists Charles Bartlett, Tom Braden, Marquis Childs, Ernest B. Furguson, Stanley Karnow, Mary McGrory, Ralph Nader, Kevin P. Phillips, Richard L. Strout, Roy Wilkins, George F. Will, Garry Wills, D. J. R. Bruckner, Vic Gold, Russel Kirk, Louis Kohlmeier, and Robert Donovan; and television journalists Bill Lawrence, Dan Rather, Walter Cronkite,[6] and Charles Collingwood.

Table 9.1 lists the index of vigorousness for each journalist and the vigorousness quotients in the separate subject matter categories. The score in "Major Issues" is a summary of the scores in the major issues subgroups, and the index of vigorousness is the sum of scores in major issues, minor issues, and nonissues weighted by 3, 2, and 1, respectively. Table 9.2 focuses on style and interprets the evaluative, potency, and activity measures according to the grading system traditional to most classrooms. Here the "gentleman's C" corresponds to the middle range of scores and indicates average performance.

HIGH RANK, LOW RANK

The index of vigorousness should be considered in much the same way as record time achieved by an athlete. The record itself stands as the upper limit of possiblity and is the standard against which all subsequent achievement is measured — until a new record is established. So it is with the index of vigorousness and the separate measures that make it up. They should be understood not in terms of what is the highest score possible but, rather, in comparative terms — how one journalist compares with another. Among the 23 journalists studied, the index of vigorousness ranged from 201 to 662, with nearly half hovering in the 400s. As a guideline, an index of 800 or more would indicate a habit of focusing almost exclusively on major issues while ignoring minor issues and nonissues.

TABLE 9.1
The Commentators/Columnists Ranked

Rank	Commentator/Columnist	Index of Vigorousness	Vigorousness by Subject Matter Category						
			Major Issues Subgroups				Major Issues	Minor Issues	Non-Issues
			Federal Government	Nixon Administration	Domestic Problems	Watergate			
1	Tom Wicker	662	89	53	53	–	195	32	13
2	Joseph Kraft	653	61	53	83	–	197	25	12
3	James J. Kilpatrick	552	47	2	36	25	110	103	16
4	Joseph Alsop	545	78	40	3	4	125	85	–
5	Clayton Fritchey	495	42	29	43	9	123	58	10
6	James Reston	493	51	42	17	5	115	69	10
7	Jack Anderson	490	87	10	31	14	142	26	12
8	David S. Broder	482	71	37	14	26	148	15	8
8	Nicholas von Hoffman	482	11	12	19	–	42	148	60
10	Evans and Novak	466	35	58	32	18	143	18	1
11	William Safire	465	–	50	–	77	127	16	52
12	Roscoe Drummond	449	33	23	58	–	114	44	19
13	Howard K. Smith	446	75	16	15	1	107	57	11
14	Nick Thimmesch	438	50	53	27	4	134	5	26
15	Eric Sevareid	436	51	31	20	1	103	49	29
16	David Brinkley	397	35	15	38	9	97	42	22
17	William F. Buckley, Jr.	382	–	3	2	42	47	112	17

18	Anthony Lewis	353	11	64	10	−1	84	48	5
19	William Raspberry	350	32	–	–	–	32	112	30
20	Frank Reynolds	330	27	7	17	–	51	70	37
21	Harry Reasoner	224	6	0	6	3	15	57	65
22	Russell Baker	219	–	–	–	−5	−5	73	88
23	Art Buchwald	201	2	7	7	–	16	37	79

Index of vigorousness = Sum of scores in major issues, minor issues, and nonissues weighted by 3, 2, and 1 respectively.

Major issues scores = Sum of scores in major issues subgroups.

– indicates no discussion delivered in this category.

141

TABLE 9.2
Report Card on Style

Rank	Commentators/ Columnist	Proportion of Attention (in percentages)*			Positive v. Negative Views	Taking a Point of View	Strong v. Weak Words	Active v. Passive Words
		Major Issues	Minor Issues	Non-issues				
1	Tom Wicker	76	20	5	-+	B	B	A
2	Joseph Kraft	80	10	10	-	D	B	A
3	James J. Kilpatrick	60	34	7	-:	B	A	B
4	Joseph Alsop	64	36	0	--:	C	A	C
5	Clayton Fritchey	56	40	4	-	A	E	B
6	James Reston	62	34	4	-:	C	C	B
7	Jack Anderson	75	21	4		C	C	C
8	David S. Broder	82	10	8	-:	C	E	B
8	Nicholas von Hoffman	18	48	34	++	A	A	B
10	Evans and Novak	78	16	7	-	B	C	D
11	William Safire	61	12	27	-	B	C	C
12	Roscoe Drummond	62	26	12	-	C	C	D
13	Howard K. Smith	62	26	12	-	B	C	D
14	Nick Thimmesch	73	5	23	-+	D	C	C
15	Eric Sevareid	53	30	17	-	C	C	C
16	David Brinkley	54	25	21	-:	B	E	C
17	William F. Buckley, Jr.	28	61	11	-+	E	B	B
18	Anthony Lewis	49	34	17	--:	A	E	E

19	William Raspberry	17	50	33	- -	D	C	C
20	Frank Reynolds	41	34	25	- -	D	C	C
21	Harry Reasoner	20	34	46	+	C	E	D
22	Russell Baker	3	48	48	- - - -	A	E	D
23	Art Buchwald	27	27	46	+	A	E	E

*Because of rounding, figures do not always total 100.

Legend: - - - - (exceptionally negative); - - - (strongly negative); - - (moderately negative); - (mildly negative); - + (balanced); + (mildly positive); + + (moderately positive).

A = exceptionally high. C = average. E = exceptionally low.
B = more than most. D = less than most.

143

Little qualification and only the strongest, most active rhetoric would be used at this level: unrelieved anger or support, always waving banners or fighting dragons, all hills and no valleys. An index in the neighborhood of 400 would indicate varying degrees of balance in some or all things: balanced attention to major issues, minor issues, and nonissues; anger, if any, balanced with pleasantries; support balanced with criticism; praise balanced with censure. Or none of the above and, instead, the middle of the road. With indexes down near 100, there is a hint of the toastmaster. Here triviality abounds and nonissues take center stage. A vast expenditure of language where the focus is on wit, wordsmanship, the illusion that work is being done, filling time and space, or escape. In literary circles they might call this level "comic relief."

Showing an index of 662, Tom Wicker, a *New York Times* syndicated columnist, holds the honor of ranking first, as the journalist whose news analysis comes closest to reflecting "uninhibited, robust, and wide-open debate on public issues." He is followed closely by the *Washington Post*'s Joseph Kraft, whose columns measured an index of 653. Nearly 100 points separated Wicker and Kraft from the rest of the field.

At the bottom of the rankings are Russell Baker and Art Buchwald, with scores of 219 and 201, respectively. Both are humorists in the classic sense and have been described as "the two top satiric columnists"[7] among contemporary writers. But their emphasis on humor, irony, and the foibles of society generally precluded serious discussion of the major controversies of the day. In the period studied, nearly half of their material focused on nonissues.[8]

To a man, the television commentators ranked in the lower half of the scale. Small wonder, then, that no one here appeared on Nixon's list of media enemies. The most vigorous television commentator was ABC's Howard K. Smith, who, with an index of 446, ranked thirteenth. Eric Sevareid of CBS was close behind with an index of 436, and NBC's David Brinkley lagged somewhat with an index of 397. It is interesting to note that Harry Reasoner, the major ABC commentator who shared the spotlight with Howard K. Smith, ranked just above the humorists. Close to bottom at twenty-first, Reasoner was more than 100 points behind colleague Frank Reynolds, who weighed in at twentieth.

UNEASY LIES THE HEAD THAT WEARS A CROWN

Just as the winner in the decathlon event of the Olympic games represents the best combination of all categories considered but not necessarily the best in each separate category, so it is with the index of vigorousness and the separate measures that it combines. More than any other news analyst, Tom Wicker was able to put it all together. But while Wicker was the most vigorous all-around journalist, he was equaled or surpassed in most of the separate categories considered. Whereas Wicker devoted 76 percent of his columns to major issues, Joseph Kraft, David Broder, and Evans and Novak devoted more; and whereas Wicker devoted only 5 percent of his columns to nonissues, Joseph Alsop, Clayton Fritchey, James Reston and Jack Anderson devoted less. When it came to taking a stand on the issues, Wicker's score was bested by Kilpatrick, Fritchey, von Hoffman, Evans and Novak, Smith, Buckley, Lewis, Baker, and Buchwald. Wicker's use of strong rather than weak words was surpassed by Kilpatrick, Alsop, and Buckley; and his use of active rather than passive words was surpassed by Kraft.

Wicker, with Jack Anderson close at his heels, was the most vigorous of all when the target was the federal government. Here, as in no other category, his star glittered. Congress, the cabinet, the courts, domestic policy, war, and defense were all fair game for the Wicker brand of strong talk, hard stands, and no-holds barred panache. But not so in articles on the Nixon White House. Here the Wicker acid cooled and was consistently less biting than that of fellow *Times* staffer Anthony Lewis, whose columns proved to offer the most vigorous presidential criticism. In the matter of Watergate, Wicker's restraint was even more dramatic as he and six others opted for avoidance and looking the other way. In the sample used in this study, not one Watergate piece appeared under the Wicker by-line. Let it be recognized, however, that except for Nixon apologist William Safire, and to a lesser extent conservative William F. Buckley, Jr., most of the analysts — newspaper and television — approached Watergate warily, with scant attention, much blandness, and much qualification.

ANATOMY OF VIGOROUSNESS

Of all the journalists — television and newspaper — David S. Broder devoted the most attention to major issues (82 percent), whereas Russell Baker devoted the least (3 percent). As explained earlier, the subject matter category scheme was based on a 1972 Gallup survey in which the public was asked to order the period's most important problems. By this standard the category "major issues" was considered to include all affairs of the federal government, the Nixon administration per se, Watergate, and such domestic problems as crime, drug abuse, busing, and inflation. The category "minor issues" was taken to include pollution, local government, protests, women's liberation, and other such areas where the crises were perceived as being less acute than those of the major issues. "Nonissues" covered such areas as natural history, travel, art, amusements, science, and others where there was little or no controversy or where interest was limited to a small segment of the population.

While Broder was commenting on Nixon's callous response to official reports of campus unrest, the bleak outlook for filling Supreme Court vacancies, and the growing desire of some Republicans to place distance between themselves and the president, Baker, as the top scorer in nonissues, was bringing chuckles with the topsy-turvy world of Ms. and marriage contracts, the replacement of traditional America with shopping centers and Football City, historical precedents for official opposition to long hair, and Everett Dirkson's Dirkson imitation. Those devoting 75 percent or more of their time to major issues were David Broder, Joseph Kraft, Evans and Novak, Tom Wicker, and Jack Anderson.

In terms of topic choice, the most frequent user of minor issues was William F. Buckley, Jr., who devoted 61 percent of his material to matters that managed to sidestep the major crises of the time. With urbane analyses rich in extravagant verbiage and the nooks and crannies of history and innuendo, he regularly focused on such topics as foreign internal affairs, conservative ideology, and historical political blunders. While the country was reeling from social unrest, war, and unemployment, Buckley's columns (their relatively vigorous attention to Watergate notwithstanding) avoided discussion of the federal government, the White House, or major domestic problems, and spoke instead of Russian faith in the inspirational leadership of its revolutionary heroes, the financial straits of American compared with European airlines, and the role of rhetoric in world diplomacy. Other heavy users of minor issues were William Raspberry, the *Washington Post* columnist who usually confined his attention to civil rights and local politics, and

Nicholas von Hoffman, who took honors for the most vigorous treatment of minor issues generally.

More than any other factor, the avoidance of trivia or other nonissues was the key to a high index of vigorousness. Among the journalists ranking as the ten most vigorous, the proportion of attention to nonissues averaged 8 percent. The average among the lower-ranking journalists was 26 percent. Front-runner Wicker discussed nonissues only 5 percent of the time, while Buchwald, who had the lowest overall index, dealt in nonissues nearly half the time. Among those journalists ranking in the top ten, only Joseph Alsop totally avoided nonissues, and only Nicholas von Hoffman, with 34 percent, dipped deep in the nonissues cookie jar. Of the television commentators, Smith devoted 12 percent of his time to nonissues; Sevareid, 17 percent; Brinkley, 21 percent; Reynolds, 25 percent; and Reasoner, a whopping 46 percent.

Scores to measure "taking a point of view" registered the frequency and intensity of expressing a position and gave equal weight to both positive and negative orientations. Here strong views, whether for or against any issue, brought high marks. Tied closely to these measures were data identifying the positive vs. negative leanings of each journalist — whether on an overall basis his positions tended to be balanced, positive, or negative, and to what extent.

Anthony Lewis and Russell Baker scored highest as journalists who most often took hard stands on the issues. Both found much to criticize, and neither was reluctant to publicize his unqualified negativism. Scoring somewhat lower but also getting high marks in expressing positions were Fritchey, who more often than not tended toward the negative, and von Hoffman and Buchwald, both of whom found more to praise than to censure. But for hedging and avoidance of controversiality, the numbers again pointed to William F. Buckley, Jr., who was sui generis in this regard. With almost legendary civility, Buckley showcased carefully honed rhetoric — robust and uninhibited, yet spectacularly neutral — to generate balance and unmatched evenhandedness.

Among the television commentators, ABC's Howard K. Smith and NBC's David Brinkley, with moderately high scores, were notable for their forthrightness in taking stands — Smith mildly negative and Brinkley considerably more so. No wonder that, in 1970, White House aide H. R. Haldeman issued a memo singling out NBC for "their almost totally negative approach to everything the Administration does."[9] This, of course, proved to be an astute observation, in light of the vigorousness measures subsequently generated in this study, for the evidence shows that NBC was substantially more negative in commentary relating to the administration than it was in any other subject matter category, and that it was substantially more negative in these discussions than each of the other networks. This record was broken only in commentary on Watergate, when CBS, through Sevareid, surpassed NBC in negativism.

Showing a relatively high level of tenacity and resoluteness, Joseph Alsop and James J. Kilpatrick were far and away the most robust in their choice of words. Other high scorers included von Hoffman, Buckley, and Wicker. Using such strong words as "ruthless," "attack," "overpower," and "deadly,"[10] these journalists differed from low scorers Brinkley, Fritchey, Broder, Baker, and Buchwald, who were more likely to soften their rhetoric with such weak words as "pathetic," "despair," "superficial," or "inadequate" and with such qualifiers as "hopes to," "appears to," "probably," or "perhaps."

Joseph Kraft was the most uninhibited. Peppering his columns with active rather than passive words, he was miles from Tom Wicker, his nearest competitor in this dimension. Emphasis on active words such as "exploit," "blast," "revive," "resist," "win," "leap," and "conspire" appears to reflect energy supportive of challenge and initiation, whereas emphasis on such passive words as "anguish," "forfeit," "abandon," "suffer," "worry," "awe," and "decay" appears to reflect submissive compliance to the status quo. By using active words the journalist inspires involvement in shaping affairs; by using the passive he implies helplessness in the face of overwhelming external forces. On balance, most of the journalists opted for active rhetoric, though Reasoner, Baker, and Evans and Novak showed a greater tendency than any of the others to select words with extremely low levels of activity. Only Anthony Lewis and Art Buchwald made a habit of using passive words.

THE TELEVISION FIRMAMENT

Of the TV networks in this period, only ABC aired commentary nightly on its evening news program. Rotating Howard K. Smith, Harry Reasoner, and sometimes Frank Reynolds to deliver what was called "Commentary," ABC differed from CBS and NBC, which featured single commentators in approximately three programs weekly. Speaking for CBS, Eric Sevareid delivered "Analysis," while NBC offered David Brinkley's "Journal." When either Sevareid or Brinkley was not available, a replacement was rarely brought in, even when the absence was for a prolonged period. At these times the news would simply go without commentary.

As the rankings show, the TV commentators were a timid lot, blazing no trails in vigorousness. Sporting scores considerably below most of their newspaper brethren, they seesawed back and forth, one with the other, each taking separate honors but each, in the end, showing up as remarkably similar to the other. Howard K. Smith, who ranked first among the commentators in the overall ratings, scored as the most vigorous in discussion of the federal government; Eric Sevareid scored as the most vigorous in discussion of the White House; and David Brinkley was the most vigorous when domestic problems were the issue. Smith, trailed closely by Brinkley, most often took the hardest position, and Sevareid used the strongest and most active language. Brinkley was the most negative, and of all the commentators only Reasoner leaned toward the positive. Smith paid more attention than the others to major issues; Reynolds, to minor issues; and Harry Reasoner took the prize for more attention to nonissues. Reynolds showed the least tendency to take a stand on the issues; Brinkley was the least robust; and Reasoner was the least active.

While the other commentators fielded the great issues with reasonable frequency — some more, some less — Reasoner's fluff made no pretenses and appeared more often than not. Specializing in inhibition, wordsmanship, and happy talk, he dwelt in the house of the great and the not-so-great nonissues of the day. For Reasoner, who devoted a full 46 percent of his time to nonissues, no trivia was off base. Never mind the war, never mind Watergate, never mind unemployment, drug abuse, or busing, Howard K. Smith was there for those sorts of issues. The Reasoner style was to tell how Christmas is almost here now that June is past, or the effect of good eating and drinking on Common Market summit talks. For more inspiring fare, there was talk of the baseball strike, the American tradition of making a buck, youth-oriented advertising, how government scandals are not new, and the fascination of knowing you don't have to be a judge to be named to the Supreme Court.

This is not to say, of course, that ABC and Reasoner had a corner on television's trivia and soft talk; Sevareid and Brinkley also drank from that cup, though to a lesser extent. For them, half and half appeared to be the rule – half the time on major issues and half on minor issues and nonissues. Comments on government, the economy, and the war, to be sure; but from Sevareid we also learned that business executives were taking courses on handling noisy reporters, that history had need to revise its estimate of Alf Landon, that getting to know other nations will help nations like each other better, that the problems of the inner man are perplexing, and that we've just staggered through a decade. Given to excessive qualification and greater reluctance than any but Reynolds to air a point of view, Sevareid was a cautious man. One columnist, commenting on his middle-of-the-road delivery, recalled, "Sevareid was so reasonable, so fair, he's often been a bore. You longed for the salt of passion, a bit of anger, cynicism, and dark humor."[11] Indeed, Sevareid himself joked about his tendency to qualify terms when he said, "If I were the new Betty Furness, I'd probably say something like, 'On present evidence and all things being equal, you can be reasonably sure if it's Westinghouse.' "[12]

Compared with Sevareid, Brinkley was equally imaginative and inconsequential in much of his topic choice, even if, as the most negative and as runner-up in expressing a point of view, he was somewhat less cautious. Without Brinkley we might never have known that Florida is a curious state and that Camden, Maine, is a livable town. It's hard not to like Shetland ponies, he told us. British scandals involve the bedroom, whereas ours tend to involve the cashbox. And then there were the questions of outrage. Why is it that those on the public payroll feel entitled to luxuries unavailable to those who pay them? And why does a country that prefers peace have so many wars?

THE MOST VIGOROUS NETWORK

In spite of Smith's leadership in the vigorousness rankings, Reasoner's triviality in combination with Reynolds' blandness cost ABC its edge on the other networks. The overall winner for this period was CBS, which ranked first as the network with the most consistently vigorous commentary. NBC ranked second, and ABC third.

When it came to watching the business of government, including Congress, the courts, and the White House, the CBS eye focused sharply and deftly, with a vigorousness unmatched by the other networks (though far less than that of most newspaper columnists). But when it came to Watergate, the big CBS machine sputtered and balked, sagging noticeably under the strain of avoidance, blandness, and uncharacteristic weakness and inhibition. NBC, on the other hand, found its stride in Watergate, where, as the least bland, the most robust, the least inhibited, and intensely negative, it easily placed at the head of the class. While all this was going on, ABC overslept and missed the main event. Exhausted from its triumphs in minor issues and nonissues, it ended up dead last as the weakest, most inhibited, least negative, least vigorous network so far as major issues were concerned, especially the White House and Watergate.

But lest we not forget, there are no laurels due television for its Watergate commentary, which at best was pale and thin. Even NBC, the television tiger here, growled less and had less bite than many newspaper columnists, who themselves did little more than sulk or stand aloof.

NOTES

1. Audience data represents rounding to the nearest million. Actual data for February 1970:

	Households	Total Persons
ABC	4,270,000	7,820,000
CBS	10,470,000	18,760,000
NBC	9,777,000	17,690,000

Source: A. C. Nielsen Company, *National Audience Demographics Reports, Nielsen Television Index* (see Chapt. 1, note 2).

2. Francis Beaumont in *Letter to Ben Johnson* (1640).

3. William Shakespeare, *Hamlet*, act I, scene 4, l. 90.

4. Because networks had essentially the same commentators over the course of the period under study, television commentators were represented by the largest number of cases.

5. Since the procedures for analysis involved reduction into assertions, 5 commentaries would have generated approximately 75 assertions and 100 words for scoring.

6. While Walter Cronkite anchored most of the CBS programs of the period, there were only two occasions in the sample when he presented the commentary.

7. Richard Weiner, *Syndicated Columnists* (New York: Richard Weiner, 1977), p. 98.

8. Baker's and Buchwald's low ranks on the vigorousness scale reflects in great measure their emphasis on humor and irony at the expense of serious discussion. However, there is also the possibility that the measuring instrument used for this study was not sufficiently sensitive to harness the vigorousness inherent in satire even though special techniques were devised to account for this genre. See chapter 5, sections "Nuts and Bolts" and "Expectations Revisited," for coding instructions and for discussion of methodological limitations.

9. White House memorandum from H. R. Haldeman to J. S Magruder, February 4, 1970, in William E. Porter, *Assault on the Media: The Nixon Years* (Ann Arbor: University of Michigan Press, 1976), pp. 266-277.

10. The words presented here as examples reflect high values in the dimensions cited; however, they may at the same time reflect values in the other two dimensions. For examples of words that reflect value in only the one dimension cited but are neutral in the other two dimensions, see chapter 8, subsections "Uninhibited?" "Robust?" and "Debate."

11. Sandy Grady, "Eric the Oracle Bows out with a Scowl," *Philadelphia Evening Bulletin*, November 17, 1977, p. 64C.

12. Ibid.

10

EXECUTIVE SUITE

My special problem is that the truer I speak the less I am believed. And the statement I make (often) which is believed least is that I felt no pressure during those years.

A network news president
writing of the Nixon period.[1]

What is the mind-set of the well-placed media executive? If his business is broadcasting, and if he's someone under the level of top-top brass, he is more than likely an obliging type with eyes darting hither and yon, searching the boss and other such heavies for signs of approval, disapproval, direction, caution, or support. He has grown comfortable with government and hobnobs with steadfast amiability as he goes about the business of being cozy and regulated. Slow to anger, he meets his government with tolerance and acceptance, rarely with suspicion, usually with compliance. But when that government lights his fuse, as it sometimes does, when it musters its troops to cross the line he has divined, he gets hopping mad. Frightened, too. He may rant and rave, spit and sputter, curse, denounce, and resolve. But when all is said and done, he usually says what has to be said and does what has to be done. Or so the data suggest.

A chronology of 359 governmentally initiated media-related events spanning the Nixon administration was submitted to a blue ribbon panel of men who were media executives during the Nixon years. The panel was responsible for rating each event in the chronology along a nine-point scale on which "0" represented perception that the event was free of any direct or indirect anti-media effort emanating from the White House, and where "1" through "8" represented perception that the event represented some degree of an effort — directly or indirectly emanating from the Nixon White House — to discredit, harass, intimidate, manipulate, or otherwise influence the news media.[2]

PROFILES OF HIGH PLACES

One kind of information generated from these ratings was an attitude profile of the executives on the panel. How people perceive their world is often a reflection of themselves. So it was assumed with these ratings, in which an executive's attitude about government initiatives was taken as a measure of his own orientation. But while it may hold a special fascination to peek furtively at the psyches of movers and shakers, several caveats are in order here. First, the ratings as recorded by the executives represented their perceptions of recalled events, events that had occurred four or more years earlier. It was assumed that these retrospective perceptions represented reliable measures of executives' attitudes at the time of the actual experience. But in fact these latter-day perceptions might have been influenced by subsequent events — writings, legal testimony, criminal convictions, the presidential resignation — that could color whatever the earlier (now irretrievable) perceptions may have been.

Second, only 19 executives participated in the study. While that number may have been sufficient for meaningful analysis of the 359 events potentially constituting the anti-media assault, it was possibly too small for dependable analysis of executive trends. (But then again, how many network news presidents could one have in a study of network news presidents?) Additionally, since only highly visible executives had been solicited in the first instance, and since those participating had necessarily volunteered their services along with approximately two hours of their time, it is possible that the participants shared a personality bias that could suggest alternative explanations for any inferences able to be drawn from these data. Nevertheless, within the context of the caveats described, let us move forward to the fascination of furtive peeks.

To enable analysis from different perspectives, the executives were assigned to one or more relevant subgroups:[3] newspaper vs. broadcast, network vs. nonnetwork, and "top-top brass." This last category, further subdivided into newspaper and broadcast, included executives with the highest level of operating responsibility: board chairmen, publishers, corporate presidents, and general managers of broadcasting stations. These executives were responsible for all facets of the operation, not just news. They were also directly responsible for the financial health of the whole organization. A president of the network news division would not be regarded as top-top brass; a president of the network would be so regarded. By grouping the executives in this way, comparative analysis was made possible. How did newspaper executives differ in their perceptions from broadcast executives? Were network executives significantly different from their nonnetwork counterparts? And how did the top-top brass differ from the junior command?

Awarding a "0" to an event indicated the executive's perception that the event was okay, business as usual, not an anti-media effort. It was assumed that the more "okay" events an executive perceived, the more tolerant he was of government behavior. And if he were to perceive whatever affronts there were as only mild instead of strong, his tolerance would be all the more convincing. Thus the mean score of an executive's total ratings (which was in great measure influenced by the proportion of zeros awarded) was considered a measure of his tolerance index. But once the executive's fuse was lit, once he deemed an event to be anti-media, the level of his perceptions as to severity was taken as an indication of his anger. An angry executive would presumably view most anti-media events as strong or very strong; one who was less angry would award so severe a rating more sparingly. Thus, the mean of the anti-media ratings ("1" through "8"), where the zeros were removed from the computations, was considered a measure of the anger index. Taken together, the tolerance and anger measures would suggest the anxiety level: high tolerance/low anger, suggestive of low anxiety; low tolerance/ high anger, suggestive of high anxiety.

The data showed that broadcast executives as a group were more tolerant of government media efforts than newspaper executives and that, of all subgroups, network broadcasters were the most tolerant. Broadcasters viewed more than 33 percent of the government's initiatives as acceptable, okay, business as usual; newspaper executives considered only 12 percent of the initiatives to be accept-able behavior by government. Network broadcasters, who awarded zeros to nearly 38 percent of the events, showed themselves slightly more permissive than their nonnetwork counterparts, who passed off 31 percent as acceptable. One could infer that newspaper execu-tives, used to a tradition of laissez-faire under government, tended to perceive anti-media intent in the slightest government effort. Broadcasters, however, with a tradition of government involvement in their affairs, tended to view government efforts with a much more lenient eye.

It is as if broadcasters, by virtue of their history of licensing and their constant negotiation with government, had grown inured to mild or moderate government interference. However, according to the anger index, once they recognized an event as having anti-media intent, broadcasters generally, and network broadcast executives in particular – normally the most tolerant group – seemed consistently to feel the most anger. Indeed, one network broadcaster who rated nearly 44 percent of the events with a "0" awarded a rating of "8" to an equal number of events. Thus this executive, with a high level of tolerance for government assault, was slow to anger. But once he did, he viewed most government efforts as calamitous. Two other broadcast executives showed similar orientations.

The top-top brass executives represented a unique subgroup. Awarding the least number of zeros, both newspaper and broad-cast top-top brass executives were very intolerant of the govern-ment relationship. In fact, with the lowest tolerance index and with a strong anger index, they showed themselves to have perceived most White House efforts with high levels of anxiety. One could infer that, as top operating officers, they were in a position to be most sensitive to attacks on their enterprises. An effort that might seem acceptable and very ordinary to another executive could easily have been identified by members of this group as an oblique effort to intimidate or manipulate. What's more, many government initiatives were made directly to this group. Threats, propositions, and com-plaints were lodged directly in the chief executive's ear. He was phoned, invited to meetings, and subpoenaed. No wonder his anxiety reached this fever pitch. Of these chief executives, top-top brass broadcasters seemed the most anxious, and the most consistently so. Of all groups they perceived more efforts as anti-media, awarded a higher proportion of "strong" and "very strong" ratings, had the lowest tolerance index, and had the lowest variability among their ratings.

OLD QUESTIONS OF WHO AND HOW MUCH

But the moral question in all this, one that has generated seemingly endless apologias and debate, focuses on the independence of news decisions from corporate control. To what extent were television news programs influenced by anxious executives at the pinnacle of the corporate structure? Or, to state it otherwise, to what extent did top-top brass broadcast executives call the shots in the newsroom?

Broadcast executives at all levels have been adamant in defending newsroom independence. Decision making, they say, is the product of news personnel enjoying editorial autonomy well insulated from outside pressure of any type. In his book *As It Happened*,[4] CBS board chairman William S. Paley vehemently denied charges that he had ordered cuts in the second part of a two-part report on Watergate that was scheduled for airing on the evening news. Whether or not the cuts were made in response to Charles Colson's phone calls to Paley and to CBS Corporate President Frank Stanton, and whether or not the cuts were ordered from the top, bottom, or middle — the record as it happened, stands: Part I of a broadcast embarrassing to the administration is aired; the administration complains to the ranking brass; part II of a potentially embarrassing broadcast is defused, despiced, and cut down to size. To document his distance from this and other suspect news decisions,[5] Paley reprinted a letter by then President of CBS News Richard S. Salant, who explained that in all his years as president of the news division he had not experienced any improper or undue interference from the chairman.

Other such declarations of independence are not uncommon. One network executive who had been president of a news division during the Nixon administration wrote at great length to this researcher to describe his experiences at that time:

> My special problem is that the truer I speak the less I am believed. And the statement I make (often) which is believed least is that I felt no pressure during those years.

During all that time, I got two telephone calls, both from Herb Klein.
. . . The first time I was angry until one of my colleagues (later my
successor) reminded me that Klein was being paid to call me and I
was being paid not to do anything about it. (And the following Saturday morning, Herb called me, woke me, early, to make amends by
telling me about something someone . . . had said, which he did like.
Apparently he felt awkward about it.) In the second instance, he
demanded a retraction. I asked for a transcript, read it carefully, got
back to Klein ten days or two weeks later and told him I was sorry I
could not oblige.

As for Colson, I never met him. As for Ziegler, I met him at Washington
press functions, duty appearances for both of us, but he never called
me about anything. As for threats to television in its other ramifications, licenses, the anti-trust action, and all the rest, I knew they
existed, mostly from what I read in newspapers and some from talk
with . . . executives outside the News Division, but no one ever suggested to me that my Division, in its interpreting, reporting or any
other activity, in any way take cognizance of these matters, by doing
something, by failing to do something, or even by doing even more than
we should otherwise have done just to show those guys.

It has been printed that Colson visited the Presidents of the three networks individually making what were taken to be veiled threats, but
. . . who was then the President of . . . made no suggestion to me as
to what any of the News programs should do, omit, or include, and in
fact did not tell me about his meeting with Colson until some time
later. This despite our close relations and long personal friendship. . . .

We did all feel, and I more than most, that Nixon was commanding
the air more than we liked. Some angry voices were raised, within our
councils, to suggest that his "requests" for air be turned down. It was
considered impolitic to do so. Because, for one thing, we had never
turned down Lyndon Johnson, who was just as insensitive to any needs
but his own, although the sense of a well-considered plan behind it all
was not as great. But this impatience with the Presidency commanding
the broadcast schedule – the sales people because it cost revenue, the
news people because Presidents oughtn't to do that, or be allowed to
– goes back to the Kennedy years and has nothing to do with what
the President said or which President it was. . . .

Most of the incidents in your sample list have to do with pressure on
broadcasting as a commercial undertaking and the implication is that
this pressure was translated into news, to reduce what was being perceived as its negative impact. And I have read enough books about
those days to conclude that all this was true. But I was never importuned

to change anything we were doing, nor did I ever make such a suggestion directly or indirectly to anyone for whose work I was responsible.

So my answer to your question, "Do White House efforts to manipulate the news media have a chilling effect on the quality of interpretive
journalism?" is no. But I am speaking only from my own experience,
and it is limited experience, sheltered by . . . and perhaps some others.[6]

Recall earlier a reference to television's breaking point[7] — that
critical level of the White House anti-media assault that was sure to
trigger a slump in television vigorousness. Now vigorousness in television commentary had always been a sometimes thing — sometimes
uninhibited, wide-open, and robust; sometimes passive, trivial, and
weak.[8] Even in the face of White House displeasure or impatience.
But let broadcast executives perceive White House fury and what
vigorousness there was died of chills and fever. Four times during
the Nixon period, broadcast executives perceived the anti-media
assault to be critical. In every instaance there was a corresponding
drop in television vigorousness across all subject matter categories.

But the story was quite different with the top-top brass broadcast executives. (With only three broadcast chief executives in our
sample, we tread here precariously and caution is advised.) With
top-top brass broadcasters there was not the same "critical level"
relationship between perceptions of government assault and television's timidity. Their anxiety index so high, the top-top brass
perceived 9 of the 23 quarters as reaching the critical level. Examination of these quarters did not reveal the swift point-to-point relationship between executive anxiety and television timidity that was
so much in evidence with lower-level broadcast executives. Here at
the top, perceptions of White House rage were out of harmony with
the actual ups and downs of the news product — unlike the situation with lower-level executives, where perceptions of White House
rage found immediate translation into change-of-pace, watered-down
commentary. Thus, as broadcast executives have consistently
claimed, there may indeed have been some insulation between
top-top brass and decision making in the newsroom.

But on standing back to take a broader view, a negative cause-
and-effect relationship between perceptions of White House fury
and television timidity was apparent at both levels of executives —
even if top-top brass was somewhat farther removed.[9] For correlation analysis, which deals in trends and patterns, revealed negative

correlations between measures of television vigorousness and the anti-media perceptions of both top-top brass and lower-level executives.[10] But while the perceptions of lower-level broadcast executives (president of the news division) were very significantly related to television timidity, the perceptions of the chief operating officers (corporate president) were slightly less so. Thus the corporate president appeared to have less affect on the news product than did the president of the news division. But to what extent the attitudes of the corporate president influenced the attitudes of the news division president — socialization mechanisms being what they are[11] — is for another study to research.

NOTES

1. Excerpt from a letter received by this researcher from a network executive who had been president of his network's news division during the Nixon period. This executive participated in this present study as a member of the panel rating the events of the chronology. To preserve his anonymity, the date of the letter is not provided.

2. See chapter 5, section "The Survey/WHAMA," for a more complete description of the executive rating procedure.

3. A total of 19 media executives participated in the study. The numbers of executives included in the various subgroups are newspaper, 4; broadcast, 15; nonnetwork broadcast, 10; network broadcast, 5; top-top brass newspaper and broadcast, 5; top-top brass newspaper, 2; top-top brass broadcast, 3.

4. William S. Paley, *As It Happened* (New York: Doubleday, 1979).

5. Cessation of "instant analysis" (analysis of a presidential speech immediately after its delivery) was announced by Paley on June 6, 1973, after the White House complained about a critical review of a key Nixon speech. This type of analysis by news commentators had been the target of one of Vice-President Agnew's earlier anti-media speeches.

6. See note 1. Ellipses (. . .) were added by this researcher to indicate removal of parts that would serve to identify the executive or that were not relevant here.

7. See chapter 1, introductory section; and for a discussion of critical levels in the White House anti-media assault (WHAMA), see chapter 6, section "Charting Storms of State."

8. See chapter 7, section "Index of Vigorousness."

9. For a caveat explaining recognized limitations of correlation analysis for assertions of causality, see chapter 8, note 3.

10. Broadcast executives' perceptions vs. television vigorousness: Pearson $r = -.47$, $p = .01$; top-top brass broadcast executives' perceptions vs. television vigorousness: Pearson $r = -.44$, $p = .02$.

11. Many studies have dealt with socialization of reporters and the attitudes of journalists as a determinant of news coverage. Of these, the most valuable are Warren Breed, "Social Control in the News Room," *Social Forces* 33 (May 1955): 326-335, a classic study of how newspaper journalists become aware of organizational policy; Lee Sigelman, "Reporting the News: An Organizational Analysis," *American Journal of Sociology* 79 (July 1973): 132-135, an analysis of how two daily newspapers in the same city came to consistently slant their news similarly, thus suggesting the existence of covert and indirect controls. Also, Ruth C. Flegel and Steven H. Chaffee, "Influence of Editors, Readers, and Personal Opinions on Reporters," *Journalism Quarterly* 48 (Winter 1971): 645-651; Robert G . Pekurny and Leonard D. Bart, " 'Sticks and Bones': A Survey of Network Affiliate Decision-making," *Journal of Broadcasting* 19 (Fall 1975): 427-437; and Ronald H. Wagenberg and Walter C. Soderlund, "The Influence of Chain-Ownership on Editorial Comment in Canada," *Journalism Quarterly* 52 (Spring 1975): 93-98.

IMPLICATIONS

11

PAST, PRESENT, AND HOLDING

Just so far as, at any point, the citizens who are to decide an issue are
denied acquaintance with information or opinion or doubt or disbelief
or criticism which is relevant to that issue, just so far the result must
be ill-considered, ill-balanced planning for the general good.

> Alexander Meiklejohn
> *Free Speech and its Relation to Self-Government*[1]

The Nixon anti-media assault was of such intensity that it was
successful to a significant extent in stifling criticism of the president
in television news commentary. To that extent the people of this
republic were ill-advised. And to that extent the political process
— including the presidential election of 1972 — was affected, perhaps
to have altered the course of history.

When a people committed to self-government is deprived of the
information necessary to decide issues, both the political system
and the people become diminished. In the United States the First
Amendment to the Constitution, by guaranteeing freedom of speech
and of press, was enacted as protection against that kind of insult
to the thinking process of the community. But while the amendment
articulates the guarantee, actual protection is more elusive. For a
people committed to a democratic system, constant evaluation and
appraisal of the systems at work are the least that is required. And
if, in the course of their affairs, the people suddenly and painfully
recognize that full flow of information and ideas is no more than
delusion, that the forces of the society they created and of the

government to which they subscribe are combining to deny them their basic decision-making tools, it is incumbent on the people to demand correction.

The case study reported here was a response to the democratic mandate for continuing evaluation and appraisal. It sought to examine the quality of "information or opinion or doubt or disbelief or criticism"[2] that the press provided at a particular time in our nation's history. Focusing on the Nixon administration, the study compared political commentary from television and newspapers, the dominant media of the American press, and assessed the ability of those media to function with integrity in the face of intense pressures to compromise.

PRESSURES ON THE PRESS

Pressures on the press are varied and often insidious. They range from the direct to the tangential, from the obviously overt to the veiled and subtle, and can emanate from political, social, or economic experience. Using one scholar's model of institutional process analysis, we see that pressures can involve authorities, patrons, management, auxiliaries, colleagues, competitors, experts, organizations, and publics.[3] More specifically, they can involve the government, capital investors, advertisers, publishers, reporters, support services, labor unions, critics, consumers, public interest groups, and, in the case of broadcasting, the affiliates.

Each of these entities has at its disposal many varieties of leverage that it can exercise in a show of power. Governments can arbitrate, regulate, threaten, and withhold information; investors and advertisers can set conditions for the supply of capital and operating funds; publishers can hire and fire, set and supervise policies; the support services can provide or withhold talent, copy, newsprint, or transportation; affiliated broadcasting stations can grant or refuse clearance to network programs; competitors can raid, scoop, set standards, or corner the market; public interest groups can support, boycott, or appeal to the authorities; labor can strike; and consumers can buy papers or not, tune in programs or not, attend to or ignore messages, and buy or not buy advertised products.

Inevitably the struggle between the press and the various interest groups finds its way to the newsroom, where the toll is often exacted in the form of revisions, additions, omissions, or deletions — full or partial — with newsroom copy as currency. The effects that these behaviors may have on the news product are many and varied, including blandness, bias, tokenism, avoidance of controversy, failure to censure government, uncritical dissemination of official doctrine, homogenization of opposing views, excessive balance to the exclusion of debate, and emphasis on spot news to the exclusion of commentary.

Of the many powers, roles, and relationships capable of affecting the news, the case study at hand focused on but one — the federal government-of-the-day. Using the Nixon administration as the time frame, the study identified and quantified the anti-media assault perceived by the press to have emanated from the White House, and it assessed the relationship of that perceived assault to the vigorousness of the period's newspaper and television commentary.

TIMID AND INTIMIDATED

Specifically the study was designed to identify and measure two hypothesized parameters of the press-government relationship during the Nixon administration: timidity and intimidation. In the first instance it sought to demonstrate television's timidity vis-à-vis newspapers in political commentary, particularly in the area of government criticism; in the second instance it sought to identify the chilling effect of White House pressure on the vigorousness of television political commentary. Analysis in both areas bore fruit; the data more than amply supported the existence of both television timidity and the chilling effect.

Television's timidity vis-a-vis newspapers was evident across all subject matter categories generally, and in major issues particularly. Inhibition, lack of robustness, avoidance of controversy, emphasis on nonissues, and exceptional balance and moderation were typical of the television style. Television was consistently more bland than newspapers in all discussions on government, but in discussion of the president, its blandness and blunted vigorousness were especially in evidence.

Further analysis revealed that White House pressures to manipulate the press succeeded handily, at least as far as television was concerned. As the White House anti-media assault became more severe, television became significantly less vigorous than newspapers in commentary regarding the White House. In fact, while television was reacting to White House pummeling with ever increasing timidity in commentary on White House affairs, newspapers were reacting to that same pummeling with ever increasing vigorousness in columns on the White House.

These findings were interpreted as evidence of the chilling effect in network television news programs – a chilling effect that during the Nixon years found its mark in television commentary pertaining to the Nixon administration and that was the direct result of administration efforts to discredit, harass, intimidate, or otherwise manipulate the press. Fluctuating in negative concert with the ups and downs of administration pressure, it came in the shape of diminished vigorousness in discussion of presidential and administration affairs, and was manifested by avoidance of Watergate as a topic of discussion, reluctance to speak in judgment of the president, emphasis on weak rather than robust language, and excessive blandness, inhibition, and qualification. All this was accompanied by characteristics of the "reverse chilling effect" in which fighting words were offered for nonissues and wherever else controversy was not a factor.

The chilling effect is a phenomenon that heretofore has been feared or suspected but never documented, much less measured; but by procedures developed for this study, it was established as an observable and measurable experience. While timidity in its various forms was identified in many categories of television commentary during this period, only one category – commentary pertaining to the Nixon administration – displayed evidence of the chilling effect. Journalistic timidity in and of itself does not demonstrate evidence of the chilling effect. But when that timidity operates in concert with muscle exerted by an outside influence, it becomes the product of intimidation. In such cases the existence of a chilling effect is clearly demonstrated.

IN PRAISE OF A FESTERING SORE

The Nixon administration's anti-media assault was presumably engineered to achieve, at the most, newspaper and television praise for administration policies and, at the very least, elimination of

newspaper and television censure of those policies. What the administration was able to gain by its efforts was a dampening of the
censure leveled by television.

Censure is a multidimensional posture grounded primarily in
negativism. It involves boldness, judgment, and expression that is
candid and sharply disapproving. To be sure, television succumbed
to administration pressure by touting commentary that was significantly less than bold, candid, and sharp. But when it came to negativism, television's dose was steady and persistent. Even in the
face of television's overall timidity in comment on the White House,
the negativism so resented by the administration was unyielding,
significantly exceeding the negativism of newspaper columnists.
We have here the stuff of censure, but not quite. For while television registered its independence by extraordinary negativism in
comment on the administration, it faltered on this crucial topic
by being less robust, less wide-open, and more inhibited than its
newspaper counterparts.

Without doubt, television's persistent negativism that refused
to go away was a festering sore to the administration. In 1970
White House aide H. R. Haldeman issued a memorandum singling
out NBC for "their almost totally negative approach to everything
the Administration does."[4] While other dimensions of television
commentary could apparently be manipulated, the negativism
appeared to have been indomitable. It was possibly television's
uncompromising resolve in this dimension that, by sparking White
House fire, contributed to the tenacity and unrelenting hostility
of Nixon's assault on the press generally.

A WHAMA index of 80 was identified as television's breaking
point.[5] When the White House anti-media assault measured 80 or
above on the WHAMA index, television vigorousness everywhere
consistently slumped below that of newspapers. Thus a raging White
House venting unbridled fury and thunder could predictably cause
a chilling effect in television commentary. But, according to the
data, a simply displeased or resentful White House was not so predictable in its ability to intimidate television. Even in the face
of persistent White House assault, television commentary would
come through with ups as well as downs, peppering its predictable
timidity in some quarters with fight and spirit in some other.[6] And
even though critical levels in the anti-media assault had an immediate chilling effect on the vigorousness of television commentary,

in every instance television's vigorousness rose shortly thereafter, perhaps to overtake that of newspapers. It was as if, in response to the assailant's blow, the victim fell, sometimes staggered and reeled for a short time thereafter, but always returned to his feet in an effort to trade blows again.

This recuperative power on the part of television, this stubborn refusal to abdicate the responsibilities with which it was entrusted — this professionalism, if you will — is what makes the fact of television's intimidation so serious. Television as it was staffed and organized during the Nixon administration had the potential of producing vigorous commentary across the board, but instead, during this crucial period, timidity and intimidation were the rule more often than not. Unlike newspapers, television is a licensed medium subject to regulatory policy determined in part by the White House. By this mechanism television, unlike newspapers, is made vulnerable to White House leverage. And when there came a time in our nation's history that the White House, with its enormous power over appointment, appropriation, legislation, and other governmental machinery, overreached the bounds of responsible authority and preyed on television's vulnerability, the chilling effect was all but inevitable.

AT ISSUE

In general this study addressed the relationship of First Amendment theory to interpretive journalism. The specific problem at issue was the ability of the government, because of the structure of broadcast regulatory policy, to affect television interpretive journalism in ways that potentially chill both critical appraisal of government and controversiality in coverage of public issues. Such a problem would not be experienced in the same way by print journalism, which is free of regulatory control.

As it relates to the press, the First Amendment is the keystone to two distinct traditions of public policy: the journalism tradition for the printed press and the regulation tradition for the broadcasting press. The former speaks to a laissez-faire regime and editorial autonomy; the latter speaks to government oversight and editorial autonomy that is couched in affirmative requirements. The journalism tradition expects that freedom from government oversight will inspire the press to responsible performance, whatever that may be; the regulation tradition defines "responsible performance" and, by government edict reinforced by government sanctions, requires it. Like its newspaper counterpart, the television press is charged by the democratic system with the same responsibilities for "uninhibited, robust, and wide-open" debate on public issues. But through legislative and judicial decision, television has been denied the level of economic and editorial independence traditionally accorded newspapers.

Over the years an elaborate structure of laws and FCC rules and regulations has evolved, stretching from engineering concerns to certain aspects of program content.[7] The pervasiveness of the government's regulation of broadcasting affairs, together with its fines and other sanctions, the massive paperwork requirements, and, not the least threatening, the potential for license denial, subjects the broadcaster to incalculable burden. That burden is sweetened considerably, of course, by the dangling carrot that often translates into enormous profits. Possessive of the profits that they are determined to keep at any cost, broadcasters learn to withstand, even ignore, the battering that their condition invites. But in the process they become vulnerable, and their very integrity is threatened.

NEW DIRECTIONS

Logic demands a new broadcast policy orientation. The principles traditionally underlying the regulation tradition must be re-evaluated for their current relevance, their tendency to compromise constitutional ideals, and their effects in practice. Does the regulation tradition, as it now stands, serve the democratic ideal? Does it invest broadcasting with a vulnerability that is lethal to its integrity as a segment of the press? By inviting government oversight of program content, does the regulation tradition in fact foster governmental management of information? Does it not encourage broadcasters to keep paramount the administration's interest rather than the enlightened national interest? And by diluting broadcasters' participation in the dynamics of a competitive market, does it not make government, rather than the public, the ultimate consumer, from the broadcasters' perspective?

That a free and vigorous press is basic to a free society is accepted as given. That a primary function of the press in a republic is surveillance and criticism of government is also accepted as given. Thus there is a fundamental flaw in our present broadcast public policy, by which the government that is to be surveyed and criticized by the television press (the dominant medium for news dissemination in this country) is at one and the same time the benefactor and the judge of that press.

In his classic analysis, *The Structure of Scientific Revolutions*,[8] Thomas S. Kuhn describes the experience of functioning under "paradigms," a term which summarizes traditions of attitudes, policy and behavior viewed by a given community as framework for present and ongoing practice. Kuhn theorizes that, at any time, when a particular paradigm ceases to be effective for the particular community — when a sense of malfunction becomes evident, when problems mount beyond reason, when anomalies are recognized and cannot be controlled despite repeated efforts — a crisis ensues, and the community becomes ripe for a "scientific revolution." At such time, he continues, debate over fundamentals occurs; prior "facts" are reevaluated; new theories are offered in competition with the older ones; and eventually the community rejects the once time-honored paradigm in favor of another that, in whole or in part, is incompatible with the older tradition. When the older paradigm is replaced by the new paradigm, now the basis for further conceptualization and standards, a scientific revolution is said to have occurred, and the community proceeds with a transformation in perspectives and a shift in professional commitments.[9]

Parallels are easily drawn between Kuhn's theoretical description and the chain of events surrounding television. In a political system dependent on the free dissemination of ideas, one cannot ignore the findings of this present study, which levy charges of "timid" and "intimidated" against our dominant medium of news and public affairs information. The sense of danger and malfunction that these findings suggest, coupled with the fact that the assumptions of television public policy have undergone little substantial change since the time of the study, leaves no doubt that television interpretive journalism functions in a crisis situation in the sense described by Kuhn. The regulation tradition as it currently exists has compromised television interpretive journalism (and, perhaps, broadcast journalism generally) by investing it with a serious and crippling vulnerability. Perhaps it is time to recognize that a "scientific revolution" is necessary and probably, to follow Kuhn's reasoning, inevitable.

To the extent that broadcasting policy continues to support competing traditions of First Amendment interpretation, the problem will continue and the threat to our republic will remain. To the extent that revised broadcasting policy mitigates or eliminates the clash points[10] by bringing the regulation tradition closer to the journalism tradition, so will television interpretive journalism be fortified for service to our society in ways supportive of the First Amendment ideal.

Pursuant to this reasoning, several state actions are worthy of note. In 1959, in the matter of *Farmers Educational Union* v. *WDAY*,[11] the Supreme Court struck at the public-trustee principle by relieving the licensee of responsibility for defamatory statements by political candidates replying under the equal opportunity provisions of section 315 of the Communications Act. In that same year Congress amended section 315 to exempt certain kinds of bona fide news programs from its otherwise strict political broadcasting requirements.[12] In 1967, when drafting its Personal Attack Rules, the FCC exempted commentary or analysis that was contained in news programs from Fairness Doctrine obligations.[13] In 1975, in the "Aspen Institute" ruling, the FCC expanded its interpretation of political broadcasting exemptions to permit broadcast of press conferences by incumbent officeholders and debates that did not include all candidates.[14] In 1976, in the matter of the "Pensions Program,"[15] the Supreme Court let stand an Appeals Court verdict that in effect removed investigative journalism from the reach of the Fairness Doctrine. In 1981 the Supreme Court opted for competitive enterprise when it upheld an FCC finding that market forces, not government, should determine what formats are used in radio programs.[16] And in 1982 a District Court held that the Communication Act's ban on editorializing by public broadcasting stations was unconstitutional.[17] By these actions Congress, the courts, and the FCC were protecting those crucial aspects of information flow that seemed particularly threatened by the interference of government regulation.

But piecemeal legislation and administrative or case law are necessarily limited to particular issues, even though in some instances they may have broader implications. If broadcasting is to play the important role our political system requires of it and that the times and modern technology have delegated to it, comprehensive congressional reappraisal of the whole regulation paradigm is imperative. Recognizing that the status quo contributes to compromise in the quality of "information or opinion or doubt or disbelief or criticism"[18] that is disseminated to the public, Congress must consider whether assumptions made half a century ago regarding broadcast policy are valid in today's communications/information environment.

Over the years Congress has regularly considered broadcast policy in piecemeal fashion by dealing with limited areas such as license renewal, public broadcasting, television violence, and monopolies, or with such specific regulations as the Fairness Doctrine and the equal opportunity provisions of political broadcasting. Rarely, since 1934, has it addressed itself to the fundamental assumptions underlying the structure of broadcast policy generally.

In 1978 Congress appeared ready to embark on that much-needed review. Draft legislation that provided for rewriting of the Communications Act was submitted to Congress by the House and the Senate subcommittees on communications. Together the bills spoke to a full-scale audit of radio, television, and nonbroadcast policy; and by upholding the banners of maximum deregulation, maximum competition, and minimum control, they challenged the integrity of the public trustee principle and other fundamental concepts of broadcast policy.[19] The debate on the issues was tangled and complex as vested and public interests clashed. But in time and with electoral sweeps that shifted personnel on Capitol Hill and in the Oval Office, the proposed omnibus rewrites were reworked, diluted, and all but laid to rest.

In 1981 the climate again appeared charged with reform as both the FCC and Congress, pushed to some degree by the courts, placed their bets on natural market forces and drastically reduced regulation of radio.[20] No longer was format an appropriate consideration in radio licensing. No longer was radio held to specific guidelines for amount of news and public affairs programming. Formal ascertainment requirements, program logging requirements, and guidelines for commercial time were also eliminated. What remained for radio were technical regulations, political broadcasting requirements, the Fairness Doctrine, generalized obligations for programming in the public interest, and periodic license renewals by traditional procedures on traditional grounds — though in a separate action the term of the radio license, which heretofore had been limited to three years, was extended to seven years. (At this time the term of license for television was extended to five years.)

Similar efforts toward broad-scale deregulation were promised "eventually" for television. Debate raged and the buck was passed as calls for sweeping reform came from high places. In 1981 the FCC formally asked Congress to abolish the Fairness Doctrine and political broadcasting requirements; and Congress, that same year, gave the green light to the FCC to consider the establishment of a lottery system for initial licensing.[21] But to date there has been little substantial change in television's regulatory environment. Thus, in television the old burdens essentially remain; and television's vulnerability to government manipulation is alive and as threatening as ever.

Enlightened self-interest requires dramatic restructuring of the regulatory policy governing television. The urgency for such restructuring does not suggest superficial measures but, rather, sweeping overhaul of both economic and First Amendment orientations. With the technological explosion in telecommunications, the doctrine of scarce resources is less relevant; it follows, therefore, that the public trustee principle is of reduced importance. Refinements in computers, satellites, cable, low-power TV, expanded use of the spectrum, interactive systems, electronic field production, home video recording, teletext, and facsimile have greatly increased the potential for more and diversified information while enhancing the public's opportunity for greater access to the media. While the multiplication of media systems in itself does not guarantee increased information flow, the potential for such is diminished to the extent that government regulatory controls prevail.

Our present system of managing television by administrative controls should be relaxed in favor of mechanisms encouraging market dynamics. Though the marketplace in media systems is increasingly characterized by concentration of ownership, distribution networks, and other economic arrangements viewed as hostile to free expression, the government's management of television in ways that potentially impinge on programming — however limited or oblique — has proved more harmful than protective. The laissez-faire interpretation of the First Amendment, as applied to the printed press, is grounded in the economics of competition, supply and demand, and other forces of a free market. However imperfect, this formula alone holds out the promise for integrity in television news programming. As Justice Douglas observed:

> What kind of First Amendment would best serve our needs as we approach the 21st century may be an open question. But the old fashioned First Amendment that we have is the Court's only guideline; and one hard and fast principle has served us through days of calm and eras of strife and I would abide by it until a new First Amendment is adopted. That means, as I view it, that TV and radio, as well as the more conventional methods for disseminating news, are all included in the concept of "press" as used in the First Amendment and therefore are entitled to live under the laissez faire regime which the First Amendment sanctions.[22]

Old assumptions in broadcast press policy that threaten the independence of news and public affairs programming must be unceremoniously discarded, and options that serve to insulate programming from government pressures must be vigorously sought. Congress at the very least must strengthen the "no censorship" parameter of present broadcast policy. With the force of legislative decree, it must guarantee for broadcasting the level of editorial autonomy that is guaranteed the printed press under the First Amendment. And stipulations restraining present or future governments from imposing restrictions, prescriptions, or requirements concerning program content must be explicit and undeniable. By these guarantees, program diversity, balance, and responsiveness to the public interest would no longer be considered the proper focus of government concern. News and public affairs program content — amount, type, or quality — would be eliminated as a criterion for licensing or for choosing between competing applicants. Fairness and political broadcasting requirements would be abandoned. And proscriptions against obscenity, indecency, fraud, deception, and other improprieties would properly be left to statutory or case law.

If Congress fails to provide this brand of free speech for the electronic press, it will be incumbent on the courts to so do by applying the First Amndment equally and in all its ramifications.

In summary, we defer to former acting FCC Chairman Robert E. Lee, who noted that our present licensing system "has evolved into a monster" that will have untoward effects "unless alternate procedures are devised."[23] The chilling effect that was detected and analyzed in this study was the practical result of television's intimidation by the White House during the Nixon presidency. It reflects abuse of presidential power that is potentially as viable today as it was in the Nixon era. For those same regulatory mechanisms that earlier fostered television's vulnerability to an aggressive White House are no less threatening today. That presidents seek to stifle criticism of their policies is inevitable. That they may succeed is dangerous.

NOTES

1. Alexander Meiklejohn, *Free Speech and Its Relation to Self-Government* (New York: Harper, 1948), p. 26.
2. Ibid.
3. George Gerbner, "Cultural Indicators: The Third Voice," in George Gerbner, Larry P. Gross and William H. Melody, eds., *Communications Technology and Social Policy* (New York: John Wiley, 1973), pp. 555-573, at 559-562.
4. See chapter 9, note 9.
5. See chapter 1, introductory comments; chapter 10, section "Old Questions of Who and How Much."
6. According to the WHAMA index, there was not a quarter when the White House failed to display some level of anti-media hostility. In spite of this continuing hostility, television commentary showed an index of vigorousness that surpassed that of newspaper columns in 9 of the 23 quarters. See Table 7.1.
7. The FCC does not routinely review program content. It will review program content in charges involving the Fairness Doctrine, section 315, and other programming violations, and in evidentiary and comparative hearings if programming has been designated an issue. However, it is empowered to review content as necessary.
8. Thomas S. Kuhn, *The Structure of Scientific Revolutions* (Chicago: University of Chicago Press, 1962).
9. An example of a "scientific revolution" in the Kuhn sense would be the replacement of the Ptolemaic tradition of astronomy (the earth is the center of the universe) with the Copernican tradition (the sun is the center of a system of planets, of which earth is one). Modern astronomy functions within the Copernican tradition.
10. For a discussion of "clash points," see chapter 1, section "Journalism Tradition vs. Regulation Tradition."
11. *Farmers Educational and Cooperative Union of America* v. *WDAY*, 360 U.S. 525 (1959).

12. 47 USCA 315 (a).

13. 47 CFR 73.123; 73.300; 73.598; 73,679.

14. *Aspen Institute*, 55 F.C.C.2d 697 (1975).

15. *National Broadcasting Company* v. *FCC*, 516 F.2d 1101 (D.C. Cir. 1974); cert. denied, 424 U.S. 910 (1976).

16. *FCC* v. *WNCN Listeners Guild*, 49 U.S.L.W. 4306 (March 24, 1981).

17. *League of Women Voters of California* v. *FCC.*, 547 F.Sup. 379 (C.D. Cal. 1982); 103 Sup.Ct. 1249 (1983), cert. granted, appeal pending.

18. Meiklejohn, *Free Speech and Its Relation to Self-Government*, p. 26.

19. For expanded discussion of the proposed legislation of 1979, see Mel Friedman, "A New Communications Act: The Debate Begins," *Columbia Journalism Review*, September/October 1978, pp. 40-43.

20. Effective April 3, 1981. Challenged in the matter of *United Church of Christ* v. *FCC*, no. 81-1032 (D.C. Cir., filed January 14, 1981).

21. The legislative broadcasting provisions — extending terms of existing broadcast licenses and establishing a lottery system for new licenses (to be implemented at FCC discretion) — were tacked onto the budget reconciliation bill, signed into law by President Reagan on August 13, 1981.

22. *Columbia Broadcasting System* v. *Democratic National Committee*, 412 U.S. 94 (1973).

23. "Market Forces Will Tune Radio Broadcasting, FCC Declares," *News Media and the Law*, June-July 1981, p. 41.

12

PRIME TIME FRINGE

The common problem, yours, mine, every one's
Is — not to fancy what were fair in life
Provided it could be, — but, finding first
What may be, then find how to make it fair
Up to our means.

Robert Browning
Men and Women[1]

While adjustments in public policy regarding television are essential if a vigorous press is to be expected, adjustments elsewhere are also of pressing importance. Our habits as media consumers, what we demand of our press, and what we're willing to forgo must of necessity be open to reevaluation. Our institutions give us what we ask of them. If, as a result of apathy, naiveté, misplaced priorities, a sense of impotence, or lack of information, we ask little, we cannot expect to get more.

THE COMMENTARY CONNECTION

In a free society the absence or presence of political commentary in the news media is not to be taken lightly; the people's right to a diversity of ideas, as guaranteed by the First Amendment, rests at the heart of self-government. Essential to both the form and the substance of a healthy republic, the free flow of ideas, vigorous and unfettered, shapes the system even as it preserves its integrity. A safety valve in time of dissension, the bread and butter of the electoral process, the grease of the democratic wheel, ideas are trump, and the opportunity for receiving them is relinquished only at great peril. The front pages of newspapers and the rat-a-tat bombardment of television summaries on news programs survey our world and inform us with pictures, facts, and figures. Information, data, clues are the stuff of ideas. But they are not ideas. Inferences, judgments, opinion, background, making connections are the fruits of information and data, and are what a free people requires of its press in addition to hard news.

Political analysis, as delivered in newspaper columns and commentaries on television news programs, is uniquely able to provide these behind-the-news reflections. When separated from the hard news, political analysis offering the journalist's rendition of what it's all about serves notice that events exist outside of themselves and that they exist in a total environment within the context of a past, a present, and a future. When it is responsible and vigorous, political analysis can focus our attention on the relevant and important; it can promote insight and stimulate perspectives never before considered; it can reinforce old attitudes or encourage new ones; and by jogging initiative, it can provoke decision and even action.

On balance and by and large, the syndicated columnists have proved to be a healthy lot doing their job somewhat as the Constitution meant them to, helped in no small measure by the enlightened editorial ecumenism of most of the country's newspapers. Among the dailies used in this study — *Boston Globe, Chicago Tribune, Los Angeles Times, Louisville Courier-Journal, Miami Herald, Milwaukee Journal, Newsday, New York Times* and *Washington Post* — the prevailing style was to publish a variety of perspectives and formats in a special section called by such titles as "Op-Ed," "Commentary," or "Perspective." These sections provided an editorial brew in which differing biases, ideologies, and passions were vented in varying combinations of editorials, political cartoons, letters from the public, and columns by syndicated journalists and others.

On any given day, a reader of one of these papers might be exposed to a liberal or conservative editorial along with any number of liberal, conservative, or middle-of-the-road columnists. For instance, the *Los Angeles Times*, in addition to several editorials, carried Alsop, Buchwald, and Kilpatrick one day; Buchwald, Evans and Novak, Alsop, and Kilpatrick the next day; and Buckley and Broder or Buchwald, Kilpatrick, and Thimmesch on other days.

Because of this mélange of perspectives, the individual syndicated columnist was free of editorial pressures for balance or conformity that might otherwise have existed. Each was free to vent his biases and persuasions as he saw fit. To paraphrase the poet William Cowper, each was monarch of all he could survey, and his right there was none to dispute.[2]

But the television commentators — alack and alas! Cautious, trivial, timid, and intimidated. Too few and too often absent. The single-commentator-per-program policy (or, indeed, the no-commentator policy) to which the networks have stubbornly clung has ill served the quality of television news — to the detriment of the American people, who more and more are relying on TV as their major source of information and ideas. While the addition of multiple voices to network news programs would be no guarantee of increased vigorousness in political commentary, such a change would have the potential of reducing individual bias and of altering the sameness evident across networks. But more important, an enlarged cast would remove the burden of balance and fairness that the "one and only" commentator apparently feels — or is given to believe — he must bear. Furthermore, a commitment to frequent and specially identified commentary on evening news programs might work to decrease the editorial baggage that, according to some critics, is increasingly creeping into hard news reports.[3]

Regulatory policy holds that broadcasters must be fair in presenting controversial issues of public importance, not necessarily in any one commentary or any one program; but opposing viewpoints must be presented somewhere in the station's total programming over a reasonable period. Newspapers suffer no such regulatory obligation regarding their news content. If, by juggling columns and editorials of varying political persuasions, the op-ed pages of a newspaper reflect balance (and they often do), it is by the grace of a responsible and enlightened editor. But even so, there are times when opposing views go unwritten in newspapers and when imbalance or unfairness is more the case. This is a risk that the Supreme Court has recognized and that, in deference to First Amendment values, it believes society must take. But neither the law nor the courts allow television news directors the luxury of such risk. The government has claimed that adherence to the principles of fairness is the sine qua non of license renewal. And over the years, lapses in fairness have subjected broadcasters to fines, costly hearings, and mild-to-severe snags at license renewal time.

Within this regulatory framework it is easy to understand why a Harry Reasoner or an Eric Sevareid or a David Brinkley could be so meticulously "fair": intricate soft-shoe maneuvers, deft tight-rope walking, flavorless concoctions of watered-down grog — all for the cause of avoiding controversiality, the law, and red faces in the executive suite. From the network point of view, having or not having commentary appears to be an exercise in strategy. The choice is clear: eliminate commentary altogether or limit it to a few well-chosen, statesmanlike types finely tuned to word design and blessed with self-control, the maturity to understand their place on the horns of a dilemma, and the stomach to play the game.

Deemphasis of vigorous political commentary on television news programs is the result of both government and industry policy. Both must share the blame, and neither can be relieved of the responsibility for new orientations if television news programs are to go about the business of doing fully what the press is supposed to do. Give them their head, a longer leash, and more players in the brass section — and the Sevareids and the Brinkleys, and even the Reasoners, might begin looking more and more like the Wickers and the Krafts.

THE PEOPLE, TOO

Not only the government and the industry, but the people too, have a responsibility in shaping their circumstances. They must throw off the shackles of indifference and uncritical allegiance to media trends. Seduction is everywhere in television news: slick production, pretty faces, movement, pace, theater. Visuals that take us to foreign shores, place us at the center of extravagant public gatherings, or allow us to glimpse the private moments of human souls. Serious journalism here, the appearance of serious journalism there, and sometimes the absence of both (the real or the sham) before we've awakened to realize our poverty.

The enormity of television's influence on our lives rejects this brand of listless inattention, for television is the medium that over 64 percent of the people use as their major news source.[4] As a people committed to a free society, we must demand the highest standard of performance from our news media. To this end we must embark on a program of aggressive vigilance whereby we seek reliable and objective information from ongoing surveillance of press performance and, when appropriate, engage the press in confrontation through whatever legal and other means are available. On a regular basis rigorous analysis by independent scientists must assess the quality, quantity, and vigorousness of political information and ideas disseminated by our media. This present study dealt only with newspapers and television, and focused on only one genre of news information (political commentary) and only one outside factor (the White House) that had the potential of causing a chilling effect. Other media and other genres might also be studied, as might other factors with the potential of causing chilled voices. Furthermore, those special factions of our body politic — political, industrial, religious, ethnic, other special interest groups, or even individuals — must assume responsibility for aggressive vigilance on their own behalf. For even at the most personal level, surveillance and, when necessary, confrontation — if based in the logic of science and objectivity — are a service to the whole society.

The public at large, the decision makers in the political arena, and the media themselves would all benefit from this kind of aggressive vigilance. By being alert to the trends and biases in news services, the public would be better able to manage its political decisions. Additionally, with real information as a basis, the focus of the public's considerable leverage would be more precise when expressing outrage or when demanding needed corrections in media performance. By having dependable, credible, and convincing evidence, the courts and the legislature would be better informed on the existing problems in media affairs, and thus could minimize the risk of incorrect policy decisions regarding those media. And last, by being apprised of its own tendencies and of biases of which it may not have been aware, the press would have an opportunity to alter its posture before its integrity was seriously compromised.

Working in concert, the government, the people, and the press share the responsibility for carrying out the mandate of the First Amendment. Building on lessons learned from past experience, we must pool our collective intelligence to protect our future. The goals we seek are difficult; they challenge our discipline, skill, imagination, and resources. But the direction is unmistakable: an independent and vigorous press, both printed and broadcast, that is not vulnerable to government intimidation. In a republic the quality of the press is a common problem, yours, mine, and everyone's. It is of compelling urgency that together we carve an environment for all facets of that press that will be conducive to performance worthy of our highest ideals.

NOTES

1. Robert Browning, "Bishop Blougram's Apology," in *Men and Women* (1855).

2. William Cowper, "Verses Supposed to be Written by Alexander Selkirk" (1782).

3. The author has expanded the methodology described in this book to measure bias in hard news and is currently pursuing research in that area.

4. See chapter 1, note 3.

APPENDIXES

APPENDIX A
CHRONOLOGY OF THE WHITE HOUSE
ANTI-MEDIA ASSAULT
DURING THE NIXON ADMINISTRATION

**January 20, 1969. *Just before Richard Nixon's inauguration as president, FBI agents and members of the Army's 116th Military Intelligence Detachment raided the offices of an underground newspaper, the* Washington Free Press. *There had been concern about plans of activities to disrupt the inauguration.*

*January 20, 1969. *Army intelligence agents posed as TV cameramen during the presidential inauguration activities in Washington.*

**January 20, 1969. *Herbert G. Klein assumed office as director of communications for the executive branch, a new position created for centralized control and coordination of media releases of all executive departments. The new office was to function in addition to that of the traditional press secretary, who spoke only for the president.*

Legend
    *Mild anti-media effort (as perceived by media executives)
    **Moderate anti-media effort (as perceived by media executives)
    ***Strong anti-media effort (as perceived by media executives)
    ****Very strong anti-media effort (as perceived by media executives)

*February 8, 1969. *The FCC announced that it was instituting an inquiry into ownership patterns of the broadcasting industry. The inquiry was to be concerned with licensees having "other large-scale business interests," conglomerates, cross-media ownerships, and multi-media ownerships.*

**March 24, 1969. *In a letter to Senator John Pastore (D., R.I.), President Nixon referred to the senator's criticism of excessive sex and violence in network programming and said he shared the "deep concern and strongly applaud your vigorous criticism of what you regard as the misuses of this great medium."*

*March 26, 1969. *Representative Harley O. Staggers (D., W.Va.), chairman of the House Commerce Committee, proposed a bill that would require broadcasters to retain all used and unused film and tape for six months, in order to support their objectivity in case of a challenge. The bill would also make it a crime to falsify news broadcasts and would make investigative news gathering and reporting that involved violation of the law a threat to license renewal.*

**April 9, 1969. *In a letter to the FCC, Richard W. McLaren, chief of the Antitrust Division of the Justice Department, referred to CATV as "the most promising means of achieving greater competition and diversity" in mass media, and supported a proposal to bar cross-ownership of television stations and CATVs in a market. Also recommended was a ban on newspaper and CATV combinations.*

**April 28, 1969. *It was announced that Richard W. McLaren, chief of the Antitrust Division of the Justice Department, in a letter to the FCC chairman, endorsed proposals under advisement that aimed at curbing network domination of television programming.*

****May 1969. *President Nixon personally authorized the use of wiretaps against 13 members of his own staff and against four* *newsmen. The taps were instituted because of concern over leaks of classified information to the press.*

*July 10, 1969. *The FCC ordered the first competitive hearing for license renewal of a network owned station: KNBC-TV, owned by NBC.*

***September 25, 1969. *Frank Shakespeare, director of the United States Information Agency and close adviser of the president, speaking to the Radio-Television News Directors Association (RTNDA) convention, charged that many broadcast journalists exhibited a disturbingly strong liberal bias.*

***September 29, 1969. *The licenses of WTOP-TV and WTOP-AM and FM, stations owned by the Washington Post Company, were challenged by a Washington group charging that the company's ownership constituted media monopoly in that area and that the newspaper's editorial views were imposed on the station.*

****October 17, 1969. *Jeb Stuart Magruder issued a memorandum to the president's chief of staff, H. R. Haldeman, entitled "The Shot-gun versus the Rifle," in which he listed "21 requests from the President in the last 31 days" for specific retributive action against the media for alleged unfair news coverage. The suggestions were designed to address the media as institutions rather than to engage in short-range attempts "to get to the media" for specific daily remarks. Among the proposals were use of the Department of Justice to investigate media anti-trust violation and to threaten antitrust action, the initiation of an official monitoring system under the auspices of the FCC, the use of the IRS to investigate returns of "various organizations that we are most concerned about," show favoritism within the media, and use of the Republican National Committee for launching major letter-writing efforts.*

**October 31, 1969. *Dean Burch, a principal adviser in Barry Goldwater's 1964 presidential campaign and the former chairman* of the Republican National Committee, was appointed chairman of the FCC.

***October 1969. *The government issued subpoenas to four Chicago newspapers, NBC news, and* Time, Life *and* Newsweek *magazines, demanding that they produce unedited files, photographs, film, and notebooks of reporters who had covered the four days of disturbances in Chicago attributed to the Weatherman faction of the Students for a Democratic Society.*

***November 4, 1969. *Meeting of H. R. Haldeman, John Ehrlichman, Ronald Ziegler, Herbert Klein, and President Nixon to discuss strategy for responding to critical network commentary following the president's television address to the nation on November 3. It was reportedly suggested that the issue be raised in a speech by Vice-President Spiro Agnew.*

****November 5, 1969. *On instructions from the White House, Dean Burch, newly appointed FCC chairman, telephoned heads of networks and asked for transcripts of their commentaries delivered after President Nixon's November 3 Vietnam speech.*

****November 13, 1969. *Vice-President Agnew, in a nationally televised address to a Republican regional conference in Des Moines, Iowa, attacked the television news media, the networks, and the "gaggle of commentators" and "self-appointed analysts" as representing a privileged and detached elite neither responsive nor responsible to the American public they are supposed to serve. He charged bias, willful distortion of the news for profit, and vast, unchecked political power, and he appealed to citizens "to defend themselves" and to assume the role of "reformer" and "crusader" by protesting and demanding a full accounting of the network stewardship of public airwaves.*

***November 14, 1969. *Dean Burch, FCC chairman, said that he did not consider Agnew's speech intimidating, that the* *vice-president's remarks were "thoughtful, provocative and deserve careful consideration by the industry and the public."*

***November 15, 1969. *Clark R. Mollenhoff, special counsel to the president, said that Agnew's speech "reflected the views of the administration."*

***November 16, 1969. *Herbert Klein, president Nixon's director of communications, said on CBS's "Face the Nation" that Agnew's speech reflected a widely held view in the top levels of the administration. He added that the criticism extended to newspapers as well as to networks.*

***November 19, 1969. *Herbert Klein, director of communications, said that the White House had asked television stations about editorial treatment at various times, both before and after presidential appearances. He considered such inquiries proper.*

****November 20, 1969. *Vice-President Agnew, in a speech to the Montgomery, Alabama, Chamber of Commerce, attacked the* New York Times *and the* Washington Post *as representing another small, self-appointed, biased elite. He singled out the* Post *as a monopolistic media baron controlling "the largest newspaper in Washington, D.C., and one of the four major television stations, and an all-news radio station, and one of the three major national news magazines." He charged these media with "all grinding out the same editorial line." Agnew rejected the idea of a press immune from official criticism and pledged stern commitment to continued watchfulness and vocal criticism.*

***November 28, 1969. *In an article published in* Life *magazine, Vice-President Agnew defended his criticism of the media by saying that he had "endured the didactic inadequacies of the garrulous in silence, hoping for the best but witnessing the worst for many months."*

***December 8, 1969. *In a press conference President Nixon, while disclaiming responsibility for Agnew's media speeches, went on to praise him for public service by addressing "in a very dignified and courageous way" the problem of unfair coverage.*

***January 2, 1970. *Greater Miami Telecasters, Inc. — a new Florida corporation headed by W. Sloan McCrea, a business partner of Nixon's long-time friend Bebe Rebozo, and composed of other friends, supporters, and former business associates of President Nixon — applied to the FCC to take over the license of Miami's WLBW-TV (renamed WPLG-TV), owned by the Post-Newsweek Corporation.*

***January 8, 1970. *Federal prosecutors in San Francisco issued subpoenas to CBS, demanding that it hand over the film, used and unused, that it had collected while putting together a program on the Black Panthers, and demanding a complete record of CBS's correspondence, internal notes, and telephone calls made in connection with the program. The program had been shown January 6 on the CBS series "60 Minutes."*

**January 12, 1970. *The FCC was reported to be considering a sharply increased schedule of fines and forfeitures, possibly up to $500,000. The current limit was $10,000.*

**January 12, 1970. *In a report released by the National Commission on the Causes and Prevention of Violence, the panel urged, among its many recommendations, that the Justice Department and the FCC use their power over mergers and licenses to avoid "greater concentration of media ownership."*

*January 17, 1970. *Senator Thomas J. McIntyre (D., N.H.) announced that he would introduce a proposal to prohibit newspaper chains from acquiring more than five newspapers and to prohibit a newspaper from owning a radio or television station in the same metropolitan area. He claimed that the bill had the backing of the Nixon administration.*

***January 29, 1970. *Federal prosecutors in San Francisco issued a second subpoena to CBS, demanding that the network turn over to the Secret Service and the FBI a complete record of all correspondence, memoranda, notes, and telephone records used to produce the Black Panthers film aired on "60 Minutes." Tapes of an interview with Eldridge Cleaver, the Panther's leader in exile, were also demanded.*

*January 1970. *As a special assistant to the president, Clay T. Whitehead, architect of the plan outlining the Office of Telecommunications Policy (OTP), sent a memorandum to FCC Chairman Dean Burch suggesting that the commission reevaluate its previously expressed position on domestic satellite services. The FCC position authorizing a Comsat-directed pilot program, had been outlined in a draft of a report and order that was submitted to the White House prior to issuance. The Whitehead memorandum proposed, instead, an "open-skies" policy that would, in effect, remove Comsat as the single supplier of services and would open the field to "any financially qualified public or private entity, including Government corporations."*

***February 1, 1970. *Representatives of* Time, Life, *and* Newsweek *magazines revealed that the government had subpoenaed unedited files and unused photographs dealing with the movements of the Weatherman faction of the Students for a Democratic Society.*

*** February 2, 1970. New York Times *reporter Earl Caldwell was subpoenaed by federal prosecutors to testify before a federal grand jury in San Francisco that was investigating the activities of the Black Panthers. Caldwell was instructed to appear with his "notes and tape recordings" regarding activities and personnel of the party.*

****February 4, 1970. *H. R. Haldeman issued a "High Priority" confidential memorandum to Jeb Magruder that singled out commentator David Brinkley for his criticism of the federal* *budget and that requested a strategy to deal quickly with NBC's "almost totally negative approach to everything the Administration does." Priority was given to mobilization of the "silent majority" into a campaign designed "to pound the magazines and the networks in counter action" — concentrating efforts on NBC,* Time, Newsweek, Life, *the* New York Times, *and the* Washington Post.

**February 5, 1970. *One day after the* New York Times, *CBS,* Time, *and* Newsweek *issued statements criticizing the government for using subpoenas to gather information about radical political groups, Attorney General John Mitchell issued a statement holding that no further subpoenas would be issued to those associated with national media without first attempting to negotiate agreement as to the scope.*

**February 6, 1970. *Chief Justice Warren E. Burger asked ABC and CBS to remove the cameras set up to cover his speech in Washington before the National Association of Attorneys General. He said that television is likely "to latch onto a speaker's most lurid phrase" and thus, in the brief time allotted, to distort the meaning.*

**February 10, 1970. *The Justice Department served a subpoena on* Fortune *magazine (owned by Time, Inc.), demanding all interview notes, tape recordings, and other documents collected in an interview with James J. Ling, a principal in a government antitrust suit.*

***February 16, 1970. *In a magazine interview Clay T. Whitehead, architect of the OTP and its soon-to-be-named director, characterized the director's role as that of communications tsar and commented that "the White House has no qualms about seeking to influence the commission [FCC] or other-so-called independent agencies."*

*February 16, 1970. *In letters to four radio stations, the FCC outlined a new policy limiting the amount of commercial time* *permissible for radio broadcasting. Failure to comply would be cause for license-renewal hearings.*

February 19, 1970. The FCC proposed a 50 percent increase in fees broadcasters pay for licenses, applications, and other FCC services.

**February 23, 1970. Mike Wallace, a CBS correspondent who worked on the January 6 Black Panthers show, reported that he was informally approached by a Justice Department press aide, who asked him to testify voluntarily before a federal grand jury in New Haven, Connecticut, investigating the activities of the Black Panthers. The producer of the show had also been asked to appear. This was the third time that the government had sought CBS data on the Panthers.*

February 24, 1970. The FCC issued a directive warning broadcasters that they faced punitive action if they failed to keep off the air songs whose lyrics tended "to promote or glorify the use of illegal drugs."

March 26, 1970. The FCC announced the "single market rule," whereby it would prohibit any new combinations of radio and television ownership in the same market.

April 2, 1970. The White House press corps was moved from quarters in the West Lobby into the opulent West Terrace Press Center. Access was forbidden to the old West Wing entrance, where incoming White House visitors could be glimpsed and sometimes interviewed.

April 6, 1970. The FCC voted to fine WUHY-FM for "indecent" programming in violation of FCC regulations. The station was charged with broadcasting "patently offensive words." This was the commission's first such action.

***May 6, 1970. In a memorandum to H. R. Haldeman, Jeb Stuart Magruder said that a team of workers was calling and writing* *the* Washington Post *on a daily basis to complain about its "childish, ridiculous and overboard" criticism of the president.*

May 7, 1970. The FCC issued its "Prime Time Rule," by which local television stations in the 50 top markets would have to fill at least one of the four nightly prime-time hours (7-11 P.M.) with independently produced material rather than network programs, network reruns, or previously broadcast movies.

****May 22, 1970. Vice-President Agnew, in a speech at a Republican fund-raising dinner in Houston, denounced by name his press critics as "the liberal news media of this country, those really illiberal, self-appointed guardians of our destiny who would like to run the country without ever submitting to the elective process as we in public office must do." He specifically named* the *New York Times,* the *Washington Post,* the *Atlanta Constitution,* the *New Republic* magazine, *I.F. Stone's Weekly, and various journalists.*

June 2, 1970. FCC Chairman Dean Burch gave testimony before a subcommittee of the House Commerce Committee in which he endorsed legislation that would cut the cost of television advertising for political candidates and repeal the "equal opportunities" requirement for the presidential and vice-presidential candidates.

***June 5, 1970. Addressing the International Federation of Newspaper Publishers in Washington, Vice-President Agnew criticized the "biased" media coverage of the Vietnam war and contended that his differences with the news media had come about "not over their right to criticize government or public officials but my right to criticize them."*

June 11, 1970. Senator J. William Fulbright (D., Ark.), chairman of the Senate Foreign Relations Committee, introduced legislation to legalize, on demand, congressional access to national television. The bill would require broadcasters to supply time to authorized representatives of Congress.

***June 25, 1970. *President Nixon invited 40 newspaper and broad-casting station executives to San Clemente for a six-hour private briefing on American operations in Indochina. The* Washington Post *and the* New York Times *were not invited.*

**June 26, 1970. *President Nixon met with newspaper and broad-cast executives at the Western White House and delivered a briefing on foreign policy.*

*June 29, 1970. *The FCC adopted rules barring common owner-ship of cable television operations and over-the-air television stations within the same community.*

**July 7, 1970. *The Republican National Committee filed a com-plaint with the FCC demanding time to reply to a CBS pro-gram called "The Loyal Opposition," one of a series of broad-casts scheduled to provide the Democratic National Committee with opportunity to counter Nixon administration policy pro-nouncements.*

***July 16, 1970. *A secret memorandum was issued by Lawrence Higby, staff assistant to H. R. Haldeman, suggesting general strategy in retribution for remarks by NBC's Chet Huntley (as quoted in* Life *magazine) that were critical of the president.*

***July 17, 1970. *A "Confidential/Eyes Only" memorandum was sent by Jeb Magruder to H. R. Haldeman and Herbert Klein, suggesting the invincibility of Huntley and therefore proposing a public examination of press objectivity and ethics generally. Specific proposals included encouragement of public debate on declining press values by making witting and unwitting use of columnists, academics, RTNDA, the National Association of Broadcasters, the vice-president, the FCC chairman, congress-men, public-interest consumer groups, and the media themselves.*

***July 23, 1970. *President Nixon gave a personal briefing to the staff of the* Washington Evening Star, *a* Post *competitor* *and a newspaper generally supportive of administration policies.*

*August 10, 1970. Attorney General John Mitchell issued guidelines barring government lawyers from seeking subpoenas to force newsmen to testify in criminal cases without his personal approval.

*August 14, 1970. The FCC held that CBS, which had allowed the Democratic National Committee free time to state its opposition to the president's policies, must give the Republican National Committee time to reply to the Democrats.

*August 14, 1970. During his visit to New Orleans, President Nixon met with southern regional news media representatives and delivered a briefing on foreign policy.

**August 18, 1970. President Nixon visited the office of the New York Daily News, *a supporter of administration policy, and delivered a briefing on foreign and domestic issues.*

*August 24, 1970. At the Western White House, President Nixon met with news executives from the western states and delivered a briefing on foreign policy.

***August 26, 1970. A memorandum was sent by Charles Colson to H. R. Haldeman, suggesting that "the other side" was beginning to understand that they were being hurt by recent FCC decisions. He continued, "I think it is time for us to generate again a PR campaign against the Democrats and CBS."

***August 28, 1970. An "Administratively Confidential" memorandum, on strategy for keeping press activity at the forefront of public discussions, was sent by Laurence Higby to Jeb Magruder. Careful monitoring and regular references to "press favoritism" by the vice-president and cabinet officers was suggested as a "continuing function."

**September 4, 1970. *A White House order established the OTP, an agency in the Executive Office of the President, with Clay T. Whitehead as director. The agency was to advise the president on all telecommunications matters, particularly on new initiatives in public policy. Having no actual powers, the office was also free of restrictions.*

**September 14, 1970. *Vice-President Agnew, in a speech to Nevada Republicans, criticized the playing on the radio of songs that contained "drug culture propaganda."*

*September 16, 1970. *During his visit to Chicago, President Nixon met with midwestern regional news media representatives and delivered a briefing on foreign policy.*

***September 23, 1970. *Charles Colson visited CBS headquarters to meet with William Paley, chairman, and Frank Stanton, president. This was one of a series of meetings between Colson and the networks.*

***September 25, 1970. *Charles Colson, special counsel to the president, issued an "Eyes Only" memorandum to H. R. Haldeman summarizing his meetings with the three network chief executives. He described them as "terribly nervous over the uncertain state of the law," "apprehensive about us," "insecure," and as responding to his increased pressure by becoming "more accommodating, cordial and almost apologetic." He described his goal as being to "dampen their ardor for putting on 'loyal opposition' type programs" and to "split the networks in a way very much to our advantage." He proposed continued careful monitoring of network news and continued official calls to protest bias. He added that he would ask FCC Chairman Dean Burch to consider issuing an interpretive ruling on the Fairness Doctrine after the Republicans became the majority on the commission.*

*September 1970. *Mark Knops, editor of an underground newspaper, was ordered to jail for refusing to divulge information* to a grand jury investigating the bombing of the Army Math Research Center at the University of Wisconsin.

***October 8, 1970. *Charles Colson called CBS executives to complain of their allegedly biased treatment of President Nixon's television address on Vietnam that had been delivered the previous evening.*

*October 12, 1970. *During his visit to Hartford, Connecticut, President Nixon met with editors, publishers, and broadcast executives from the northeastern states and delivered a briefing on foreign policy.*

***October 19, 1970. *Vice-President Agnew criticized the press for circulating "libelous mouthings" of his opponents. He described himself as a victim of a "hate" campaign that the press perpetuated by its failure to subject the remarks to careful scrutiny.*

**November 9, 1970. *President Nixon invited nine columnists of a "conservative or moderate inclination" to a 70-minute background briefing on his plans for appointing a southern conservative to the Supreme Court.*

**November 20, 1970. *In a speech at Honolulu before the Associated Press Managing Editors Association, Vice-President Agnew contended that his criticism of the news media achieved its purpose by encouraging the media to examine itself critically. He described the American news profession as "the fairest and finest journalistic complex in the entire world."*

**December 1, 1970. *It was reported that an army agent masqueraded as a reporter for the* Richmond Times Dispatch *to obtain information on the Southern Christian Leadership Conference.*

**December 3, 1970. *The FCC refused to renew licenses of five radio stations owned by Star Stations, Inc. The reasons cited* *included political favoritism, news slanting, and trying to influence an audience rating company.*

***December 11, 1970. *A memorandum from Jeb Stuart Magruder to H. R. Haldeman listed action taken to denounce the news media following a presidential press conference. According to the memo, "Ten telegrams have been drafted by Buchanan. They will be sent to* Time *and* Newsweek *by 20 names around the country from our letter-writing system." Additionally, an op-ed page statement for the* New York Times *was being drafted; Herbert Klein was suggested as the "best signatory" for the statement.*

**January 1971. *It was reported that in Wichita, Kansas, press credentials had been given to local policemen during a visit by Vice-President Agnew in October 1970.*

**February 25, 1971. *Hearings by the House Armed Services Committee were interrupted as its chairman, Representative F. Edward Hébert (D., La.), denounced the CBS documentary "The Selling of the Pentagon," which had been broadcast February 23, as a "vicious piece of propaganda" that left him "with an emptiness in his stomach, nausea." The documentary had charged the Pentagon with untoward public relations practices and with spending $30 million dollars a year to polish its image with the public.*

***March 18, 1971. *Vice-President Agnew, addressing a Republican club in Boston, questioned the ethics and credibility of the CBS documentary "The Selling of the Pentagon." He referred to the program as a "subtle but vicious broadside against the nation's defense establishment."*

***March 19, 1971. *Senator Robert Dole (R., Kan.), chairman of the Republican National Committee, accused all three networks, but particularly CBS, of biased news coverage.*

***March 22, 1971. *Pressure from the executive branch resulted in a change of format of the "Dick Cavett Show." An assistant to Herbert Klein, the president's director of communications, called the producer of the show and requested that a government spokesman for the controversial supersonic transport plane be featured as the sole guest on the show, in light of recent guests who had been anti-SST. The producer reported that the White House request contained "a suggestion that ABC was in violation of the fairness doctrine."*

***March 1971. *President Nixon and some staff members met with William Paley, chairman of CBS, and a delegation of the network's top executives in one of a series of unannounced meetings with major networks. According to Charles Colson, one of the participants, the major thrust of the talk was network policy issues that involved the federal government, but President Nixon addressed the news coverage problem indirectly several times.*

**April 7, 1971. *Under the chairmanship of Representative Harley Staggers (D., W.Va.), the Special Subcommittee on Investigations of the House Interstate and Foreign Commerce Committee subpoenaed from CBS "all film, workprints, outtakes, soundtape recordings, written scripts and/or transcripts utilized in whole or in part" for the controversial documentary "The Selling of the Pentagon," which was critical of the Defense Department's expenditures for public relations.*

****April 29, 1971. *During a private conversation while at CBS to tape an interview, John Ehrlichman, assistant to the president, suggested to CBS News President Richard Salant that correspondent Dan Rather be removed from the White House press corps and reassigned elsewhere. "Rather has been jobbing us," Ehrlichman is reported to have said. "Aren't you going to open a bureau in Austin where Dan could have a job?" He then went on to suggest that Rather be given a year's vacation.*

**May 8, 1971. *Addressing the White House Correspondents' Association, President Nixon remarked that Vice-President Agnew* had three television sets in his bedroom — one for ABC, one for NBC, and one standing in the corner.

*May 18, 1971. In a Washington speech Chief Justice Warren Burger, primarily criticizing lawyers who disrupted the decorum of the court, extended his remarks to include overzealous journalists. In particular, he said, "Editorials tend to become shrill with invective, and political cartoons are savagely reminiscent of a century past."

**May 22, 1971. Senator Sam J. Ervin (D., N.C.) reported that the FCC was checking all license applications against a computerized list of 11,000 persons deemed suspicious characters by such agencies as the Justice Department, IRS, CIA, and House Committee on Internal Security.

*May 25, 1971. In Birmingham, Alabama, President Nixon met with southern media representatives and delivered a background briefing on domestic policy initiatives.

**May 26, 1971. The House Special Investigations Subcommittee, probing the production of the CBS television documentary "The Selling of the Pentagon," issued a new subpoena to CBS that insisted on outtakes of the film and demanded that Dr. Frank Stanton, president of CBS, appear personally.

***June 1, 1971. In a speech to radio station owners, Vice-President Agnew criticized the media for reacting to the administration's "constructive" criticism with a "frenzy about intimidation and repression." He argued that media "attempts to portray the government as anxious to control or suppress the news media" would "backfire."

**June 13, 1971. The White House barred Judith Martin, a columnist for the Washington Post, from covering Tricia Nixon's wedding. Martin, who had previously previewed Tricia's upcoming television tour of the White House, had described her as "dressed *like an ice cream cone" with the potential of giving "neatness and cleanliness a bad name."*

***June 14, 1971. *The Pentagon issued a statement indicating its concern about the* New York Times*'s June 13 printing of the Pentagon Papers, articles based on a secret Pentagon report. Referring to "the disclosure of publication of highly classified information affecting national security," the Pentagon noted that it had called the matter to the attention of the Justice Department.*

****June 14, 1971. *About two hours before press time for the edition scheduled to carry the third installment of the Pentagon Papers, Assistant Attorney General Robert C. Mardian telephoned the* New York Times *to request that publication be halted. He warned that court action would follow noncompliance.*

****June 14, 1971. *Attorney General John Mitchell sent a telegram to the* New York Times *notifying it that the first two installments of the Pentagon Papers, published June 13 and 14, contained information relating to national defense, and as such had violated provisions of the Espionage Act of 1917. He requested a halt to further publication and return of the documents. The telegram was received one hour before press time.*

****June 14, 1971. *An FBI investigation was begun, seeking the source that gave the* New York Times *the secret Pentagon report. Daniel Ellsberg was the principal object of the investigation.*

****June 15, 1971. *In the face of the* New York Times*'s refusal to halt publication of the Pentagon Papers, the Justice Department filed a civil suit against the newspaper, seeking a permanent injunction against publication of the articles.*

*June 18, 1971. *In Rochester, New York, President Nixon met with media executives and delivered a background briefing on domestic policy initiatives.*

****June 18, 1971. *In the face of the* Washington Post*'s publication of an installment of the classified Pentagon Papers, the Justice Department filed a civil suit seeking an injunction to restrain publication of the articles in that paper.*

****June 22, 1971. *After publication in the* Boston Globe *of one and a half pages of the Pentagon study, the Justice Department sought and obtained a restraining order against further publication of such articles in that paper.*

****June 26, 1971. *At the request of the Justice Department, the Supreme Court issued a restraining order against the* St. Louis Post-Dispatch *after the newspaper refused to voluntarily halt publication of material from the classified Pentagon study.*

*June 28, 1971. *President Nixon announced formation of a high-level administration committee charged with developing comprehensive policy, and ultimately legislation, with regard to cable television. OTP director Clay Whitehead was named chairman. The FCC was advised to continue with its deliberations on cable.*

**June 29, 1971. *In view of CBS's refusal to turn over the raw materials used to produce the documentary "The Selling of the Pentagon," the Special Investigations Subcommittee voted 5-0 in favor of requesting the House to issue a contempt citation against CBS and its president, Dr. Frank Stanton.*

***June 29, 1971. *U.S. Attorney for the District of Massachusetts telephoned the* Christian Science Monitor *to request that the newspaper voluntarily halt publication of two articles on the Pentagon report that were scheduled for publication.*

****June 1971. *On orders from President Nixon, the White House "Plumbers" unit was authorized by Attorney General John N. Mitchell. Among their responsibilities was the tapping of phones of at least two reporters for the* New York Times.

****July 1, 1971. *In a press release Attorney General John N. Mitchell issued a statement that the Justice Department would prosecute "all those who have violated federal criminal laws" in connection with the disclosure of the classified Pentagon study. A spokesman for the Justice Department said that the statement was intended to show that the Supreme Court's ruling of June 30, which held for the* New York Times *and the* Washington Post *in their right to publish, did not affect subsequent criminal suits against lawbreakers.*

**July 1, 1971. *The full House Commerce Committee voted, 25-13, to support the subcommittee's request for a contempt citation against CBS and its president, Dr. Frank Stanton, for failure to produce raw materials from the documentary "The Selling of the Pentagon."*

***July 5, 1971. *In a speech delivered in Singapore, Vice-President Agnew charged the American press with unintentionally assisting the North Vietnamese by some of their coverage of the Indochina war.*

*July 6, 1971. *In Kansas City, Missouri, President Nixon met with news media executives and delivered a background briefing on domestic policy initiatives.*

***July 12, 1971. *A federal grand jury in Boston was reported to be investigating possible criminal charges against the* New York Times, *the* Washington Post, *and the* Boston Globe *in connection with their publication of the Pentagon Papers. In addition the grand jury was reportedly considering criminal charges against Neil Sheehan, the* Times *reporter credited with a major role in the preparation of the articles.*

***July 13, 1971. *According to Charles Colson, the White House intervened to produce sufficient votes to defeat the House contempt citation against CBS and Dr. Frank Stanton in the matter of "The Selling of the Pentagon" documentary. Colson* noted that Haldeman had ordered him to "get something for it."

*July 13, 1971. *By a vote of 226-181, the House refused to approve a contempt citation against CBS and its president, Dr. Frank Stanton, for their failure to produce outtakes and other raw materials used in the production of the controversial documentary "The Selling of the Pentagon."*

**July 15, 1971. *Representative Hastings Keith (R., Mass.) introduced a bill to curb broadcast editing "excesses." Under this bill staged incidents, juxtaposition, and "spontaneous" interviews would be prohibited.*

*July 21, 1971. *William F. Buckley, Jr., editor in chief of the* National Review, *a conservative publication supportive of administration policies, admitted that his publication of a series of government memorandums based on the Pentagon study and purported to be information not published by the* New York Times *and the* Washington Post, *was in reality a hoax. The documents had been created by the editors to show the public that "forged documents would be widely accepted as genuine provided their content was inherently plausible."*

**July 23, 1971. *OTP Director Clay T. Whitehead met with broadcasters, cable representatives, and copyright owners, and reportedly made it clear that the White House intended to take a central role in the formulation of cable regulation.*

**July 26, 1971. *It was reported that FCC Chairman Dean Burch had been summoned to several unannounced meetings at the White House relative to cable-regulation policy. He met with OTP Director Clay Whitehead, White House Director of Communications Herbert Klein, and Charles Colson, special counsel to the president.*

***August 19, 1971. *Charles Colson telephoned CBS President Frank Stanton to complain about Daniel Schorr's on-air comments* *of August 17, when, in an analysis on the evening news, he suggested that President Nixon's promise of support for Catholic schools was in fact based on no concrete program and seemed to be nothing more than political rhetoric.*

****August 19, 1971. *On orders from Lawrence Higby, assistant to H. R. Haldeman, the FBI began an investigation of Daniel Schorr by questioning his bosses at CBS, his friends, and his neighbors.*

****August 19, 1971. *CBS correspondent Daniel Schorr was called to the White House for a meeting with Patrick Buchanan and others who rebutted Schorr's on-air comments critical of the administration stand on support for Catholic schools.*

***September 2, 1971. *It was reported that FBI agents had questioned State Department personnel in a probe regarding unauthorized news leaks relative to a* New York Times *story on the SALT talks.*

**September 2, 1971. *At a press briefing State Department spokesman Robert J. McCloskey admitted that certain topics had been designated off limits in discussion with reporters. Such topics included the president's proposed trip to China and the South Vietnamese presidential elections.*

*September 25, 1971. *In Portland, Oregon, President Nixon engaged in a question-and-answer session at a media briefing for northwestern editors, publishers, and broadcast executives.*

***September 27, 1971. *In a speech to the International Association of Chiefs of Police, Vice-President Agnew accused the news media of giving wide currency to "radical left" ideas and of trying to make the prisoners' revolt at the state prison in Attica, New York, into "yet another cause celebre in the pantheon of radical revolutionary propaganda."*

***October 6, 1971. *After press screenings of a telecast that was part of the public broadcasting program series "Great American Dream Machine" and was critical of the FBI, FBI Director J. Edgar Hoover sent a letter to PBS denying the charges and informing it that the FBI had "referred this matter to the Department of Justice."*

***October 14, 1971. *A memorandum was sent by Jack Caulfield to John Dean, referring to the investigative series published in the Long Island daily* Newsday *on the business activities of President Nixon's close friend Charles Rebozo. The memo proposed that the series be discredited by an "oblique" leak suggesting an affiliation among the Kennedys,* Newsday, *and the* Los Angeles Times *(the dominant paper of the group that owned* Newsday*). The leak would be "a sort of alert that we are aware."*

***October 20, 1971. *Speaking before the National Association of Educational Broadcasters, OTP Director Clay T. Whitehead criticized the Corporation for Public Broadcasting and the Public Broadcasting Service for their centralized network structure. He approved of some form of financial recognition for stations reflecting the "bedrock of localism," and warned that if public broadcasting didn't change its direction, "permanent financing will always be somewhere off in the distant future."*

***October 29, 1971. *As part of an ongoing investigation into alleged criminal activity, a federal grand jury subpoenaed the financial records of the Beacon Press shortly after it announced its intention to publish the complete text of the Pentagon Papers.*

**November 14, 1971. *The White House denied a press pass, on security grounds, to Thomas K. Forcade, the Washington representative for the Underground Press Syndicate.*

***November 1971. *Charles Colson telephoned CBS President Frank Stanton to complain about correspondent Daniel Schorr's treatment of government-labor affairs.*

**December 1, 1971. *A memorandum from Donald Wilson responded to John Dean's inquiry about the prospects of an antitrust action against the* Los Angeles Times *based on their proposed new "street edition" that could purportedly stifle competition in southern California. Prospects of successful action were judged improbable because of lack of supporting evidence.*

*December 18, 1971. *A State Department spokesman insisted on putting himself on "background" in spite of a warning by a* Washington Post *reporter, Stanley Karnow, that according to his paper's guidelines, he could not participate under such circumstances. The reporter and sympathizers walked out of the briefing.*

*December 25, 1971. *In support of the "background" briefing, White House Press Secretary Ronald Ziegler quoted President Nixon as saying that nonattributable information is "a problem for the journalistic community to solve."*

***December 1971. *Herbert Klein, White House communications director, met with the heads of the three networks in New York. According to network executives, there were passing references to the amount of prime time programming produced by the networks, mention of the possibility of an antitrust suit, and the suggestion that forces in the administration favored an antitrust suit as punitive action related to news coverage.*

*January 6, 1972. *The FTC petitioned the FCC to require broadcasters to give free time for counteradvertising to commercials discussing controversial issues of public importance.*

***January 12, 1972. *OTP Director Clay Whitehead, in a speech over National Public Radio, said, "There is a real question as to whether public television, particularly the national federally funded part of public television, should be carrying public affairs, news commentary and that kind of thing."*

January 17, 1972. *White House Press Secretary Ronald Ziegler said that steps had been taken, at President Nixon's direction, to prevent leaks to the press of information on national security matters.*

January 31, 1972. *Senator Sam J. Ervin (D., N.C.) reported that the administration had refused his request to permit officials involved in the FBI investigation of CBS newsman Daniel Schorr to testify at a hearing of the Constitutional Rights Subcommittee.*

January 1972. *On a television talk show OTP Director Clay Whitehead, in referring to public broadcasting, expressed reservations about using federal funds to underwrite public affairs programming. He questioned the principle of "taking the tax-payer's money and using it to express controversial points-of-view which are going to be opposite of the point of view of many citizens."

January 1972. *Robert Greene, head of the* Newsday *team investigating for the Rebozo series, was informed by the New York State Internal Revenue Division that, at the request of federal authorities, his 1970 income tax return was to be audited.

*February 3, 1972. *The FCC announced new rules regulating the future extension of cable television. The new policy would promote growth of cable television from rural areas into the smaller cities but would restrict its growth in the major metropolitan markets.***

February 7, 1972. *OTP Director Clay T. Whitehead reported to the House Commerce Committee that the administration would not consider any permanent financing of noncommercial broadcasting.*

*February 8, 1972. *Hearings were held on a proposed 142 percent second-class postal rate increase — a move that would greatly affect the economics of many magazines and newspapers.***

***February 1972. *Martin Schram, Newsday's correspondent who had regularly reported on presidential trips, was stricken from the list of correspondents accompanying President Nixon to Peking. It was made clear in high-level, off-the-record conversations that the reason for this denial was the investigative series on Charles Rebozo that that paper had published.*

***February 1972. *When the* Boston Globe *was excluded from the presidential trip to Peking, Ronald Ziegler explained to the* Globe's *bureau chief that there were three criteria for the selection. When the journalist protested that the* Globe *did meet all those criteria, Ziegler replied, "Well, there must be other standards." When pressed with the query, "What standards?" Ziegler answered, "We wish we had two more seats. You almost made it."*

**March 1972. *A Twentieth Century Fund task force report revealed examples of police posing as journalists and of such government practices as raiding the offices of an underground newspaper.*

***April 8, 1972. *Speaking at a meeting of the California GOP Assembly, Vice-President Agnew referred to the liberal eastern press and political critics of the administration as "demogogues" who pandered to "the Leftist radical mob" by denigrating the armed forces and the police agencies.*

***April 11, 1972. *Speaking in Washington at a meeting of the GOP's Capitol Hill Club, Vice-President Agnew charged that "latter-day Goebbels of the radical left" were writing anti-administration bias into reference books. His office later said that he was specifically referring to the* Encyclopaedia Britannica *and the 1970* Collier's Encyclopedia Yearbook.

***April 14, 1972. *The Antitrust Division of the Department of Justice filed suit against NBC, CBS, and ABC television networks, charging monopolization of prime time entertainment programming and use of their control to obtain valuable financial interests in such programs.*

*April 20, 1972. Members of the American Society of Newspaper Editors attending the society's annual meeting in Washington were guests of President and Mrs. Nixon at a reception at the White House.

**April 21, 1972. Speaking in Washington at a meeting of the American Society of Newspaper Editors, Vice-President Agnew assailed the New York Times as "an early and ardent advocate of getting America into Vietnam [that is now] doing public penance regularly by scourging the President who is getting us out."

***April 28, 1972. Speaking at a bar association meeting in California, FBI Interim Director L. Patrick Gray said that the media were "becoming too much a part of the culture of disparagement which threatens to destroy all respect for established institutions." His charges of "partisan bias and prejudice" in reporting and editing were specifically directed at NBC, CBS, the New York Times, and the Washington Post.

***May 3, 1972. In a speech at Charleston, South Carolina, Vice-President Agnew referred to the Pulitzer Prizes awarded to the New York Times for printing the Pentagon Papers and to Jack Anderson for disclosure of administration procedures during the India-Pakistan war. He said the journalism awards "demeaned" the Pulitzer Prizes.

***May 4, 1972. In an interview on public television, Patrick Buchanan denounced the liberal bias of the networks and said that if they continued to "freeze out" opposing points of view, they were "going to find something done in the area of antitrust type action." He was also critical of "instant analysis" following presidential addresses.

*May 18, 1972. Representative Harley O. Staggers (D., W.Va.), chairman of the House Commerce Committee, began hearings on staging of news events for television cameras. He deplored the FCC's failure to issue guidelines on news rigging.

**May 22, 1972. *The White House held a briefing for a small group of reporters and stressed the administration's concern over articles on Vietnam by* New York Times *reporter Anthony Lewis. The* Times *was not invited.*

**June 1, 1972. *In a House debate conservatives complained that the Corporation for Public Broadcasting had concentrated on public affairs and cultural programs at the expense of educational programs, and that news programs and personnel were biased toward the liberal view.*

***June 1, 1972. *John Mitchell, campaign manager for President Nixon, sent a telegram praising the pressmen at the* New York Times *who delayed publication of the newspaper for 15 minutes to protest a two-page advertisement calling for impeachment of President Nixon because of his Indochina war policy. While praising the "patriotism and responsibility" of the pressmen, Mitchell accused the* Times *of "irresponsibility."*

*June 8, 1972. *The FCC implemented rules by which networks would be barred from acquiring any financial or proprietary rights to any program they did not exclusively produce. They would also be barred from distributing programs to independent stations.*

**June 15, 1972. *In a television interview, when asked why the president did not hold more press conferences, John Ehrlichman replied that reporters ask "a lot of flabby and fairly dumb questions and it really doesn't elucidate very much."*

*June 22, 1972. *In a Senate debate Senator Howard H. Baker, Jr. (R., Tenn.), questioned the propriety of a nude ballet and an anti-war program, both aired on public television.*

*June 27, 1972. *President and Mrs. Nixon hosted a reception at the White House for 200 radio and television news anchormen and radio personalities and their wives who were attending an administration briefing.*

***June 30, 1972. *President Nixon vetoed a two-year, $115 million appropriation for the Corporation for Public Broadcasting (CPB). In his veto message he expressed concern over centralization of the system, and indicated he had been influenced by the "public and legislative" debate over the program content and the criticism of CPB's trend to focus on public affairs.*

***June 1972. *The administration reportedly expressed displeasure with the political content of such Public Broadcasting System (PBS) public affairs programs as William F. Buckley, Jr.'s, "Firing Line," "Black Journal," and "Washington Week in Review," and with such news personnel as Peter Lisagor, Sander Vanocur, and Robert MacNeil. The latter two were to anchor productions from the new National Public Affairs Center for Television (NPACT).*

**June 1972. *President Nixon entertained a group of 30 local station owners and executives at dinner in the White House. At this time he reportedly promised to support legislation stabilizing license renewal and expressed his disapproval of some recent attacks on advertising.*

**August 9, 1972. *Patrick Buchanan, in an interview with the* New York Times, *claimed that "at the express instructions of President Nixon, the White House's three years of intermittent conflict with the press has come to at least a temporary halt."*

**August 10, 1972. *John W. Macy, Jr., resigned as president of the Corporation for Public Broadcasting. His resignation was reported to have resulted from a dispute with the Nixon administration over the future direction of public broadcasting.*

***August 20, 1972. *In an interview in the* New York Times, *Patrick Buchanan suggested that the primary role of the media is to support and assist the government in carrying out its purposes. "The idea of the press playing the role of loyal opposition," he said, "is a lot of malarkey."*

**August 30, 1972. *President Nixon signed into law the bill that his administration had recommended for the public broadcasting system. The measure called for a one-year, $45 million appropriation — $20 million less than the bill that the president had vetoed one month earlier.*

***August 1972. *Ronald Ziegler, replying by letter to Daniel Schorr's request for an official explanation of the FBI investigation that had been conducted, wrote that Schorr had been briefly under consideration for the job of assistant to the chairman of the Council on Environmental Quality.*

*September 4, 1972. *President and Mrs. Nixon hosted a reception at their California home for reporters covering the Western White House. Spouses were invited.*

**September 14, 1972. *President Nixon wrote to the Screen Actors Guild, supporting their position that television reruns represent an economic threat to the film industry and that television networks, by excessive use of reruns, were failing to serve the public interest. He pledged to "explore whatever regulatory recommendations are in order."*

**September 15, 1972. *Speaking publicly, OTP Director Clay Whitehead referred to the "spreading blight of re-runs" and high profits at the networks.*

***September 15, 1972. *At a meeting with CBS President Frank Stanton, Charles Colson charged CBS with extreme anti-administration bias. Colson claimed that, according to a White House analysis, CBS was broadcasting almost three times as much pro-McGovern as pro-Nixon material.*

****September 15, 1972. *In a conversation at the White House involving the president, H. R. Haldeman, and John Dean, the president said, "The main thing is the* Post *is going to have damnable, damnable problems out of this one. They have a* *television station . . . and they're going to have to get it renewed. Does [the radio station] come up too? . . . it's going to be goddam active here . . . well, the game has to be played awfully rough. . . ."*

***September 28, 1972. *Before the program's theme had faded, White House communications director Herbert Klein called NBC to protest reporter Catherine Mackin's analysis on the NBC "Nightly News" that was critical of the Nixon campaign style. Klein "demanded a retraction."*

**October 6, 1972. *The FCC asked the ABC and CBS networks to respond to charges uncovered in the House Commerce Committee hearings regarding staging of news events between 1968 and 1971. There were six charges against CBS and three against ABC.*

*October 10, 1972. *President and Mrs. Nixon hosted a reception at the White House for state and national newspaper association officers and their spouses.*

***October 25, 1972. *Denying the* Washington Post *report linking H. R. Haldeman with a secret campaign fund used to finance political espionage, White House Press Secretary Ronald Ziegler referred to the* Post *story as a "political effort," "character assassination," and "the shoddiest type of journalism."*

***November 4, 1972. *Charles Colson phoned CBS Board Chairman William Paley, to complain about a two-part report on the break-in at Democratic headquarters in the Watergate building. The first part of the report had been aired on November 3. Colson complained that the report was too close to election and appeared as an effort to embarrass the president.*

***November 5, 1972. *Charles Colson telephoned CBS President Frank Stanton to ask about plans for part 2 of the Watergate report, scheduled for the next day. Colson reportedly said,*

"Whether the report was fair or not, it should not have been broadcast at all."

***November 13, 1972. *Charles Colson, addressing the New England Society of Newspaper Editors, argued that the* Washington Post *and CBS were arrogant elitists who employed tactics similar to those of Senator Joseph McCarthy in the 1950s, in that they engaged in "the identical kind of unproven innuendo they found so shocking 20 years ago." He referred to Ben Bradlee, editor of the* Post, *as a "self-appointed leader of a tiny fringe of arrogant elitists" in journalism.*

***November 17, 1972. *A memorandum sent by Charles Colson to Presidential Counsel John Dean suggested evidence that could be used to "destroy" the credibility of columnist Jack Anderson.*

****November 1972. *According to CBS testimony, Charles Colson telephoned CBS President Frank Stanton and described a five-point plan of administration action against the television networks: government subsidies to CATV; action on limiting reruns; renewal troubles for network-owned stations; a proposal to license networks; and divestiture of network-owned stations. The plan was to "bring them to their knees in the marketplace, Wall Street and Madison Avenue."*

****November 1972. *At a meeting with a CBS attorney, Charles Colson reportedly made such remarks as "Sandy, the only way you'll improve relations with the Administration is if you dismantle CBS" and "When we get through with you guys, they'll be jumping off the thirty-second floor."*

***December 15, 1972. *Dorothy McCardle, society reporter for the* Washington Post *and a regular member of the White House press pool, was denied admission to the White House to cover a reception.*

***December 17, 1972. *Dorothy McCardle,* Washington Post *reporter, was again excluded from the press pool that was to cover White House church services. The rumored word was that the* Post *would not be admitted to White House social events until after January 20, 1973 — Inauguration Day.*

***December 18, 1972. *OTP Director Clay T. Whitehead, addressing the Indianapolis chapter of Sigma Delta Chi, criticized local broadcasting station owners for abdicating responsibility for programming in favor of network dominance. He warned that "Station managers and network officials who fail to act to correct imbalance or consistent bias from the networks — or who acquiesce by silence — can only be considered willing participants to be held accountable by the broadcasters' community at license-renewal time." He urged the affiliates to take action against the "intellectual plugola" imposed by the networks, and disclosed administration plans for legislation revising license renewal procedures. The new legislation would make local stations responsible for the objectivity of network news programs.*

***December 19, 1972. *In a regular press briefing Ronald Ziegler rejected the long-held practice of automatic representation of all Washington papers at White House functions and announced that in the future, the* Washington Post *would be subject to a "fairer and broader" basis for selection of pool reporters — this in spite of the fact that he did not "hold a great deal of respect for the journalistic approach" of the* Post.

***December 19, 1972. *John F. Lawrence, chief of the Washington bureau of the* Los Angeles Times, *was jailed for several hours for refusing to turn over to the U.S. District Court tape recordings of an interview with Alfred Baldwin, a witness in the case involving the break-in at Democratic party headquarters in the Watergate building. The* Times *had published articles based on that interview.*

*December 20, 1972. *At President Nixon's direction, Attorney General Richard G. Kleindienst said the administration would* *seek legislation forbidding television blackouts of sporting events for which all tickets had been sold.*

**December 20, 1972. *In an interview with the Associated Press, President Nixon made several critical comments about television news commentators: "I could go up the wall watching TV commentators. I don't. . . . Decision-makers can't be affected by current opinion, by TV barking at you and commentators banging away with the idea that World War III is coming because of the mining of Haiphong."*

****January 8, 1973. *The IRS secretly subpoenaed the telephone records of the Washington bureau of the* New York Times.

**January 31, 1973. *Federal agents arrested and briefly imprisoned Les Whitten, Jack Anderson's assistant and a principal in developing the series touching on documents stolen from the Bureau of Indian Affairs. The charge was receiving, concealing, and retaining stolen government property.*

****January 1973. *The license of WJXT-TV — the Post-Newsweek-owned station in Jacksonville, Florida, and a CBS affiliate — was challenged by three groups. Principals in two of the groups were reported to be Nixon associates.*

***February 1, 1973. *The* St. Louis Post-Dispatch *disclosed that the Justice Department had issued secret subpoenas in 1971 for the telephone records of the* Post-Dispatch, *Knight Newspapers, and Leslie H. Whitten, an associate of syndicated columnist Jack Anderson.*

***February 5, 1973. *Jack Nelson, a reporter for the* Los Angeles Times, *testified in hearings before a subcommittee of the House Judiciary Committee that the Department of Justice tried to suppress his interview with Alfred Baldwin, a government witness in the Watergate case. The Justice Department had threatened to take away Baldwin's immunity from prosecution if the tapes of the interview were not released to them.*

**February 20, 1973. *Agriculture Secretary Earl L. Butz criticized the "big city newspapers and urban press" for sensationalizing price increases by reporting "grossly unfair and phony" statistical interpretations of the Wholesale Price Index.*

***February 26, 1973. *In connection with civil suits, subpoenas were issued for 12 reporters and news executives to relinquish to the Committee to Re-Elect the President their notes and other private material relating to articles published on the Watergate affair. Among those subpoenaed were personnel from the* Washington Post, *the* Washington Star-News, *the* New York Times, *and* Time *magazine.*

***March 5, 1973. Time *magazine charged that by White House order the FBI, over a period of more than two years, tapped the telephones of "six or seven" newsmen in order to track news leaks in the executive staff. According to the article, when FBI Director J. Edgar Hoover balked at using the wiretaps, he was ordered by Attorney General Mitchell to follow White House orders.*

***March 14, 1973. *The White House sent to Congress a proposal for revision of the Federal Criminal Code that included an Official Secrets Act making it a crime to publish any national defense information, and revision of the Espionage Act that would prohibit publications that might prejudice interests of the United States.*

**March 14, 1973. *In a letter to both houses of Congress, OTP Director Clay Whitehead announced that the administration had proposed legislation that would increase the terms of broadcast licenses from three to five years and would establish guidelines on broadcast performance in the local public interest.*

**March 14, 1973. *H. R. Haldeman and CBS Chairman William Paley met at the White House on the day of the CBS reception honoring the outgoing president, Frank Stanton, and the incoming*

president, Arthur Taylor. The two agreed to get to know each
other better and to hold further meetings.*

**March 14, 1973. *At an informal meeting at the White House,
John Ehrlichman welcomed Arthur Taylor, who was to replace
Frank Stanton as president of CBS. Referring to past troubles
with the networks, Ehrlichman expressed hope that things
would go better in the future.*

*March 22, 1973. *The FCC voted to investigate alleged obscenity
on radio and television stations. An administration law judge
with subpoena powers would conduct the investigation.*

**March 23, 1973. *OTP Director Clay T. Whitehead asked the FCC
to study ways to require networks to use fewer reruns or repeat
programs during prime time.*

***April 12, 1973. *White House officials Clay Whitehead, Patrick
Buchanan, and John Ehrlichman reportedly contacted at least
four CPB board members to persuade them to vote against the
CPB-PBS compromise agreement scheduled to be placed before
the board the following day.*

**April 21, 1973. *A warrant was issued by the United States Attorney's office in South Dakota for the arrest of Thomas Oliphant, a*
Boston Globe *reporter accompanying a private plane dropping
food and medical supplies to Indians marooned at Wounded
Knee, site of a militant Indian-government confrontation.*

**April 30, 1973. *After delivering his first major speech about
the Watergate affair, President Nixon walked into the White
House press room and said, "We've had our difference in the
past, and just continue to give me hell when you think I'm
wrong. I hope I'm worthy of your trust." He then shook hands
with newsmen and photographers.*

***May 3, 1973. *It was reported that the phones of at least two
reporters for the* New York Times *were tapped by members*

of the Nixon administration in connection with the Pentagon
Papers. The taps were reportedly authorized by former Attorney
General John N. Mitchell in June 1971, and supervised by
Watergate conspirators E. Howard Hunt and G. Gordon Liddy,
who were operating independently of the FBI, the agency
normally responsible for electronic surveillance.

***May 4, 1973. A CBS news team that had managed to gain en-
trance to the Indian compound at Wounded Knee, South Dakota,
was taken into custody by federal authorities, and their cameras
and film seized. After much argument the crew and their gear
were released.

***May 4, 1973. Press credentials of three print journalists, includ-
ing one from the New York Times, were confiscated while the
journalists were covering the Indian uprising at Wounded Knee.
After a confrontation with an FBI agent, the credentials were
returned, but the journalists were ordered to leave the scene.

***May 8, 1973. Vice-President Agnew referred to the "techniques"
used by the media in Watergate reporting as "a very short jump
from McCarthyism." Describing the press as "overzealous" on
Watergate, he criticized it for printing "a great amount of hear-
say" and material from unnamed sources.

****May 11, 1973. The New York Times reported that, beginning
in 1969, the Nixon administration ordered wiretaps placed
on telephones of reporters from three newspapers. The article
identified, by name, two reporters for the New York Times,
one Washington-based correspondent for the Sunday Times
of London, and unidentified reporters from the Washington
Post.

****May 16, 1973. The White House acknowledged that in May
1969, President Nixon personally authorized the use of wiretaps against 13 administration aides and four newsmen. The taps
were placed because of leaks of classified documents.

***May 24, 1973. *Before an audience of recently returned prisoners of war, President Nixon affirmed the government's right and duty to impose secrecy in national security matters and denounced "those who steal secrets and publish them in the newspapers."*

**June 1, 1973. *The* New York Times *disclosed that, just before the Nixon inauguration in 1969, FBI agents and members of the Army's 116th Military Intelligence Detachment raided the offices of an underground newspaper, the* Washington Free Press. *There had been concern about plans of activities to disrupt the inauguration.*

*June 6, 1973. *Amid rumors that his authority had substantially eroded, Herbert Klein resigned as director of communications for the executive branch. Ronald Ziegler was named as his successor.*

***June 14, 1973. *It was reported that in May 1971 the White House received information from wiretaps on Pentagon Papers defendant Daniel Ellsberg and* New York Times *reporters Neil Sheehan and Tad Szulc. According to the report, the wiretap information was received in the White House one month before the Pentagon Papers were published in the* New York Times, *and one month before the White House "Plumbers" group was set up on orders from President Nixon.*

***June 26, 1973. *The U.S. Information Agency (USIA) announced that foreign newsmen would no longer be permitted to use USIA facilities to broadcast programs on the Watergate case to television stations abroad.*

****June 26, 1973. *Testifying before Senator Ervin's Senate Select Committee on Presidential Campaign Activities, former Presidential Counsel John W. Dean revealed that H. R. Haldeman had ordered an FBI investigation of CBS newsman Daniel Schorr. He also said that, after an article unfavorable to Nixon's friend*

Bebe Rebozo appeared in Newsday, *he (Dean) was given "instructions that one of the authors of the article should have some problems" with the Internal Revenue Service. Dean admitted that he had arranged that the writer be subjected to an income tax audit.*

***June 27, 1973. *Testifying before Senator Ervin's Senate Select Committee, John Dean submitted in evidence lists of Nixon's "political enemies." On a master list of 550 were the names of 56 "media enemies."*

**August 20, 1973. *Entering a hall in New Orleans before speaking to the Veterans of Foreign Wars, President Nixon turned around abruptly, grabbed Press Secretary Ronald Ziegler, shoved him toward the newsman following, and said, "I don't want any press with me and you take care of it." The reporters were directed to use another entrance.*

***August 22, 1973. *In a press conference President Nixon strongly defended Vice-President Agnew and deplored "convicting him in the headlines and on television before he's had a chance to present his case in court." The president also included "some members of the press . . . some members of television" among those who were exploiting the Watergate issue to keep him from doing his job.*

***September 5, 1973. *In a press conference President Nixon referred to himself as being "attacked in every way" on television for four months. He described the attack as "by innuendo, by leak, by frankly, leers and sneers of commentators."*

**September 7, 1973. *In confirmation hearings on his nomination as secretary of state, Henry Kissinger defended wiretapping as necessary to stop leaks to the press.*

***September 26, 1973. *The Senate Watergate Committee released memoranda disclosing an operation in which letters and telegrams* *drafted by White House aides would be signed by other people and sent to opinion leaders throughout the country. The leaders included editors, publishers, and business leaders.*

**October 5, 1973. *Attorneys for Vice-President Agnew issued subpoenas to reporters and news organizations for testimony and for "all writings and other forms of record (including drafts)" reflecting on leaks relating to the Agnew case with the Justice Department.*

**October 25, 1973. *A spokesman for the National Association of Manufacturers admitted to having been contacted by a White House aide who suggested "we might want to make a comment" following the presidential press conference.*

**October 25, 1973. *An official of the Veterans of Foreign Wars disclosed that a White House aide had asked him to make a statement of support for President Nixon following the presidential news conference originally scheduled for that day.*

**October 26, 1973. *In a conversation with a CBS reporter shortly before he entered a press conference, President Nixon said, "Cronkite's not going to like this tonight, I hope."*

***October 26, 1973. *During a news conference President Nixon said, "I have never seen such outrageous, vicious, distorted reporting in 27 years of public life"; and when asked why he was so angry with reporters, he replied, "Don't get the impression that you arouse my anger. You see, one can only be angry with those he respects."*

**October 29, 1973. *Gerald Warren, deputy press secretary, lectured reporters on responsibility during a lengthy briefing, and justified the president's critical remarks about the press at the October 26 news conference.*

***October 29, 1973. *Patrick Buchanan, on a CBS morning talk show, referred to the October 26 press conference as a "bullring,"* *and demanded that all possible legal means should be employed to force networks to more responsible reporting. Suggesting antitrust action, he went on to say, "Every legal and constitutional means ought to be considered" to break up network dominance of broadcast journalism.*

October 30, 1973. *In an NBC interview David Eisenhower, President Nixon's son-in-law, contended that the "irresponsibility" of the media had been "matched by the irresponsibility of the people they may quote."*

***October 31, 1973.** *The office of Senator Lowell Weicker (R., Ct.) released a series of private White House memoranda that had come into possession of the Ervin Committee, which was investigating the Watergate affair. A good many of these memos contained details of White House proposals to counteract the media in 1969 and 1970.*

***November 5, 1973.** *The* Washington Post *reported that it had access to a White House memorandum calling for a campaign of "pestering" the* Post *and its publisher, Katharine Graham.*

***November 5, 1973.** *The* New York Times *reported that the White House had been compiling a list of "sins" committed by the media against President Nixon. Included on the list were 19 television items considered unfavorable to the president that were aired the first weekday following the firing of Archibald Cox, the special Watergate prosecutor.*

November 24, 1973. *Addressing a rally in Albuquerque, New Mexico, White House aide Bruce Herschensohn criticized the media as a "kangaroo court" whose "verdict is very clear from the outset."*

*November 29, 1973.** *The FCC eased the length of time of the Prime Time Access Rule by barring network programs from local stations only between 7:30 and 8:00 P.M. The use of specific program types for this half-hour period was directed.*

**November 30, 1973. *The* Washington Star-News *reported that about 40 full-time reporters, free-lance journalists, and correspondents were stationed abroad as regular undercover contacts who were paid for supplying data to the CIA.*

**December 3, 1973. *The FCC ruled that NBC had violated the Fairness Doctrine in its September 1972 documentary "Pensions: The Broken Promise," and ordered corrective programming.*

**December 7, 1973. *The White House declined to cooperate with the National News Council in its proposed investigation of the charges of "outrageous, vicious and distorted reporting" made by President Nixon at his news conference of October 26. The council had sought a bill of particulars.*

*December 1973. *The Nixon family flew to San Clemente for the Christmas holiday on a commercial flight, without informing or providing space for the media.*

***January 2, 1974. *The Justice Department asked the FCC to deny the license renewal for newspaper-owned broadcasting stations in Des Moines, Iowa, and St. Louis, Missouri, on the basis that renewal "would perpetuate the high degree of concentration in the dissemination of local news and advertising." The St. Louis station was owned by the* Post-Dispatch, *a long-time Nixon critic, and the Des Moines station by Cowles Communications (the* Des Moines Register), *which reversed its customary Nixon support during the Watergate affair.*

*January 7, 1974. *The FCC announced a new policy requiring television stations to display program logs (including announcements, advertising, news, and entertainment programming) for public inspection and reproduction in convenient community locations.*

**January 11, 1974. *A new White House requirement was instituted whereby presidential aides were to report all press contacts to*

White House Press Secretary Ronald Ziegler. According to Ziegler, the new practice, instituted because "source stories have been getting somewhat out of hand," would produce more comment on the record and less on background.

*January 16, 1974. *Under the chairmanship of OTP Director Clay Whitehead, the administration issued a major study of cable television with policy recommendations concerning its development. The recommendations placed great emphasis on minimum government involvement, proposed common carrier status for cable, and proposed that TV networks, local broadcasters, and newspapers be permitted to enter the cable industry as operators or as programmers.*

***February 1, 1974. *White House Press Secretary Ronald Ziegler said at a news briefing that a new White House press policy would be instituted, whereby questions on Watergate would be turned aside in order to concentrate on "the business of government."*

**February 12, 1974. *Attending the ninetieth birthday celebration of Alice Roosevelt Longworth, President Nixon, commenting on her longevity, said, "If she had spent all her time reading the [Washington] Post or the [Washington] Star-News, she would have been dead by now." He continued by contending that Mrs. Longworth kept aloof from the great issues "which the Post, unfortunately, seldom writes about in a responsible way."*

**February 18, 1974. *Speaking before a rally in Huntsville, Alabama, President Nixon criticized news reporting in Washington as partisan and having a tendency to concentrate on the reporting of bad news.*

***March 8, 1974. *In a radio address to Congress, President Nixon disclosed his plans to draft a federal law that would make it easier for public officials and public figures to sue the media* *for libel. The reform measure would weaken the impact of the Supreme Court decisions that, since 1964, had outlined a rigid standard for libel recovery.*

July 25, 1974. The FCC began three days of hearings on a proposal to ban joint ownership of newspapers and television stations.

August 9, 1974. When the president entered the East Room of the White House to bid good-bye to the executive office staff, the audience rose to applaud him at length. He opened his remarks by saying, "I think the record should show that this is one of those spontaneous things that we always arrange whenever the President comes in to speak. And it will be so reported in the press — and we don't mind, because they've got to call it as they see it."

APPENDIX B
CODING PROCEDURES:
STEP-BY-STEP EXAMPLE

Full text of
"The Other Prisoners"
by Tom Wicker

New York Times
September 28, 1971

Like the policeman, the prison guard is a much-maligned man. To prisoners, they are all "pigs"; to many others they represent everything brutal and insensitive in American society. No doubt that view is warranted, in many cases; but as a general indictment it is grossly unfair.

As a result of the uprising at Attica, and the bloody crushing of it, the prison guard is at the moment more in the public eye than ever before. In fact, school children in the once placid town of Attica — where the prison is the primary employer — have been complaining to reporters that it is untrue that their fathers and brothers are cruel and brutal to prisoners.

Actually, the worst faults of the Attica prison can hardly be laid to its guards; at worst, they are the instruments of an inhuman system, and at best — as many showed in the aftermath of the uprising — they may understand more of the prisoner's grim plight than do high state officials.

In the first place, neither at Attica nor elsewhere are guards well-trained for their demanding, difficult and dangerous jobs. To refer to these men as "corrections officers" is an exercise in euphemism. Most qualify for their positions by passing a civil service examination and a physical, not by going through even as much training as most city policemen receive.

Statistics show that most guards have a low level of general education, with 16 percent of them not having completed high school. They are paid commensurately, with 79 per cent earning less than $8,000 a year. Thus, it is too much to expect that many of these men will have a sophisticated understanding of social issues, or that their handling of prisoners will reflect sensitive psychological approaches; society just doesn't seek out men of those qualities to guard its prisoners.

Moreover, the prison guard's job is highly dangerous and many of these men — particularly in a time like the present, when there is widespread unrest among prisoners — spend their working days and nights in something near terror. They know that prisoners almost anywhere, if led by determined men, can stage the kind of revolt that erupted at Attica; so guards are constantly subject to being held hostage, as well as to the hourly dangers of working among desperate and hostile men.

At the same time, of course, prisoners are substantially in the power of guards at most times, and since many guards are insensitive and brutal, the prisoners, too, live in fear. Men who fear other men usually come to hate them, so in these vast and gloomy fortresses, where everything is largely hidden from the public, fear and hatred mount in an ever-tightening circle. This hideous atmosphere can almost be touched and felt, as if it were tangible, in many prisons.

So, as a Utah state prison guard told Wallace Turner of The New York Times, the guards are in jail with the prisoners. It is a situation that is always ripe for violence; and when, as at Attica, there is also present in its most virulent form the racial animosity that so divides American society today, these prisons are little more than explosives waiting to be set off.

Moreover, ample history from the earliest times shows that a master-slave relationship is more corrupting for the master than for the slave. To have absolute power over another human being can bring out the worst in a man — just as, in some cases, abject slaves have been known to rise to heights of character and nobility. When guards have nagging fear for their own safety, when they are irritated and frustrated by the conditions in which they work, when they find prisoners in their power, with no one to see — in such cases, even good family men and churchgoers can be corrupted into physical brutality.

None of this is meant to suggest that guards have no personal moral responsibility for their own conduct; nor is it meant as a justification for the excesses that some observers and prisoners allege New York state prison guards even now are visiting upon the recaptured Attica rebels.

Thesis Statement But if American society is going to tolerate a prison system designed primarily to cage animals, and if the men who operate it are going to be recruited from the lowest educational levels, paid the minimum and pitted physically against the inmates in Darwinian struggle for survival, then nobody should expect much in the way of "corrections" or "rehabilitation."

We get from our guards, that is, just about what we ask and just about what we pay for.

CODING PROCEDURES IN BRIEF
(see Chapter 5 for details)

1. Sentences are transcribed into an exhaustive set of evaluative assertions comprising subject/verb/complement, where the subject is an attitude object (AO_1) and the complement is either a common meaning term (*cm*) or another attitude object (AO_2).

2. Symbolic designations are substituted for attitude objects (AO_1 and AO_2), and significant verbs and *cm* terms of the complement are italicized. Source and mode of expression are identified. (See in "Thesis Statement-Assertion Sheet" at "Legend" for explanation.)

3. AO symbols and significant words in verb and complement are transcribed to assertion chart. Significant words are assigned numerical values in terms of evaluative, potency, and activity dimensions as found in the *Stanford Political Dictionary*. Where the significant word is missing from the dictionary, a synonym based on context is substituted (synonym indicated in parentheses).

4. Verb values are corrected according to source identification and are weighted by values for modes of expression. Corrected values are recorded on the assertion chart.

5. Assertions are grouped according to AO_1 and values are transcribed onto evaluation computation chart, where assertions involving *cm* complements are listed separately from assertions involving AO_2 complement.

6. For each group of attitude objects, the evaluative, potency, and activity values for all *cm* judgments are averaged to generate AO_{cm}.

7. When AO_{cm} has been generated for all attitude objects, these values are transcribed onto the evaluation computation chart in AO_2 column as appropriate.

8. Finally, for each group of attitude objects, the evaluative, potency, and activity values for all assertions are averaged to generate AO_{total}. The AO_{total} values for each attitude object become the data for further computation and analysis.

THESIS STATEMENT-ASSERTION SHEET

Commentary #	N 1137
Quarter	11
Network/Newspaper	New York Times
Commentator/Columnist	Tom Wicker
Date	9/28/71
Coder	MAL

Thesis Statement: But if American society is going to tolerate a prison system designed primarily to cage animals, and if the men who operate it are going to be recruited from the lowest educational levels, paid the minimum and pitted physically against the inmates in Darwinian struggle for survival, then nobody should expect much in the way of "corrections" or "rehabilitation."

Source Identification   S

Assertions

BB   FD
American society/*tolerates*/prison system
                                    N

FD   BB
Prison system/is *tolerated* by/society
                                    N

FD
Prison system/is *designed*/to *cage*
                                    D

FD
Prison system/*cages*/*primarily*
                                    D

FD
Prison system/is like *caging*/*animals*
                                    M

FD
Prison guards/are *recruited*/from *lowest*
                                    N

FD
Prison guards/are *educated*/at *lowest*
                                    N

Assertions

FD
Prison guards/are *paid*/*minimum*
                                    N

FD
Prison guards/are *pitted*/*against*
                                    N

FD
Prison guards/*struggle*/for *survival*
                                    N

FD
Prison guards/*struggle*/at *Darwinian* level
                                    N

CC
One/should *expect*/*not much*
                                    N

CC
One/should *expect*/*no correction*
                                    N

CC
One/should *expect*/*no rehabilitation*
                                    N

Legend:
  Source Identification:
    S   = Words are those of commentator
    Q_1 = Words are quoted from an outside source but are perceived as agreeing with commentator
    Q_2 = Words are quoted from an outside source but are perceived as disagreeing with commentator
  Attitude Object Designation: Attitude objects are identified by symbol placed above
    FG   = Federal Government   FW = Watergate
    FGP   = Nixon Administration   BB = Minor Issues
    FD   = Domestic Problems   CC = Nonissues
  Mode of Expression: Identified in lower right hand corner of each block
    X   = Aspiration   D = Indicative
    N   = Normative   M = Comparative
    P   = Probability   V = Imperative
    T   = Interrogative

ASSERTION CHART FOR THESIS STATEMENT

Coder MAL

Commentary # N 1137
Quarter 11
Network/Newspaper New York Times
Commentator/Columnist Tom Wicker
Date 9/28/71

1 S	2 ME	2w	3 AO	4 Connector	4d E	4d P	4d A	C(4d) E	C(4d) P	C(4d) A	5 cm or AO2	5d E	5d P	5d A
S	N	.5	BB	tolerates	2	0	-2	1	0	-1	FD	-2	2	2
S	N	.5	FD	tolerates	2	0	-2	1	0	-1	BB	0	2	0
S	D	1	FD	designed	0	0	1	0	0	1	cage (imprison)	-2	2	0
S	D	1	FD	cages (imprisons)	-2	2	2	-2	2	2	primarily	-2	2	0
S	M	1	FD	cages (imprisons)	-2	2	2	-2	2	2	animals (beasts)	-2	0	0
S	N	.5	FD	recruited	1	0	2	.5	0	1	lowest	0	0	0
S	N	.5	FD	educated	0	0	1	0	0	.5	lowest	-2	0	0
S	N	.5	FD	paid	0	0	1	0	0	.5	minimum	0	-3	0
S	N	.5	FD	pitted (combat)	-2	2	3	-1	1	1.5	against	-2	1	0
S	N	.5	FD	struggle	-3	3	3	-1.5	1.5	1.5	survival	3	1	1
S	N	.5	FD	struggle	-3	3	3	-1.5	1.5	1.5	Darwinian (monumental)	2	3	0
S	N	.5	CC	expect	0	0	-2	0	0	-1	not much	0	-2	0
S	N	.5	CC	expect	0	0	-2	0	0	-1	no correction	-2	-2	0
S	N	.5	CC	expect	0	0	-2	0	0	-1	no rehabilitation (no restoration)	-1	-1	0

1 = Source.
2 = Mode of expression.
2w = Mode of expression weight.
3 = Standardized attitude object designation.
4 = Connector.
4d = Connector/dictionary score: evaluative, potency, activity.
C(4d) = Corrected connector score.
5 = Complement (evaluative common meaning term: attitude object-2).
5d = Complement (common meaning term) score.

EVALUATION COMPUTATION CHART FOR
THESIS STATEMENT: DOMESTIC PROBLEMS

Quarter	11		
AO	FD		
AO_{cm}	−.694	.833	.805
AO_{total}	−.575	.750	.675

cm Judgments									AO_2 Judgments			
1	*2*			*3*			*4*		*5*	*6*		
AO	(C) Connector			cm			(C) Connector		AO_2	Computed Value		
	E	*P*	*A*	*E*	*P*	*A*	*E*	*P*	*A*		*E*	*P*	*A*
FD	0	0	1	−2	2	2	1	0	−1	BB	0	0	0
	−2	2	2	0	2	0							
	−2	2	2	−2	2	0							
	.5	0	1	−2	2	0							
	0	0	.5	−2	0	0							
	0	0	.5	0	−3	0							
	−1	1	1.5	−2	0	0							
	−1.5	1.5	1.5	3	1	1							
	−1.5	1.5	1.5	2	3	0							

Legend:

AO_{cm} = Mean of scores in *cm* judgments.

AO_{cm} are entered in column 6 as appropriate.

AO_{total} = Mean of scores in *cm* and AO_2 judgments.

EVALUATION COMPUTATION CHART FOR THESIS STATEMENT: MINOR ISSUES

Quarter	11
AO	BB
AO_{cm}	0 0 0
AO_{total}	.153 .417 −.098

	cm Judgments								AO_2 Judgments		

1 AO	*2* (C) Connector			*3* cm			*4* (C) Connector		*5* AO_2	*6* Computed Value		
	E	P	A	E	P	A	E	P	A		E	P	A
BB							1	0	−1	FD	−.694	.833	.805

Legend:

AO_{cm} = Mean of scores in *cm* judgments.
AO_{cm} are entered in column 6 as appropriate.
AO_{total} = Mean of scores in *cm* and AO_2 judgments.

EVALUATION COMPUTATION CHART FOR THESIS STATEMENT: NONISSUES

Quarter	11
AO	CC
AO_{cm}	−.5 −.833 −.5
AO_{total}	−.5 −.833 −.5

	cm Judgments								AO_2 Judgments		

1 AO	*2* (C) Connector			*3* cm			*4* (C) Connector		*5* AO_2	*6* Computed Value		
	E	P	A	E	P	A	E	P	A		E	P	A
CC	0	0	−1	0	−2	0							
	0	0	−1	−2	−2	0							
	0	0	−1	−1	−1	0							

Legend:

AO_{cm} = Mean of scores in *cm* judgments.
AO_{cm} are entered in column 6 as appropriate.
AO_{total} = Mean of scores in *cm* and AO_2 judgments.

APPENDIX C
SUPPLEMENTARY TABLES

TABLE C.1
"UNINHIBITED?"
Comparison in Activity Means: By Subject Matter Category
(newspaper columns vs. television commentary)

Hypothesis: Television was more inhibited than newspapers.

Subject Matter Category	Inhibition		
	Z Score	Probability (1-tailed)	Significance
Major issues subgroups			
Federal government	1.02	.15	
Nixon administration	−.56	.29	
Domestic problems	1.32	.09	
Watergate	1.61	.05	*
Government (Fed/Admin/Wtrgt)	1.01	.16	
President (Admin/Wtrgt)	.01	.50	
Major issues	1.70	.04	*
Minor issues	.48	.31	
Nonissues	1.02	.15	

Legend: Mann-Whitney *U* Test
    $*p \leqslant .05$.

Notes: An asterisk in the significance column indicates that hypothesis has been demonstrated.

        Negative Z score indicates television was less inhibited than newspapers.

TABLE C.2
"ROBUST?"
Comparison of Potency Means: By Subject Matter Category
(newspaper columns vs. television commentary)

Hypothesis: Television was less robust than newspapers.

Subject Matter Category	Lack of Robustness		
	Z Score	Probability (1-tailed)	Significance
Major issues subgroups			
Federal government	.72	.24	
Nixon administration	1.13	.13	
Domestic problems	1.73	.04	*
Watergate	.85	.20	
Government (Fed/Admin/Wtrgt)	1.34	.09	
President (Admin/Wtrgt)	1.71	.04	*
Major issues	2.09	.02	*
Minor issues	.18	.43	
Nonissues	2.09	.02	*

Legend: Mann-Whitney *U* Test
    $*p \leqslant .05$.

Note: An asterisk in the significance column indicates that hypothesis has been demonstrated.

TABLE C.3

"WIDE-OPEN?"

Comparison of Proportionate Attention to Subject Matter Category (newspaper columns vs. television commentary)

Hypothesis: Television devoted proportionately less attention than newspapers to issues of public importance.

Subject Matter Category	Less Proportionate Attention		
	Z Score	*Probability (1-tailed)*	*Significance*
Major issues subgroups			
Federal government	.44	.33	
Nixon administration	1.07	.14	
Domestic problems	1.29	.10	
Watergate	1.93	.03	*
Government (Fed/Admin/Wtrgt)	.39	.35	
President (Admin/Wtrgt)	1.36	.09	
Major issues	.85	.20	
Minor issues	−.54	.30	
Nonissues	−1.69	.04	#

Legend: Mann-Whitney *U* Test
    $*p \leqslant .05$.
    $\#p \leqslant .05$ but the direction is other than hypothesized.

Notes: An asterisk in the significance column indicates that hypothesis has been demonstrated.

    Negative Z score indicates television devoted proportionately more attention than newspapers to issues of public importance.

TABLE C.4
"DEBATE?"

Comparison of Evaluative Absolute Means:
By Subject Matter Category
(newspaper columns vs. television commentary)

Hypothesis: Television was less likely than newspapers to express a point of view.

Subject Matter Category		Reluctance to Debate	
	Z Score	Probability (1-tailed)	Significance
Major issues subgroups			
Federal government	.94	.17	
Nixon administration	1.41	.08	
Domestic problems	−1.15	.13	
Watergate	−.29	.39	
Government (Fed/Admin/Wtrgt)	.67	.25	
President (Admin/Wtrgt)	2.03	.02	*
Major issues	.73	.23	
Minor issues	−.65	.26	
Nonissues	1.33	.09	

Legend: Mann-Whitney U Test
   $*p \leqslant .05$.

Notes: An asterisk in the significance column indicates that hypothesis has been demonstrated.

   Negative Z score indicates television was more likely than newspapers to express a point of view.

TABLE C.5

"DEBATE?" (Positive or Negative Emphasis)
Comparison of Evaluative Means: By Subject Matter Category
(newspaper columns vs. television commentary)

Hypothesis: Television was less likely than newspapers to emphasize positive or negative views.

Subject Matter Category	Emphasis on Positive or Negative		
	Z Score	Probability (1-tailed)	Significance
Major issues subgroups			
Federal government	−1.45	.07	
Nixon administration	1.61	.05	*
Domestic problems	.95	.48	
Watergate	.74	.23	
Government (Fed/Admin/Wtrgt)	.08	.47	
President (Admin/Wtrgt)	1.41	.08	
Major issues	.44	.33	
Minor issues	−1.57	.06	
Nonissues	2.16	.02	*

Legend: Mann-Whitney *U* Test
    p ⩽ .05.

Notes: An asterisk in the significance column indicates that hypothesis has been demonstrated.
      Positive Z score indicates television tended to emphasize negative views.
      Negative Z score indicates television tended to emphasize positive views.

TABLE C.6
Impact of White House Anti-media Assault on Newspaper/Television Vigorousness
(correlation of WHAMA with vigorousness quotient)

	Newspapers			Television		
	r	p (1-tailed)	Significance	r	p (1-tailed)	Significance
Index of vigorousness	−.15	(.12)		−.15	(.13)	
All issues combined (unweighted)	−.10	(.16)		−.10	(.16)	
Major issues subgroups						
Federal government	−.20	(.09)		−.17	(.11)	
Nixon administration	.35	(.03)	*	−.31	(.04)	*
Domestic problems	−.24	(.07)		.21	(.08)	
Watergate	−.12	(.19)		−.29	(.10)	
Government (Fed/Admin/Wtrgt)	−.04	(.21)		−.32	(.03)	*
President (Admin/Wtrgt)	.26	(.12)		−.33	(.03)	*
Major issues	−.15	(.12)		−.18	(.10)	
Minor issues	.01	(.24)		.10	(.17)	
Nonissues	.16	(.11)		.13	(.14)	

Statistic: Pearson's product-moment correlation.

*$p \leq .05$.

244

TABLE C.7
Impact of White House Anti-media Assault on Newspaper/Television Blandness
(correlation of WHAMA with vigorousness quotient)

	Newspapers			Television		
	r	p (1-tailed)	Significance	r	p (1-tailed)	Significance
All issues combined (unweighted)	−.11	(.15)		−.36	(.03)	*
Major issues subgroups						
Federal government	.16	(.12)		.18	(.11)	
Nixon administration	.08	(.18)		.06	(.20)	
Domestic problems	.18	(.10)		.02	(.24)	
Watergate	.07	(.21)		.03	(.24)	
Government (Fed/Admin/Wtrgt)	−.04	(.22)		.31	(.04)	*
President (Admin/Wtrgt)	−.08	(.18)		.04	(.22)	
Major issues	−.03	(.23)		.44	(.009)	**
Minor issues	−.05	(.21)		−.12	(.15)	
Nonissues	−.27	(.06)		.06	(.20)	

Statistic: Pearson's product-moment correlation.
*$p \leq .05$.
**$p \leq .01$.

TABLE C.8
Chilling Effect of the White House Anti-media Assault on Television Commentary, by Vigorousness
(correlation of WHAMA with television/newspaper difference scores, by vigorousness quotient: television scores minus newspaper scores)

	r	p (1-tailed)	Significance
All issues combined (unweighted)	−.01	(.24)	
Major issues subgroups			
Federal government	−.03	(.22)	
Nixon administration	−.46	(.01)	**
Domestic problems	.33	(.03)	*
Watergate	−.01	(.25)	
Government (Fed/Admin/Wtrgt)	−.18	(.11)	
President (Admin/Wtrgt)	−.37	(.02)	*
Major issues	−.04	(.22)	
Minor issues	.05	(.21)	
Nonissues	.01	(.24)	

Statistic: Pearson's product-moment correlation.
    *$p \leqslant .05$.
    **$p \leqslant .01$.

TABLE C.9
Chilling Effect of the White House Anti-media Assault
on Television Commentary, by Blandness
(correlation of WHAMA with television/newspaper difference scores, by blandness quotient: television scores minus newspaper scores)

	r	p (1-tailed)	Significance
All issues combined (unweighted)	−.41	(.01)	**
Major issues subgroups			
Federal government	.43	(.01)	**
Nixon administration	−.09	(.17)	
Domestic problems	−.09	(.17)	
Watergate	−.04	(.23)	
Government (Fed/Admin/Wtrgt)	.44	(.01)	**
President (Admin/Wtrgt)	−.09	(.17)	
Major issues	.52	(.01)	**
Minor issues	−.10	(.16)	
Nonissues	−.28	(.05)	

Statistic: Pearson's product-moment correlation.
    $*p \leqslant .05$.
    $**p \leqslant .01$.

GLOSSARY

Activity dimension. The dimension in the content analysis procedures that ranges along a continuum from active to passive.

Assertion. A linguistic construction in which an attitude object is associated with or dissociated from a complement via a verbal connector.

Attitude object. A sign with evaluative meanings that vary extremely with the persons producing or receiving it.

Blandness quotient. A statistic in the content analysis procedures that averages the relative frequencies of neutral scores in the evaluative dimension, the neutral and weak scores in the potency dimension, and the neutral and passive scores in the activity dimension.

Chilling effect. A significant reduction, in measures over time, and in light of influence by an outside factor, of the vigorousness of journalistic coverage of public issues, where a target population is measured against a comparable population used as a standard.

Chronology of the White House anti-media assault during the Nixon administration. A chronological listing of the Nixon administration's anti-media efforts as perceived by men who were media executives during the Nixon presidency.

Chronology of governmental media and media-related events during the Nixon administration. A chronological listing of events perceived by the researcher as potential anti-media efforts emanating from the Nixon White House.

Commentary. Formal, considered, media-disseminated discourse on news and public affairs in which analysis, interpretation, and/or opinion are identified as such, developed and completed within a single segment of space or time separated from regular news coverage, and presented as the editorial responsibility of a single, named, nationally recognized professional journalist.

Common meaning. Signs having evaluative meanings that vary minimally with the persons producing or receiving them.

Difference scores. See Television/newspaper difference scores.

Doctrine of scarcity. The premise that the electromagnetic spectrum, the essential natural resource for broadcast frequencies, is limited in space and thus has the potential for scarcity.

Evaluative dimension. The dimension in the content analysis procedures that ranges along a continuum from positive to negative.

First Amendment theory. The constellation of interpretations, definitions, prescriptions, and proscriptions that articulates the American commitment to freedom of expression.

Government. The full spectrum of federal official entities and policy-making personnel, encompassing the executive, legislative, and judicial branches as well as the independent regulatory agencies.

Government-of-the-day. The agencies and personnel perceived by the press to speak for the White House.

Index of vigorousness. A statistic in the content analysis procedures that sums the weighted vigorousness quotients of major issues, minor issues, and nonissues.

Index of White House anti-media assault. A statistic that represents a quantified summary of the volume and intensity of anti-media efforts by the Nixon White House, as perceived by media executives during the Nixon presidency.

Interpretive journalism. The type of professionally processed, mass-disseminated news and public affairs coverage that includes subjectivity (inference, judgments, and/or advocacy) in addition to, or instead of, objectivity (factual reports).

Journalism. News and public affairs information prepared and disseminated by the press.

Journalism tradition. A body of First Amendment theory that is rooted in libertarian philosophy and that speaks to editorial autonomy for the press and no government restraint prior to dissemination, but to post-dissemination punishment for certain stipulated transgressions.

Language intensity. A statistic in the content analysis procedures that sums the mean of the absolute values of the evaluative dimensions with the means of the potency and the activity dimensions.

Major issues. Those topics identified by 1972 public opinion surveys as representing issues of the highest importance to our citizenry.

Minor issues. Those topics identified by 1972 public opinion surveys as representing issues of less importance to our citizenry than those considered, at the time, to represent acute crises or most pressing situations.

Nixon administration. The government-of-the-day during the Nixon presidency (January 20, 1969 through August 9, 1974).

Nonissues. Those topics identified by 1972 public opinion surveys as representing issues of limited interest, or little or no controversiality, or of value to only a small segment of our citizenry.

Paradigm. A tradition of attitudes, policy, and behavior that is viewed by a given community as a framework for present and ongoing practice.

Potency dimension. The dimension in the content analysis procedures that ranges along a continuum from strong to weak.

Press. Those mass media — both print and broadcasting — that serve to gather, process, and disseminate news and public affairs information to the public.

Public policy. The body of directives embodying the values of a society as perceived and articulated by its governors.

Public press policy. The body of governmental decisions relative to the activity of the press.

Public trustee principle. The central assumption of broadcast regulatory policy in the United States, which holds that the broadcaster is a "public trustee" who is permitted private gain from use of the publicly owned electromagnetic spectrum so long as he uses that property according to the "public interest, convenience and necessity."

Regulation tradition. A body of First Amendment theory that is rooted in the philosophy of social responsibility and permits affirmative action by government to ensure the people's right to know.

Reverse chilling effect. Increased vigorousness in discussions of one or more subject matter categories when, over the same period of time and under the same general circumstances, one or more other subject matter categories meet the criteria set forth for determining the existence of the "chilling effect."

Standardized attitude object. A designation in a category scheme of six classes of attitude objects that subsumes all relevant attitude objects under study in the content analysis.

Stanford Political Dictionary. A dictionary assigning values along three dimensions — evaluative, potency, and activity — to nearly 4,000 words perceived as relevant to political documents.

Television/newspaper difference scores. For use in chilling effect analysis, vigorousness scores reflecting the comparison of two populations in which vigorousness measures of the population used as a standard (newspapers) are subtracted from vigorousness measures of the target population (television).

Thesis statement. A single sentence that expresses the dominant idea of a discourse.

Vigorousness. The quality of interpretive journalism that approximates "uninhibited, robust and wide-open" debate on public issues, where "uninhibited" means free from constraints; "robust," strong and powerful; "wide-open," of sufficient quantity; "debate," discourse defending or attacking a given proposition; and "public issues," controversial matters of public importance.

Vigorousness quotient. A statistic in the content analysis procedures that weights the language intensity of a class of standardized attitude objects with its relative frequency.

Watergate. The battery of charges against the Nixon administration that includes but is not limited to the June 17, 1972, break-in at the Democratic National Committee's headquarters in the Watergate office building and the "cover-up" that followed.

Watergate affairs. Pervasive and blatant White House immorality and criminality that includes but is not limited to the June 17, 1972, break-in at the Democratic National Committee's headquarters in the Watergate office building, the "cover-up" that followed, related court and congressional proceedings, and the president's resignation.

WHAMA. The acronym for index of White House anti-media assault.

White House anti-media assault. A campaign of anti-media efforts by the government-of-the-day.

White House anti-media efforts. Those efforts by the government-of-the-day perceived by media executives as representing intent — directly or indirectly — to discredit, harass, intimidate, manipulate, or otherwise influence the news media.

White House media efforts. Those efforts by the government-of-the-day directed to or involving use of the media.

BIBLIOGRAPHY

Abel, John D., Charles Clift III, and Fredric A. Weiss.
  1970. "Station License Revocations and Denials of Renewal, 1934-1969."
    Journal of Broadcasting 14 (Fall):411-421.

Adams, William, and Fay Schreibman, eds.
  1978. *Television Network News: Issues in Content Research.* Washington,
    D.C.: George Washington University.

Altschull, J. Herbert.
  1973. "The Journalist and Instant History: An Example of Jackal Syn-
    drome." *Journalism Quarterly* 53, no. 3 (Autumn):489-496.

Ames, William E., and Dwight L. Teeter.
  1971. "Politics, Economics, and the Mass Media." In Ronald T. Farrar and
    John D. Stevens, eds. *Mass Media and the National Experience.* New
    York: Harper and Row.

Anderson, Jack.
  1974. *The Anderson Papers.* New York: Ballantine Books.

Arieff, Irwin.
  1977. "Profits or a Free Press: The Effects of Broadcast Regulation." *Wash-
    ington Journalism Review* 1 (October):40-44.

Arkin, Herbert, and Raymond R. Colton.
  1963. *Tables for Statisticians.* 2nd ed. New York: Barnes and Noble.

Ashmore, Harry S.
  1973. *Fear in the Air.* New York: W. W. Norton.

Association of Radio News Analysts.
  1954. *History, Constitution, and Membership: 1942-1954.* New York:
    ARNA.

Atwood, L. Erwin, and Gerald L. Grotta.
  1973. "Socialization of News Values in Beginning Reporters." *Journalism
    Quarterly* 50 (Winter):759-761.

Babbie, Earl R.
  1973. *Survey Research Methods.* Belmont, Calif.: Wadsworth.

Backstron, Charles H., and Gerald D. Hursh.
    1963. *Survey Research*. Evanston, Ill.: Northwestern University Press.

Bagdikian, Ben H.
    1971a. *The Information Machines: Their Impact on Men and the Media*. New York: Harper and Row.

    1971b. "What Did We Learn?" *Columbia Journalism Review*, September/October, pp. 45-50.

    1972. *The Effete Conspiracy and Other Crimes of the Press*. New York: Harper and Row.

    1973. "Election Coverage '72: The Fruits of Agnewism." *Columbia Journalism Review*, January/February, pp. 9-23.

Balutis, Alan P.
    1976. "Congress, the President and the Press." *Journalism Quarterly* 53 (Autumn):509-515.

Barcus, Francis E.
    1960. "A Bibliography of Studies of Radio and Television Program Content, 1928-1958." *Journal of Broadcasting* 4 (Fall):355-369.

Barnouw, Erik.
    1975. *Tube of Plenty: The Evolution of American Television*. New York: Oxford University Press.

Barrett, Marvin, ed.
    1969. *The Alfred I. duPont-Columbia University Survey of Broadcast Journalism 1968-1969*. New York: Grosset and Dunlap.

    1970. *The Alfred I. duPont-Columbia University Survey of Broadcast Journalism 1969-1970: Year of Challenge, Year of Crisis*. New York: Grosset and Dunlap.

    1971. *The Alfred I. duPont-Columbia University Survey of Broadcast Journalism 1970-1971: A State of Siege*. New York: Grosset and Dunlap.

    1973. *The Alfred I. duPont-Columbia University Survey of Broadcast Journalism 1971-1972: The Politics of Broadcasting*. New York: Thomas Y. Crowell.

1975. *The Fifth Alfred I. duPont-Columbia University Survey of Broadcast Journalism: Moment of Truth?* New York: Thomas Y. Crowell.

Barron, Jerome A.
1961. "The Federal Communications Commission's Fairness Doctrine: An Evaluation." *George Washington Law Review* 30:1. Also in Donald M. Gillmor and Jerome A. Barron. *Mass Communication Law.* 2nd ed. St. Paul, Minn.: West Publishing, 1974. Pp. 801-803.

1964. "In Defense of 'Fairness': A First Amendment Rationale for Broadcasting's "Fairness" Doctrine." *University of Colorado Law Review* 31:46-48. Also in Donald M. Gillmor and Jerome A. Barron. *Mass Communication Law.* 2nd ed. St. Paul, Minn.: West Publishing, 1974. Pp. 803-804.

1967. "Access to the Press — A New First Amendment Right." *Harvard Law Review* 80:1641. Also in Donald M. Gillmor and Jerome A. Barron. *Mass Communication Law.* 2nd ed. St. Paul, Minn.: West Publishing, 1974. Pp. 553-572.

1975. *Freedom of the Press for Whom? The Right of Access to Mass Media.* Bloomington: Indiana University Press.

Bartlett, John.
1955. *Bartlett's Familiar Quotations.* 13th ed. Boston: Little, Brown.

Becker, Lee B.
1976. "Two Tests of Media Gratifications: Watergate and the 1974 Election." *Journalism Quarterly* 53 (Spring):28-33, 87.

Berelson, Bernard.
1952. *Content Analysis in Communication Research.* New York: Hafner. Repr. 1971.

Berelson, Bernard, and Morris Janovitz, eds.
1966. *Reader in Public Opinion and Communication.* 2nd ed. New York: The Free Press.

Bernstein, Carl, and Bob Woodward.
1974. *All the President's Men.* New York: Warner.

Besterman, Theodore.
1965. *A World Bibliography of Bibliographies.* 4th ed. 4 vols. Lausanne, Switzerland: Societas Bibliographica.

Blum, Eleanor.
  1972. *Basic Books in the Mass Media*. Urbana: University of Illinois Press.

Bobrow, Davis B.
  1974. "Mass Communication and the Political System." In W. Phillips
    Davison and Frederick T. C. Yu, eds. *Mass Communication Research*.
    New York: Praeger. Pp. 93-121.

Bosmajian, Haig A., ed.
  1971. *The Principles and Practice of Freedom of Speech*. Boston: Houghton
    Mifflin.

Bower, Robert T.
  1973. *Television and the Public*. New York: Holt, Rinehart, and Winston.

Broadcasting.
  1976. "From Fighting Bob to the Fairness Doctrine." 5 (January):46-68,
    at 50.

Brechner, Joseph L.
  1970. "A Statement on the 'Fairness Doctrine.'" In John M. Kittross and
    Kenneth Harwood, eds. *Free and Fair*. Philadelphia: Association for
    Professional Broadcasting Education. Pp. 143-152.

Breed, Warren.
  1955. "Social Control in the News Room." *Social Forces* 33 (May):326-335.

Brown, Les.
  1971. *Televi$ion: The Business Behind the Box*. New York: Harcourt
    Brace Jovanovich.

Buckalew, James K.
  1969-1970. "News Elements and Election by Television News Editors."
    Journalism of Broadcasting 14 (Winter):47-54.

Budd, Richard W., Robert K. Thorp, and Lewis Donohew.
  1967. *Content Analysis of Communications*. New York: Macmillan.

Bush, Chilton R.
  1960. "A System of Categories for General News Content." *Journalism
    Quarterly* 37 (Spring):206-210.

Byrne, Gary C.
  1969. "Mass Media and Political Socialization of Children and Preadults."
    Journalism Quarterly 46 (Spring):140-144.

Campbell, Donald T., and Julian C. Stanley.
  1963. *Experimental and Quasi-Experimental Designs for Research*. Chicago: Rand McNally.

Cater, Douglas.
  1959. *The Fourth Branch of Government*. Boston: Houghton Mifflin.

  1972. "The Politics of Public TV." *Columbia Journalism Review*, July/August, pp. 8-15.

Chafee, Zecharia, Jr.
  1941. *Free Speech in the United States*. Cambridge, Mass.: Harvard University Press.

  1947. *Government and Mass Communications: A Report from the Commission on Freedom of the Press*. Chicago: University of Chicago Press.

Chaffee, Steven H.
  1972. "The Interpersonal Context of Mass Communication." In F. Gerald Kline and Phillip J. Tichenor, eds. *Current Perspectives in Mass Communication Research*. Beverly Hills, Calif.: Sage. Pp. 95-120.

Chaffee, Steven H., L. Scott Ward, and Leonard P. Tipton.
  1970. "Mass Communication and Political Socialization." *Journalism Quarterly* 47:647-659, 666.

Clark, David G.
  1968. "H. V. Kaltenborn and His Sponsors: Controversial Broadcasting and the Sponsor's Role." *Journal of Broadcasting* 12 (Fall):309-321.

Clarke, Peter, and Lee Ruggels.
  1970. "Preferences Among News Media for Coverage of Public Affairs." *Journalism Quarterly* 47:464-471.

Clayes, Stanley A., and David G. Spencer.
  1972. *Contexts for Composition*. 3rd ed. New York: Appleton-Century-Crofts.

Clift, Charles III, Frederic A. Weiss, and John D. Abel.
  1971. "Ten Years of Forfeitures by the Federal Communications Commission." *Journal of Broadcasting* 15 (Fall):379-385.

Coase, R. H.
  1959. "The Federal Communications Commission." *Journal of Law and Economics* 2 (October):1-40.

1974. "The Market for Goods and the Market for Ideas." *American Economic Review* 64 (May). Reprint no. 28 of the American Economic Association.

Coffey, Philip J.
1975. "Measure of Bias in Reporting of Political News." *Journalism Quarterly* 52 (Autumn):551-553.

Cohen, Jacob.
1968. "Multiple Regression as a General Data-analytic System." *Psychological Bulletin* 70, no. 6:426-443.

Cole, Richard R., and Donald Lewis Shaw.
1974. "'Powerful' Verbs and 'Body Language': Does the Reader Notice?" *Journalism Quarterly* 51 (Spring):62-66.

Columbia Journalism Review.
1974. "Has the Press Done a Job on Nixon? Report on Two Panels Re-examining the Problem of Fairness." January/February, pp. 50-58.

Commission on Freedom of the Press.
1947. *A Free and Responsible Press*. Chicago: University of Chicago Press.

Cooney, Stuart.
1969-1970. "An Annotated Bibliography of Articles on Broadcasting Law and Regulation in Law Periodicals 1920-1955." *Journal of Broadcasting* 14, pt. 2 (Winter):133-146.

Cornwell, Elmer E., Jr.
1976. "The President and the Press: Phases in the Relationship." In L. John Martin, ed. "The Role of the Mass Media in American Politics." *Annals of the American Academy of Political and Social Science* 427 (September):53-54.

Crosby, Harry H., and George F. Estey.
1968. *College Writing: The Rhetorical Imperative*. New York: Harper and Row.

Crouse, Timothy.
1973. *The Boys on the Bus*. New York: Random House.

Culbert, David Holbrook.
1976. *News for Everyman: Radio and Foreign Affairs in Thirties America*. Westport, Conn.: Greenwood Press.

Cusack, Mary Ann.
    1963-1964. "The Emergence of Political Editorializing in Broadcasting."
    Journal of Broadcasting 8 (Winter):53-62.

Danielson, Wayne A.
    1966. "Content Analysis in Communication Research." In Ralph O. Naf-
    ziger and David M. White, eds. *Introduction to Mass Communications
    Research*. 2nd ed. Baton Rouge: Louisiana State University Press.
    Pp. 180-206.

Danielson, Wayne, and G. C. Wilhoit, Jr.
    1967. *A Computerized Bibliography of Mass Communication Research
    1944-1964*. New York: Magazine Publishers Association.

Davis, Hal, and Galen Rarick.
    1964. "Functions of Editorials and Letters to the Editor." *Journalism
    Quarterly* 41 (Winter):108-109.

Davison, W. Phillips, and Frederick T. C. Yu, eds.
    1974. *Mass Communication Research: Major Issues and Future Directions*.
    New York: Praeger.

De Mott, John.
    1973. " 'Interpretative' News Stories Compared with 'Spot' News." *Journal-
    ism Quarterly* 50 (Spring):102-108.

Deutsch, Karl W.
    1963. *The Nerves of Government: Models of Political Communication and
    Control*. New York: Free Press.

Deutschmann, Paul J.
    1959. *News-page Content of Twelve Metropolitan Dailies*. New York:
    E. W. Scripps.

Devol, Kenneth S., ed.
    1976. *Mass Media and the Supreme Court: The Legacy of the Warren
    Years*. 2nd ed. New York: Hastings House.

Dexter, Lewis Anthony, and David Manning White, eds.
    1964. *People, Society and Mass Communications*. New York: Free Press.

Diamond, Edwin.
    1973. "Fairness and Balance in the Evening News." *Columbia Journalism
    Review*, January/February, pp. 22-23.

1974a. "Psychojournalism: Nixon on the Couch." *Columbia Journalism Review*, March/April, pp. 7-11.

1974b. "TV and Watergate: What Was, What Might Have Been." In Michael C. Emery and Ted Curtis Smythe, eds. *Readings in Mass Communication*. 2nd ed. Dubuque, Iowa: Wm. C. Brown. Pp. 393-396.

Dobrovir, William A., Joseph D. Gebhardt, Samuel J. Buffone, and Andra N. Oakes.
1974. *The Offenses of Richard M. Nixon: A Guide for the People of the United States of America*. New York: Quadrangle/The New York Times Book Co.

Dominick, Joseph R., Alan Wurtzel, and Gut Lometti.
1975. "Television Journalism vs. Show Business: A Content Analysis of Eyewitness News." *Journalism Quarterly* 52 (Summer):213-218.

Drossman, Evan, and Edward W. Knappman, eds.
1974. *Watergate and the White House: July-December 1973*. Vol. II. New York: Facts on File.

Efron, Edith.
1971. *The News Twisters*. Los Angeles: Nash Publishing.

Emerson, Thomas I.
1966. *Toward a General Theory of the First Amendment*. New York: Random House.

1970. *The System of Freedom of Expression*. New York: Random House.

1971. "Where We Stand: A Legal View." *Columbia Journalism Review*, September/October, pp. 34-44.

Emery, Edwin.
1976. "Changing Role of the Mass Media in American Politics." In John L. Martin, ed. "Role of the Mass Media in American Politics." *Annals of the American Academy of Political and Social Science* 427 (September):84-94.

Emery, Michael C., and Ted Curtis Smythe, eds.
1974. *Readings in Mass Communication: Concepts and Issues in the Mass Media* 2nd ed. Dubuque, Iowa: Wm. C. Brown. 3rd ed., 1976.

Emery, Walter B.
  1971. *Broadcasting and Government: Responsibilities and Regulation.* 2nd ed. East Lansing: Michigan State University Press.

Epstein, Edward Jay.
  1973. *News from Nowhere.* New York: Random House.

  1975. *Between Fact and Fiction: The Problem of Journalism.* New York: Random House.

Ernst, Morris L.
  1946. *The First Freedom.* New York: Macmillan.

Evarts, Dru, and Guido H. Stempel III.
  1974. "Coverage of the 1972 Campaign by TV, News Magazines and Major Newspapers." *Journalism Quarterly* 51 (Winter):645-648, 676.

Fang, Irving E.
  1977. *Those Radio Commentators!* Ames: Iowa State University Press.

Farrar, Ronald T., and John D. Stevens, eds.
  1971. *Mass Media and the National Experience: Essays in Communications History.* New York: Harper and Row.

Federal Communications Commission.
  1949. *In the Matter of Editorializing by Broadcast Licensees.* 13 FCC 1246.

  1964. *Applicability of the Fairness Doctrine in the Handling of Controversial Issues of Public Importance.* 29 Fed. Reg. 10415.

  1974. *Fairness Doctrine and Public Interest Standards: Fairness Report Regarding Handling of Public Issues.* 39 Fed. Reg. 26372.

The Federalist (1787-1788).
  1955. *Selections.* Chicago: The Great Books Foundation.

Festinger, Leon.
  1966. *A Theory of Cognitive Dissonance.* Stanford, Calif.: Stanford University Press.

Finlay, D. J., O. R. Holsti, and R. R. Fagen.
  1967. *Enemies in Politics.* Chicago: Rand McNally.

Flegel, Ruth C., and Steven H. Chaffee.
    1971. "Influence of Editors, Readers, and Personal Opinions on Reporters."
    Journalism Quarterly 48 (Winter):645-651.

Flynn, Patrick H.
    1970. "Countervailing Power in Network Television." *Journal of Broadcasting* 14 (Summer):297-305.

Ford, Frederick W.
    1970. "The Fairness Doctrine." In John M. Kittross and Kenneth Harwood,
    eds. *Free and Fair*. Philadelphia: Association for Professional Broadcasting Education. Pp. 119-131.

Fowler, Joseph S., and Stuart W. Showalter.
    1974. "Evening Network News Selection: A Confirmation of News Judgment." *Journalism Quarterly* 51 (Winter):712-715.

Francois, William E.
    1978. *Mass Media Law and Regulation*. 2nd ed. Columbus, Ohio: Grid.

Frank, Robert S.
    1973. *Message Dimensions of Television News*. Lexington, Mass.: D. C.
    Heath.

Frankel, Max.
    1971. "The 'State Secrets' Myth." *Columbia Journalism Review*, September/October, pp. 22-26.

Franklin, Marc A.
    1977. *Cases and Materials on Mass Media Law*. Mineola, N.Y.: The Foundation Press.

Freedom of Information Center.
    1975a. *Index: FOI Reports*. Freedom of Information Center Report no.
    341. Columbus: School of Journalism, University of Missouri.

    1975b. *Annotated Bibliography* Freedom of Information Center Report
    no. 344. Columbus: School of Journalism, University of Missouri.

French, John W., and William B. Michael.
    1966. *Standards for Educational and Psychological Tests and Manuals*.
    Washington, D.C.: American Psychological Association.

Friedenthal, Jack H., and Richard J. Medalie.
1959. "Impact of Federal Regulation on Political Broadcasting: Section 315 of the Communications Act." *Harvard Law Review* 72 (January):445.

Friedman, Mel.
1978. "A New Communications Act: The Debate Begins." *Columbia Journalism Review*, September/October, pp. 40-43.

Friendly, Fred W.
1967. *Due to Circumstances Beyond Our Control* . . . New York: Vintage Books.

1973. "The Campaign to Politicize Broadcasting." *Columbia Journalism Review*, March/April, pp. 9-18.

1976. *The Good Guys, the Bad Guys and the First Amendment: Free Speech vs. Fairness in Broadcasting.* New York: Random House.

Funkhouser, G. Ray.
1973. "Trends in Media Coverage of the Issues of the '60s." *Journalism Quarterly* 50 (Autumn):533-538.

Gandy, Oscar H., Jr., Susan Miller, William L. Rivers, and Gail Ann Rivers.
1975. *Media and Government: An Annotated Bibliography.* Stanford, Calif.: Institute for Communication Research.

Gates, Gary Paul.
1978. *Air Time: The Inside Story of CBS News.* New York: Harper and Row.

Geller, A., D. Kaplan, and Harold D. Lasswell.
1942. "An Experimental Comparison of Four Ways of Coding Editorial Content." *Journalism Quarterly* 19 (December):362-370.

George, Alexander L.
1959. "Quantitative and Qualitative Approaches to Content Analysis." In Ithielde Sola Pool, ed. *Trends in Content Analysis.* Urbana: University of Illinois Press. Pp. 7-32.

Georgetown Law Journal.
1973. *Media and the First Amendment in a Free Society.* Amherst: University of Massachusetts Press.

Gerbner, George.
    1973. "Cultural Indicators: The Third Voice." In George Gerbner, Larry
        P. Gross, and William H. Melody, eds. *Communication Technology
        and Social Policy*. New York: John Wiley. Pp. 555-573.

Gerbner, George, Larry P. Gross, and William H. Melody, eds.
    1973. *Communication Technology and Social Policy*. New York: John
        Wiley.

Gerbner, George, Ole R. Holsti, Klaus Krippendorff, William J. Paisley, and
Philip J. Stone, eds.
    1969. *The Analysis of Communication Content: Developments in Scientific
        Theories and Computer Techniques*. New York: John Wiley.

Gideon, Seymour.
    1942. "The Relationship of the Press to Government and to the People."
        Journalism Quarterly 19 (March):51-57.

Gieber, Walter.
    1955. "Do Newspapers Over-play 'Negative' News?" *Journalism Quarterly*
        32 (Summer):311-318.

Gillmor, Donald M., and Jerome A. Barron.
    1974. *Mass Communication Law: Cases and Comment*. 2nd ed. St. Paul,
        Minn.: West Publishing.

Goldberg, Henry, and Michael Couzens.
    1978. " 'Peculiar Characteristics': An Analysis of the First Amendment
        Implications of Broadcast Regulation." *Federal Communications Law
        Journal* 31, no. 1 (Winter):1-50.

Gompertz, Kenneth.
    1969-1970. "A Bibliography of Articles About Broadcasting in Law Period-
        icals." *Journal of Broadcasting* 14, pt. 2 (Winter):83-132.

Green, Maury.
    1969. *Television News: Anatomy and Process*. Belmont, Calif.: Wadsworth.

Gregg, James E.
    1965. "Newspaper Editorial Endorsements and California, 1948-1962."
        Journalism Quarterly 42 (Autumn):532-538.

Hachten, William A.
    1968. *The Supreme Court on Freedom of the Press: Decisions and Dissents*.
        Ames: Iowa State University Press.

Halberstam, David.
1972. *The Best and the Brightest*. New York: Random House.

Harwood, Kenneth A.
1961. "A World Bibliography of Selected Periodicals on Broadcasting."
Journal of Broadcasting 5 (Summer):251-278.

1972. "A World Bibliography of Selected Periodicals on Broadcasting."
Revised. *Journal of Broadcasting* 16 (Spring):131-146.

Hayakawa, S. I.
1964. *The Language in Thought and Action*. New York: Harcourt Brace
Jovanovich. Excerpted in Stanley A. Clayes and David G. Spencer.
Contexts for Composition. 3rd ed. New York: Appleton-Century-
Crofts, 1972. Pp. 5-19.

Hazard, William R.
1962-1963. "On the Impact of Television's Pictured News." *Journal of
Broadcasting* 7 (Winter):43-51.

Head, Sydney W., ed.
1976. *Broadcasting in America: A Survey of Television and Radio*. 3rd ed.
Boston: Houghton Mifflin.

Heider, Fritz.
1946. "Attitudes and Cognitive Organization." *Journal of Psychology*
21:107-112.

Hentoff, Nat.
1974. "Woodward, Bernstein and 'All the President's Men.'" *Columbia
Journalism Review*, July/August, pp. 10-13.

Herschensohn, Bruce.
1976. *The Gods of Antenna*. New Rochelle, N.Y.: Arlington House.

Hickey, Neil.
1977. "Is Television Doing Its Investigative Reporting Job?" *TV Guide*
25 (April 2):2-6.

Hiebert, Ray Eldon, and Carlton Spitzer, eds.
1968. *The Voice of Government*. New York: John Wiley.

Hofstetter, C. Richard.
1976. *Bias in the News: Network Television Coverage of the 1972 Election
Campaign*. Columbus: Ohio State University Press.

Holsti, Ole R.

1966. "External Conflict and Internal Consensus: The Sino-Soviet Case." In Philip J. Stone, Dexter C. Dumphy, Marshall S. Smith, and Daniel M. Ogilvie, eds. *The General Inquirer*. Cambridge, Mass.: M.I.T. Press. Pp. 343-358.

1967. "Cognitive Dynamics and Images in the Enemy." In D. J. Finlay, O. R. Holsti, and R. R. Fagen, eds. *Enemies in Politics*. Chicago: Rand McNally. Pp. 25-96.

1968. "Content Analysis." In Gardner Lindzey and Elliot Aronson, eds. *The Handbook of Social Psychology*. Vol. II. *Research Methods*. Reading, Mass.: Addison-Wesley. Pp. 596-692.

1969a. "A Computer Content-Analysis Program for Analysing Attitudes: The Measurement of Qualities and Performance." In George Gerbner, Ole R. Holsti, et al., eds. *The Analysis of Communication Content*. New York: John Wiley. Pp. 355-380.

1969b. *Content Analysis for the Social Sciences and Humanities*. Reading, Mass.: Addison Wesley.

Holsti, Ole R., P. Terrence Hopmann, and John D. Sullivan.

1973. *Unity and Disintegration in International Alliances: Computer Studies*. New York: John Wiley.

Hopmann, P. Terrence.

1969. "International Conflict and Cohesion in International Political Coalitions: NATO and the Communist System During the Postwar Years." Unpublished Ph.D. dissertation, Stanford University. In *Dissertation Abstracts International* sec. A, 30:3526, 3527.

Howell, Rex G.

1970. "Fairness . . . Fact or Fable?" In John M. Kittross and Kenneth Harwood, eds. *Free and Fair*. Philadelphia: Association for Professional Broadcasting Education. Pp. 133-142.

Howe, Quincy.

1957. "The Rise and Fall of the Radio Commentator." *The Saturday Review*, October 26, 1957.

Hulteng, John L.

1976. *The Messenger's Motives*. Englewood Cliffs, N.J.: Prentice-Hall.

Hyman, Herbert H.
   1974. "Mass Communication and Socialization." In W. Phillips Davison
   and Frederick T. C. Yu, eds. *Mass Communication Research*. New
   York: Praeger. Pp. 36-65.

Hynds, Ernest C.
   1975. *American Newspapers in the 1970s*. New York: Hastings House.

Johnson, Haynes.
   1974. "Watergate: The American Press' Finest Hour?" In Michael C. Emery
   and Ted Curtis Smythe, eds. *Readings in Mass Communication*. 2nd ed.
   Dubuque, Iowa: Wm. C. Brown. Pp. 389-393.

Johnstone, John W. C.
   1976. "Organizational Constraints on Newswork." *Journalism Quarterly*
   53 (Spring):5-13.

Jones, William K.
   1976. *Cases and Materials on Electronic Mass Media: Radio, Television
   and Cable*. Mineola, N.Y.: The Foundation Press.

Joseph, Ted.
   1973. "How White House Correspondents Feel About Background Briefings." *Journalism Quarterly* 50 (Autumn):509-516.

Kahn, Frank J.
   1973. *Documents of American Broadcasting*. 2nd ed. New York: Appleton-
   Century-Crofts. 3rd ed., 1978.

   1974. "The Quasi-Utility Basis for Broadcast Regulation." *Journal of Broadcasting* 18 (Summer):259-276.

Kaid, Lynda Lee, Keith R. Sanders, and Robert O. Hirsch.
   1974. *Political Campaign Communication: A Bibliography and Guide to
   the Literature*. Metuchen, N.J.: Scarecrow Press.

Katz, Elihu.
   1971. "Platforms and Windows: Broadcasting's Role in Election Campaigns." *Journalism Quarterly* 48 (Summer):304-314.

Katz, Elihu, Jay G. Blumler, and Michael Gurevitch.
   1974. "Uses of Mass Communication by the Individual." In W. Phillips
   Davison and Frederick T. C. Yu, eds. *Mass Communication Research*.
   New York: Praeger. Pp. 11-35.

Keogh, James.
    1972. *President Nixon and the Press*. New York: Funk and Wagnalls.

Kittross, John M.
    1978. *A Bibliography of Theses and Dissertations in Broadcasting: 1920-1973*. Washington, D.C.: Broadcast Education Association.

Kittross, John M., and Kenneth Harwood, eds.
    1970. *Free and Fair: Courtroom Access and the Fairness Doctrine*. Philadelphia: Association for Professional Broadcasting Education.

Klapper, Joseph T.
    1960. *The Effects of Mass Communication*. New York: The Free Press.

Kline, F. Gerald.
    1972. "Theory in Mass Communication Research." In F. Gerald Kline and Phillip J. Tichenor, eds. *Current Perspectives in Mass Communication Research*. Beverly Hills, Calif.: Sage. Pp. 17-40.

Kline, F. Gerald, and Phillip J. Tichenor, eds.
    1972. *Current Perspectives in Mass Communication Research*. Beverly Hills, Calif.: Sage.

Knappman, Edward, ed.
    1973. *Watergate and the White House: June 1972-July 1973*. Vol. I. New York: Facts on File.

    1974. *Government and the Media in Conflict/1970-74*. New York: Facts on File.

Knappman, Edward, and Evan Drossman, eds.
    1974. *Watergate and the White House: January/September 1974*. Vol. III. New York: Facts on File.

Knight, Robert P., and Alfred Delahaye, eds.
    1972. "Articles on Mass Communication in U.S. and Foreign Journals." *Journalism Quarterly* 49 (Spring):200-211.

    1973. "Articles on Mass Communication in U.S. and Foreign Journals." *Journalism Quarterly* 50 (Autumn):612-623.

Knoll, Steve.
    1972. "When TV Was Offered the Pentagon Papers." *Columbia Journalism Review*, March/April, pp. 46-48.

Knower, Franklin.
　　1967. "Graduate Theses and Dissertations on Broadcasting: 1963-1966." *Journal of Broadcasting* 11 (Spring):153-181.

Krasnow, Erwin G., and Lawrence D. Longley.
　　1978. *The Politics of Broadcast Regulation*. 2nd ed. New York: St. Martin's Press.

Krieghbaum, Hillier.
　　1956. *Facts in Perspective*. Englewood Cliffs, N.J.: Prentice-Hall.

　　1972. *Pressures on the Press*. New York: Thomas Y. Crowell.

Krippendorff, Klaus.
　　1969. "Models of Messages: Three Prototypes." In George Gerbner, Ole R. Holsti, et al., eds. *The Analysis of Communication Content*. New York: John Wiley. Pp. 69-106.

Kuhn, Thomas S.
　　1962. *The Structure of Scientific Revolutions*. Chicago: University of Chicago Press.

Kwong, Chan Ying, and Kenneth Starck.
　　1976. "The New York *Times*' Stance on Nixon and Public Opinion." *Journalism Quarterly* 53 (Winter):723-727.

Ladd, Bruce.
　　1968. *Crisis in Credibility*. New York: New American Library.

Laing, Robert B., and Robert L. Stevenson.
　　1976. "Public Opinion Trends in the Last Days of the Nixon Administration." *Journalism Quarterly* 53 (Summer):294-302.

Lang, Kurt, and Gladys Engel Lang.
　　1973. "Televised Hearings: The Impact Out There." *Columbia Journalism Review*, November/December, pp. 52-57.

Lantz, Gerald A.
　　1975. "Beardsley's Aesthetics and Evaluative Assertion Analysis: Basis for a Content Analysis of a Selected Sample of Recent American Film Criticism by Selected Critics." Unpublished master's thesis, Temple University.

Lashner, Marilyn A.

1976a. "Privacy and the Public's Right to Know." *Journalism Quarterly* 53 (Winter):679-688.

1976b. "The Role of Foundations in Public Broadcasting, Part I: Development and Trends." *Journal of Broadcasting* 20 (Fall):529-547.

1977a. "The Role of Foundations in Public Broadcasting, Part II: The Ford Foundation." *Journal of Broadcasting* 21 (Spring):235-254.

1977b. "Broadcasting and the Separate Traditions of First Amendment Theory." *Congressional Record*, 95th Cong., 1st sess. (July 29):S13142-13144; (August 1):E5001-5003.

1977c. "A Free Electronic Press: The Key to a Vigorous Republic." *Feedback* 19 (November):1-4.

1979. "The Chilling Effect of a White House Anti-media Assault on Political Commentary in Network Television News Programs: Comparison of Newspaper and Television Vigorousness During the Nixon Administration." Unpublished Ph.D. dissertation, Temple University.

Lasswell, Harold.

1966. "The Structure and Function of Communication in Society." In Bernard Berelson and Morris Janovitz, eds. *Reader in Public Opinion and Communication*. 2nd ed. New York: The Free Press. Pp. 178-190.

Lasswell, Harold, and associates.

1942. "The Politically Significant Content of the Press: Coding Procedures." *Journalism Quarterly* 19 (March):12-23.

Latham, Aaron.

1974. "How 'The Washington Post' Gave Nixon Hell." In Michael C. Emery and Ted Curtis Smythe, eds. *Readings in Mass Communication*. 2nd ed. Dubuque, Iowa: Wm. C. Brown. Pp. 377-389.

Le Duc, Don R., and Thomas A. McCain.

1970. "The Federal Radio Commission in Federal Court: Origins of Broadcast Regulatory Doctrines." *Journal of Broadcasting* 14, 4 (Fall): 393-410.

Lee Jae-won.

1972. "Editorial Support and Campaign News: Content Analysis by Q-Method." *Journalism Quarterly* 49 (Winter):710-716.

Lerner, Daniel.
    1971. "Effective Propaganda: Conditions and Evaluation." In Wilbur Schramm and D. F. Roberts, eds. *The Process and Effects of Mass Communication.* Urbana: University of Illinois Press. Pp. 480-489.

Leroy, David J., and Christopher H. Sterling, eds.
    1973. *Mass News: Practices, Controversies, and Alternatives.* Englewood Cliffs, N.J.: Prentice-Hall.

Levy, Leonard W., ed.
    1960. *Legacy of Suppression.* Cambridge, Mass.: Harvard University Press.

    1966. *Freedom of the Press from Zenger to Jefferson.* New York: Bobbs-Merrill.

Levy, Sheldon G.
    1968. "Multidimensional Content Analysis of Editorials." *Journalism Quarterly* 45 (Winter):634-640.

Lewis, Finlay.
    1973. "Some Errors and Puzzles in Watergate Coverage." *Columbia Journalism Review*, November/December, pp. 26-32.

Lewis, J. David.
    1969-1970. "Programmer's Choice: Eight Factors in Program Decision-Making." *Journal of Broadcasting* 14 (Winter):71-82.

Lichty, Laurence W., and David J. Leroy.
    1972. "Missing the Newscaster: Reactions to the 1967 AFTRA Strike." *Journal of Broadcasting* 16 (Spring):175-184.

Lindzey, Gardner, and Elliot Aronson, eds.
    1968. *The Handbook of Social Psychology.* Vol. II. *Research Methods.* Reading, Mass.: Addison-Wesley.

Lipsky, Abbott B., Jr.
    1976. "Reconciling *Red Lion* and *Tornillo*: A Consistent Theory of Media Regulation." *Stanford Law Review* 28 (February):563-588.

Liroff, David Benjamin.
    1970. "A Comparative Content Analysis of Network Evening News Programs and Other National News Media in the United States." Unpublished Ph.D. dissertation, Northwestern University.

Locke, John.
  1689. *A Letter Concerning Toleration.* Rev. and ed. by Mario Montuori. The Hague: Martinus Nijhoff, 1963.

  1690. *Essay Concerning Human Understanding.* Abridged and ed. by A. S. Pringle-Pattison. Oxford: Clarendon Press, 1924; repr. 1947.

Loevinger, Lee.
  1964. "The Role of Law in Broadcasting." *Journal of Broadcasting* 8 (Spring):113-126.

Loory, Stuart H.
  1974. "The CIA's Use of the Press: A 'Mighty Wurlitzer.'" *Columbia Journalism Review*, September/October, pp. 9-18.

Lowry, Dennis T.
  1971a. "Agnew and the Network TV News: A Before/After Content Analysis." *Journalism Quarterly* 48 (Summer):205-210.

  1971b. "Gresham's Law and Network TV News Selection." *Journal of Broadcasting* 15 (Fall):397-408.

  1974. "Measures of Network News Bias in the 1972 Presidential Campaign." *Journal of Broadcasting* 18 (Fall):387-402.

MacDougall, Curtis D.
  1964. *The Press and Its Problems.* Dubuque, Iowa: Wm. C. Brown.

Mahoney, Fabia Harris.
  1970. "White House Press Corps Attitudes Toward Press Relations of the Nixon Administration." Unpublished master's thesis, Temple University.

Maines, Patrick D., and John C. Ottinger.
  1973. "Network Documentaries: How Many, How Relevant?" *Columbia Journalism Review*, March/April, pp. 36-42.

Marcuse, Herbert.
  1965. "Repressive Tolerance." In Robert Paul Wolff, Barrington Moore, Jr., and Herbert Marcuse. *A Critique of Pure Tolerance.* Boston: Beacon Press. Pp. 81-117.

Markham, James W., and Guido H. Stempel III.
  1957. "Analysis of Techniques in Measuring Press Performance." *Journalism Quarterly* 34 (Spring):187-190.

Marnell, William H.
   1973. *The Right to Know: Media and the Common Good*. New York: Seabury Press.

Martin, L. John, ed.
   1976. "Role of the Mass Media in American Politics." *Annals of the American Academy of Political and Social Science* 427 (September).

Matlon, Ronald, and Irene R. Matlon.
   1975. *Index to Journals in Communication Studies Through 1974*. Falls Church, Va.: Speech Communication Association.

McCartney, James.
   1973. "The Washington 'Post' and Watergate: How Two Davids Slew Goliath." *Columbia Journalism Review*, July/August, pp. 8-22.

McClenghan, Jack Sean.
   1973. "Effect of Endorsements in Texas Local Elections." *Journalism Quarterly* 50 (Summer):363-366.

McCombs, Maxwell.
   1967. "Editorial Endorsement: A Study of Influence." *Journalism Quarterly* 44 (Autumn):545-548.

   1972. "Mass Communication in Political Campaigns: Information, Gratification, and Persuasion." In F. Gerald Kline and Phillip J. Tichenor, eds. *Current Perspectives in Mass Communication Research*. Beverly Hills, Calif.: Sage. Pp. 169-194.

McCombs, Maxwell, and Donald Shaw.
   1972. "The Agenda-Setting Function of the Media." *Public Opinion Quarterly* 36 (Summer):176-187.

McCoy, Ralph E.
   1968. *Freedom of the Press: An Annotated Bibliography*. Carbondale: Southern Illinois University Press.

McGuire, Delbert.
   1967. "Democracy's Confrontation: The Presidential Press Conference I." *Journalism Quarterly* 44 (Winter):638-644.

McLeod, Jack, and Garrett J. O'Keefe, Jr.
   1972. "The Socialization Perspective and Communication Behavior." In F. Gerald Kline and Phillip J. Tichenor, eds. *Current Perspectives*

in Mass Communication Research. Beverly Hills, Calif.: Sage. Pp. 121-168.

Meadow, Robert G.
    1973. "Cross-Media Comparison of Coverage of the 1972 Presidential Campaign." *Journalism Quarterly* 50 (Autumn):482-488.

Meiklejohn, Alexander.
    1948. *Free Speech and Its Relation to Self-Government*. New York: Harper.

Metz, Robert.
    1975. *CBS: Reflections in a Bloodshot Eye*. New York: Signet.

Midgley, John.
    1976. "American Politics and the Press: A View from Abroad." In L. John Martin, ed. "Role of the Mass Media in American Politics." *Annals of the American Academy of Political and Social Science* 427 (September):104-113.

Mill, John Stuart.
    1859. *On Liberty*. Chicago: The Great Books Foundation, 1955.

Milton, John.
    1644. *The Areopagitica*. Chicago: The Great Books Foundation, 1955.

Minow, Newton N.
    1964. *Equal Time: The Private Broadcaster and the Public Interest*. Edited by Lawrence Laurent. New York: Atheneum.

Minow, Newton N., John Bartlow Martin, and Lee M. Mitchell.
    1973. *Presidential Television*. New York: Basic Books.

Mintz, Morton.
    1972. "Auditing the Media: A Modest Proposal." *Columbia Journalism Review*, November/December, pp. 20-24.

Molotch, Harvey, and Marilyn Lester.
    1974. "News as Purposive Behavior: On the Strategic Use of Routine Events, Accidents and Scandals." *American Sociological Review* 39.

Mott, Frank Luther.
    1962. *American Journalism*. 3rd ed. New York: Macmillan.

Myers, David S.
    1974. "Editorials and Foreign Affairs in the 1972 Presidential Campaign."
    Journalism Quarterly 51 (Summer):251-257, 296.

Nafziger, Ralph O., and David M. White, eds.
    1966. *Introduction to Mass Communications Research*. 2nd ed. Baton
    Rouge: Louisiana State University Press.

Nail, Dawson B.
    1976. "Not Full-Fledged Heirs." Sigma Delta Chi. Pp. 17-20.

Nam, Sunwoo.
    1971. "Editorials as an Indicator of Press Freedom in Three Asian Coun-
    tries." *Journalism Quarterly* 48 (Winter):730-740.

National Press Club.
    1973. *The Press Covers Government: The Nixon Years from 1969 to Water-
    gate*. Washington, D.C.: Department of Communication, the American
    University.

Nelson, Harold L.
    1966. *Freedom of the Press from Hamilton to the Warren Court*. Indianapo-
    lis: Bobbs-Merrill.

Nelson, Harold L., and Dwight L. Teeter, Jr.
    1973. *Law of Mass Communications: Freedom and Control of Print and
    Broadcast Media*. 2nd ed. Mineola, N.Y.: The Foundation Press.

Nixon, Raymond B., and Robert L. Jones.
    1956. "The Content of Non-competitive vs. Competitive Newspapers."
    Journalism Quarterly 33 (Summer):299-314.

Nixon, Richard M.
    1962. *Six Crises*. Garden City, N.Y.: Doubleday.

    1978. *RN, The Memoirs of Richard Nixon*. New York: Grosset and Dunlap.

Noll, Roger G., Morton J. Peck, and John J. McGowan.
    1973. *Economic Aspects of Television Regulation*. Washington, D.C.: The
    Brookings Institution.

Nord, David Paul.
    1977. "First Steps Toward a Theory of Press Control." *Journalism History*
    41 (Spring):8-13.

North, Robert C., Ole R. Holsti, M. George Zaninowich, and Dina A. Zinnes.
   1963. *Content Analysis: A Handbook with Applications for the Study of International Crisis*. Evanston, Ill.: Northwestern University Press.

Novak, M.
   1971. "The Inevitable Bias in Television." In Marvin Barrett, ed. *The Alfred I. duPont-Columbia University Survey of Broadcast Journalism 1969-1970*. New York: Grosset and Dunlap. Pp. 121-132.

Osgood, Charles E.
   1959. "The Representation Model and Relevant Research Methods." In Ithiel de Sola Pool, ed. *Trends in Content Analysis*. Urbana: University of Illinois Press. Pp. 33-88.

Osgood, Charles E., Sol Saporta, and Jum C. Nunnally.
   1956. "Evaluative Assertion Analysis." *Litera* 3:47-102.

Osgood, Charles E., G. J. Suci, and Percy H. Tannenbaum.
   1957. *The Measurement of Meaning*. Urbana: University of Illinois Press.

Osgood, Charles E., and Percy H. Tannenbaum.
   1955. "The Principle of Congruity in the Prediction of Attitude Change." *Psychological Review* 62:42-55.

Owen, Bruce M.
   1975. *Economics and Freedom of Expression*. Cambridge, Mass.: Ballinger.

Owen, Bruce M., David Waterman, and Andrew Wechsler.
   1973. *Mass Communication and Economics: A Bibliography*. Stanford, Calif.: Center for Research in Economic Growth.

Padover, Saul K., ed.
   1943. *The Complete Jefferson*. New York: Duell, Sloan and Pearce.

Paley, William S.
   1979. *As It Happened*. New York: Doubleday.

Parl, Boris.
   1967. *Basic Statistics*. Garden City, N.Y.: Doubleday.

Pekurny, Robert G., and Leonard D. Bart.
   1975. "'Sticks and Bones': A Survey of Network Affiliate Decision-Making." *Journal of Broadcasting* 19 (Fall):427-437.

Perry, James M.
1973. *Us and Them: How the Press Covered the 1972 Election*. New York: Clarkson N. Potter.

Petrick, Michael J.
1976. " 'Equal Opportunities' and 'Fairness' in Broadcast Coverage of Politics." In L. John Martin, ed. "Role of the Mass Media in American Politics." *Annals of the American Academy of Political and Social Science* 427 (September):73-83.

Pool, Ithiel de Sola, ed.
1959. *Trends in Content Analysis*. Urbana: University of Illinois Press.

Pool, Ithiel de Sola, Wilbur Schramm, Frederick W. Frey, Nathan Maccoby, and Edwin B. Parker, eds.
1973. *Handbook of Communication*. Chicago: Rand McNally.

Porter, William E.
1976. *Assault on the Media: The Nixon Years*. Ann Arbor: University of Michigan Press.

Powers, Ron.
1977. *The Newscasters*. New York: St. Martin's Press.

Powers, Ron, and Jerrold Oppenheim.
1972. "Is TV Too Profitable?" *Columbia Journalism Review*, May/June, pp. 7-13.

Powledge, Fred.
1971. *The Engineering of Restraint: The Nixon Administration and the Press*. Washington, D.C.: Public Affairs Press.

President's Task Force on Communications Policy.
1968. *Bibliography [on Communications Policy]*. Springfield, Va.: National Technical Information Service, U.S. Department of Commerce.

Price, Warren C., and Calder M. Pickett.
1970. *An Annotated Journalism Bibliography: 1958-68*. Minneapolis: University of Minnesota Press.

Pride, Richard A., and Gary L. Wamsley.
1972. "Symbol Analysis of Network Coverage of Laos Incursion." *Journalism Quarterly* 49 (Winter):635-640, 647.

Rather, Dan.
　　1977. *The Camera Never Blinks*. New York: William Morrow.

Reedy, George E.
　　1976. "The President and the Press: Struggle for Dominance." In L. John
　　Martin, ed. "Role of the Mass Media in American Politics." *Annals of
　　the American Academy of Political and Social Science* 427 (September):
　　65-72.

Richardson, Gerald Alan.
　　1967. "A Comparison of the Osgood Technique and a Modified Technique
　　for the Analysis of Evaluative Assertions in Message Content." Unpub-
　　lished master's thesis, University of Washington. Described in Gerald
　　A. Lantz. "Beardsley's Aesthetics and Evaluative Assertion Analysis."
　　Unpublished master's thesis, Temple University. Pp. 12-13.

Ripley, Joseph M.
　　1964-1965. "Policies and Practices Concerning Broadcasts of Controversial
　　Issues." *Journal of Broadcasting* 9 (Winter):25-32.

Rivers, William L.
　　1965. *The Opinionmakers*. Boston: Beacon Press.

　　1970. *The Adversaries: Politics and the Press*. Boston: Beacon Press.

Rivers, William L., and Michael J. Nyhan, eds.
　　1973. *Aspen Notebook on Government and the Media*. Palo Alto, Calif.:
　　Aspen Institute Program on Communications and Society.

Rivers, William, Wallace Thompson, and Michael J. Nyhan, eds.
　　1977. *Aspen Handbook on the Media: 1977-79 Edition: A Selective Guide
　　to Research, Organizations and Publications in Communications*. 3rd
　　ed. New York: Praeger Special Studies.

Robbins, J. C.
　　1972. "Deciding First Amendment Cases: Part I." *Journalism Quarterly*
　　49 (Summer):263-270.

Roberts, Donald F.
　　1963. "Communication and Children: A Development Approach." In Ithiel
　　de Sola Pool, Wilbur Schramm, et al., eds. *Handbook of Communica-
　　tion*. Chicago: Rand McNally. Pp. 174-215.

Robinson, John P.
    1972. "Perceived Media Bias and the 1968 Vote: Can the Media Affect Behavior After All?" *Journalism Quarterly* 49 (Summer):239-246.

    1974. "The Press as King-Maker: What Surveys from Last Five Campaigns Show." *Journalism Quarterly* 51 (Winter):587-594.

    1976. "The Press and the Voter." In L. John Martin, ed. "Role of the Mass Media in American Politics." *Annals of the American Academy of Political and Social Science* 427 (September):95-103.

Robinson, Michael J.
    1977. "Television and American Politics: 1956-1976." *The Public Interest* 48 (Summer).

Rogers, Everett M.
    1973. "Mass Media and Interpersonal Communication." In Ithiel de Sola Pool, Wilbur Schramm, et al., eds. *Handbook of Communication*. Chicago: Rand McNally. Pp. 290-310.

The Roper Organization.
    1977. "Changing Public Attitudes Toward Television and Other Mass Media 1959-1976." New York: Television Information Office.

Rousseau, Jean-Jacques.
    1762. *The Social Contract*. Books 1 and 2. Chicago: The Great Books Foundation, 1966.

Routt, Edd.
    1974. *Dimensions of Broadcast Editorializing*. Blue Ridge Summit, Pa.: TAB Books.

Royal Commission on the Press.
    1947-1949. "The Standard by Which the Press Should be Judged." In *Report of the Royal Commission on the Press*, pp. 100-106. Reprinted in Bernard Berelson and Morris Janovitz, eds. *Reader in Public Opinion and Communication*. 2nd ed. New York: The Free Press, 1966. Pp. 535-542.

Rucker, Bryce W.
    1968. *The First Freedom*. Carbondale: Southern Illinois University Press.

Rudner, Richard S.
  1966. *Philosophy of Social Science*. Englewood Cliffs, N.J.: Prentice-Hall.

Sanderson, Arthur Marshall.
  1963. "A Modification of Evaluative Assertion Analysis and Its Application
    to Selected Editorials on Federal Social Security in the *New York Times*
    and the *Chicago Tribune* During the First Twenty-five Years of the Pro-
    gram." Unpublished Ph.D. dissertation, University of Iowa. Described
    in Gerald A. Lantz. "Beardsley's Aesthetics and Evaluative Assertion
    Analysis." Unpublished master's thesis, Temple University. P. 12.

Sasser, Emery L., and John T. Russell.
  1972. "The Fallacy of News Judgment." *Journalism Quarterly* 49 (Spring):
    280-284.

Schiller, Herbert I.
  1973. *The Mind Managers*. Boston: Beacon Press.

Schorr, Daniel.
  1974. "The FBI and Me." *Columbia Journalism Review*, November/Decem-
    ber, pp. 8-14.

  1977. *Clearing the Air*. Boston: Houghton Mifflin.

Schramm, Wilbur, and Janet Alexander.
  1973. "Broadcasting." In Ithiel de Sola Pool, Wilbur Schramm, et al., eds.
    Handbook of Communication. Chicago: Rand McNally. Pp. 577-618.

Schramm, Wilbur, and D. F. Roberts, eds.
  1971. *The Process and Effects of Mass Communication*. Urbana: University
    of Illinois Press.

Schwartz, Alan U.
  1977. "Danger: Pendulum Swinging." *The Atlantic Monthly* 239 (Febru-
    ary):29-34.

Sears, David O., and Richard E. Whitney.
  1973. "Political Persuasion." In Ithiel de Sola Pool, Wilbur Schramm, et
    al., eds. *Handbook of Communication*. Chicago: Rand McNally. Pp.
    253-289.

Selltiz, Clair, Marie Jahoda, Morton Deutsch, and Stuart W. Cook.
  1959. *Research Methods in Social Relations*. Rev. 1-vol. ed. New York:
    Holt, Rinehart, and Winston.

Shaw, Donald T., and Michael L. Bishop.
　　1972. "Editorial Function and Societal Stress." *Journalism Quarterly* 49 (Autumn):582-585.

Shaw, Eugene F.
　　1972. "The Press and Its Freedom: A Pilot Study of an American Stereotype." *Journalism Quarterly* 49 (Spring):31-42, 60.

Shostick, Herschel.
　　1975. "The Structural Dimensions of Television Editorial Effectiveness." *Journalism Quarterly* 52 (Spring):37-43, 60.

Siebert, Fred S., Theodore B. Peterson, and Wilbur Schramm.
　　1956. *Four Theories of the Press*. Urbana: University of Illinois Press.

Siegel, Sidney.
　　1956. *Nonparametric Statistics for the Behavioral Sciences*. New York: McGraw-Hill.

Sigal, Leon V.
　　1974. *Reporters and Officials: The Organization and Politics of Newsmaking*. Lexington, Mass.: D. C. Heath.

Sigelman, Lee.
　　1973. "Reporting the News: An Organizational Analysis." *American Journal of Sociology* 79 (July):132-135.

Simmons, Steven J.
　　1978. *The Fairness Doctrine and the Media*. Berkeley: University of California Press.

Small, William J.
　　1970. *To Kill a Messenger: Television News and the Real World*. New York: Hastings House.

　　1972. *Political Power and the Press*. New York: W. W. Norton.

Smith, Bruce Lannes, Harold D. Lasswell, and Ralph D. Casey.
　　1946. *Propaganda, Communication, and Public Opinion: A Comprehenisve Reference Guide*. Princeton: Princeton University Press.

Smith, Bruce Lannes, and Chitra M. Smith.
　　1956. *International Communication and Political Opinion: A Guide to the Literature*. Princeton: Princeton University Press.

Smith, R. Franklin.
1962. "The Nature and Development of Commentary." *Journal of Broadcasting* 6 (Winter):11-22.

Smith, Robert R.
1965. "The Origins of Radio Network News Commentary." *Journal of Broadcasting* 9 (Spring):113-122.

Spector, N. J.
1970. "The Impact of the Editorial Page on a Municipal Referendum." *Journalism Quarterly* 47 (Winter):762-766.

Sperry, Robert.
1967-1968. "A Selected Bibliography of Works on the Federal Communications Commission." *Journal of Broadcasting* 12 (Winter):83-93.

1970. "A Selected Bibliography of Works on the Federal Communications Commission, 1967-1969 Supplement." *Journal of Broadcasting* 14 (Summer):377-389.

1975. "A Selected Bibliography of Works on the FCC and OTP: 1970-1973." *Journal of Broadcasting* 19 (Winter):55-113.

Stempel, Guido H., III.
1962. "Content Patterns of Small and Metropolitan Dailies." *Journalism Quarterly* 39 (Winter):88-90.

1973. "Effects on Performance of a Cross-Media Monopoly." *Journalism Monographs* no. 29 (June 1973).

Sterling, Christopher H.
1974. "Periodicals, Annuals and Directories on Mass Communications." Philadelphia: Department of Radio-Television-Film, Temple University. Mimeographed.

1976. "A Selective Guide to the Literature of Broadcasting." In Sydney W. Head, ed. *Broadcasting in America*. 3rd ed. Boston: Houghton Mifflin. Pp. 511-550.

1978. "Broadcasting and Mass Communication: A Survey Bibliography." Philadelphia: Department of Radio-Television-Film, Temple University. Mimeographed.

Sterling, Christopher H., and Timothy R. Haight.
    1978. *The Mass Media: Aspen Institute Guide to Communication Industry Trends*. New York: Praeger.

Sterling, Christopher, H., and John M. Kittross.
    1978. *Stay Tuned: A Concise History of American Broadcasting*. Belmont, Calif.: Wadsworth.

Stevenson, Robert L.
    1977. "Studying Communications Across Cultures." *Communication Research* 4 (January):113-127.

Stevenson, Robert L., Richard A. Eusenger, Barry M. Feinberg, and Alan B. Kotok.
    1973. "Untwisting *The News Twisters*: A Replication of Efron's Study." *Journalism Quarterly* 50 (Summer):211-219.

Stone, Philip J., Dexter C. Dumphy, Marshall S. Smith, and Daniel M. Ogilvie, eds.
    1966. *The General Inquirer: A Computer Approach to Content Analysis*. Cambridge, Mass.: M.I.T. Press.

Stone, Vernon.
    1977. "News Directors and Problems Surveyed." *RTNDA Communicator* 31 (March):5-10.

Stone, Vernon A., and Thomas L. Beell.
    1975. "To Kill a Messenger: A Case of Congruity." *Journalism Quarterly* 52 (Spring):111-114.

Tebbel, John.
    1969. *The Compact History of the American Newspaper*. New York: Hawthorn.

Tuber, Richard.
    1969-1970. "An Annotated Bibliography on Broadcast Rights, 1920-1955." *Journal of Broadcasting* 14, pt. 2 (Winter):147-156.

Tuchman, Gaye.
    1972. "Objectivity as Strategic Ritual: An Examination of Newspapermen's Notion of Objectivity." *American Journal of Sociology* 77:660-679.

    1978. *Making News*. New York: The Free Press.

Tucker, St. George, ed.
    1803. *Blackstone's Commentaries on the Laws of England (1765-1769)*.
    Philadelphia: Birch and Small.

The Twentieth Century Fund.
    1972. *Press Freedoms Under Pressure*. New York: The Twentieth Century
    Fund.

    1973. *A Free and Responsive Press*. New York: The Twentieth Century
    Fund.

Ungar, Sanford J.
    1972. *The Papers and the Papers*. New York: E. P. Dutton.

U.S. Congress, House Committee on Interstate and Foreign Commerce, Subcommittee on Communications.
    1977. *Option Papers*. Washington, D.C.: U.S. Government Printing Office.

Von Hoffman, Nicholas.
    1976. "TV Commentators: Burbles from Olympus." *Columbia Journalism
    Review*, January/February, pp. 9-13.

Wagenberg, Ronald H., and Walter C. Soderlund.
    1975. "The Influence of Chain-Ownership on Editorial Comment in Canada."
    Journalism Quarterly 52 (Spring):93-98.

Walters, Robert.
    1974. "What Did Ziegler Say, and When Did He Say It?" *Columbia Journal-
    ism Review*, September/October, pp. 30-35.

Webb, Eugene J., Donald T. Campbell, Richard D. Schwartz, and Lee Sechrest.
    1966. *Unobtrusive Measures: Nonreactive Research in the Social Sciences*.
    Chicago: Rand McNally.

Weiner, Richard.
    1977. *Syndicated Columnists*. New York: Richard Weiner.

Westley, Bruce H., Charles E. Higbie, Timothy Burke, David J. Lippert, Leonard
Maurer, and Vernon A. Stone.
    1963. "The News Magazines and the 1960 Conventions." *Journalism
    Quarterly* 40 (Autumn):525-531, 647.

Wicker, Tom.
    1971. "The Greening of the Press." *Columbia Journalism Review*, May/
    June, pp. 7-12.

Windhauser, John W.
1973. "Content Patterns of Editorials in Ohio Metropolitan Dailies." *Journalism Quarterly* 50 (Autumn):562-567.

Witcover, Jules.
1971. "Two Weeks That Shook the Press." *Columbia Journalism Review*, September/October, pp. 7-15.

1973. "How Well Does the White House Press Perform?" *Columbia Journalism Review*, November/December, pp. 39-43.

Wolf, Frank.
1973. *Television Programming for News and Public Affairs*. New York: Praeger.

Wolff, Robert Paul, Barrington Moore, Jr., and Herbert Marcuse.
1965. *A Critique of Pure Tolerance*. Boston: Beacon Press.

Woodward, Bob, and Carl Bernstein.
1976. *The Final Days*. New York: Simon and Schuster.

Wright, Charles R.
1964. "Functional Analysis and Mass Communication." In Lewis Anthony Dexter and David Manning, eds. *People, Society and Mass Communications*. New York: Free Press. Pp. 91-109.

1975. *Mass Communication: A Sociological Perpsective*. 2nd ed. New York: Random House.

Yu, Frederick Teh-Chi.
1951. "The Treatment of China in Four Chicago Daily Newspapers: July 1 Through December 31, 1949." Unpublished Ph.D. dissertation, State University of Iowa.

Zuchman, Harvey L., and Martin J. Gaynes.
1977. *Mass Communications Law in a Nutshell*. St. Paul, Minn.: West Publishing.

INDEX

Abel, John D., 17
activity dimension, 249
"actual malice test," 35
"ad hoc balancing," 35
Agnew, Spiro: anti-media effort, 196; Dean Burch and, 190-91; *Life* magazine and, 191; media critiques, 47; *New York Times* and, 191;
Alien Act, 21
Allen, James E., 73
Alsop, Joseph: rank, 140; style, 142
Altschull, Herbert J., 47
American Bond and Mortgage v. *United States*, 26
American Broadcasting Corporation (ABC), news analysts, 150
American Society of Newspaper Editors, 213
Anderson, Jack: and India-Pakistan war, 213; rank, 140; White House and, 5-6
anxiety index broadcasters, 159
Armed Services Committee (U.S. House of Representatives), 201
Ashmore, Harry, 57, 63
"Aspen Institute," 173
assertion, 249
Associated Press Managing Editors Association, 200
Atlanta Constitution, 196
attitude object, 249
Austro-German Telegraphic Union, 35
"bad tendency test," 34
Bagdikian, Ben: and Nixon strategy, 61; public affairs and, 46; Watergate and, 59

Bailey, Thomas A., 51; commentators and, 47
Baker, Howard, Jr., 214
Baker, Russell, 86; rank, 141; style, 143, 146
Baldwin, Alfred, 219-20
Barker, Bernard, 64
Barron, Jerome A., 50
Bartlett, Charles, 139
Beacon Press, 209
Bernstein, Carl, 61
Bill of Rights, 21
Bingham, Barry, Jr., 73
Black, Hugo LaFayette, 25; laissez-faire policy, 8
"Black Journal," 215
Blackmun, Harry Andrew, 30
Black Panthers, 193; CBS and, 192
blandness, by intimidation, 130-32
blandness quotient, 249; of TV subjects, 116-17
Boston Globe, 205
Braden, Tom, 139
Bradlee, Benjamin C., 62
Brandeis, Louis Dembitz, 34; laissez-faire and, 8
Breed, Warren, 161
Brinkley, David: H. R. Haldeman and, 193-94; "Journal," 76; rank, 140; style, 142; White House and, 6
broadcasting: executives, 155-56; policy orientation, 171-77; regulatory policy, 12-15, 181-82
broadcasting stations, licensing, 10-11. *See also specific station*
Broder, David, 5-6; rank, 140; style, 142.
Bruckner, D. J. R., 139
Buchanan, Patrick, 213; CPB and, 222

Buchwald, Art, 86; rank, 141; style, 143
Buckley, William F., Jr., 59; labor dispute, 48; rank, 140; style, 142, 147
Buffone, Samuel J., 64
Burch, Dean, 193; Spiro Agnew and, 190-91; cable regulation policy, 207; Barry Goldwater and, 189-9(
Burger, Warren Earl, 30; ABC and, 194; CBC and, 194; lawyers and, 203
Burke, Edmund, 53
Butz, Earl L., 221
Byrne, W. Matthew, 60

Caldwell, Earl, 193
"Canuck letters," 64
Carter, Boake, 39
CATV, 188
censorship: commentary, 169; Communications Act and, 12; First Amendment and, 24
Chaffee, Steven H., 161
Chancellor, John, 32
Chandler, Otis, 73
Chapin, Dwight, 64
Childs, Marquis, 139
chilling effect, 1; reverse, 129-30; WHAMA and, 128-29
Christian Science Monitor, 205
Clift, Charles, III, 17
Coase, R. H., 15
Coding Manual, 80; assertion formation and, 86
Collier's Encylopedia Yearbook, 212
Collingwood, Charles, 139
Colson, Charles, 198, 217; "Selling of the Pentagon" and, 206; Vietnam and, 200
Columbia Broadcasting System (CBS): Black Panthers and, 192; news analysts, 150-51

commentary, 44-48; inhibition of, 115; Personal Attack Rules, 48; robustness of, 115-20; timidity of, 70; Watergate, 119
Committee to Re-elect the President (CREEP), 64
common meaning, 250
communication, Lasswell's function of, 42
Communications Act of 1934, 26; First Amendment and, 27
Cook, Fred J., 29
Corporation for Public Broadcasting (CPB), 215
Coughlin, Father Charles Edward, 48
CPB. *See* Corporation for Public Broadcasting (CPB)
CREEP. *See* Committee to Re-elect the President
Criminal Code, 16
Cronkite, Walter, 32
Crosby, Harry H., 95; thesis statement and, 80
Crouse, Timothy, 57; White House and, 61

Dahlberg, Kenneth, 64
Davis, Elmer, 39; public opinion and, 48
Dean, John, 57
Democratic National Committee, 197
Dennis v. *United States*, 34
Diamond, Edwin, 65
"Dick Cavett Show," 202
Dobrovir, William A., 60
doctrine of scarcity, 250; vs. unlimited resources, 10
Dole, Robert, 201
Dombrowski v. *Pfister*, 1
Donovan, Robert, 139
Douglas, William Orville, 176; First Amendment and, 25; laissez-faire and, 8

Drummond, Roscoe: rank, 140; style, 142
Duke, Paul, 73
Dunlamp, Wallace, 73

editorial autonomy, vs. government management of information, 11-12
Efron, Edith, 42-44
Ehrlichman, John, 190
Eisenhower, David, 227
Ellsberg, Daniel, 60; Pentagon Papers and, 224
Emerson, Thomas I., 35
Encyclopedia Britannica, 212
Environmental Quality, Council on, 216
Ervin Committee, 227
Ervin, Sam J., 211; Senate Select Committee, 224
Espionage Statute of 1917, 22-23
Estey, George F., 95; thesis statement, 80
evaluative dimension, 250
Evans, M. Stanton, 48
Evans, Rowland, 138; foreign newspapers and, 47; rank, 140; style, 142
expectations, 90-92
expression, modes of, 89

Fairness Doctrine, license renewal and, 12
Farmers Educational Union v. *WDAY*, 173
Federal Communications Commission (FCC), 48; licensing, 11; "prime time rule," 196; "single market rule," 195; v. *Pacifica Foundation*, 16
Federal Criminal Code, 221
Federal Radio Commission (FRC), 26
Federal Radio Commission v. *Nelson*

Brothers, 26
Fenno, John, 45
"Firing Line," 215
First Amendment: Communications Act of 1934 and, 27; dichotomy of, 25; Justice Douglas and, 25; Nixon administration and, 5
Fisher, Charles, 44, 50
Flegel, Ruth C., 161
Forcade, Thomas K., 209
Foreign Relations Committee (Senate), 196
Fortune, 194
Fourth Estate, 53
Frank, Reuven, 73
Frankfurter, Felix, 27
FRC. *See* Federal Radio Commission
Freedom of Information Act, Nixon and, 57
Freedom of the Press, Commission on, 41
Freneau, Philip, 46
Friendly, Fred, 36; Red Lion and, 30
Fritchey, Clayton, 138; rank, 140; style, 142; White House and, 5-6
Fulbright, J. William, 196
Furguson, Ernest B., 139

Gibbons, Floyd, 48
Gillmor, Donald M., 50
Gitlow v. *New York*, 34
Gold, Daniel E., 73
Gold, Vic, 139
Goldwater, Barry, 189
government: information management vs. editorial autonomy, 11-12; press relationship, 167-68; television intimidation by, 71
Graham, Katharine, 57; White House and, 227
Gray, L. Patrick, 213
Greater Miami Telecasters, Inc., 192

Greene, Robert, 211

Halberstam, David, 46; John Kennedy and, 56
Haldeman, H. R., 189-90; media and, 201
Hargis, Rev. Billy James, 29
Harwood, Kenneth, 36
Hebert, F. Edward, 201
Herschensohn, Bruce, 227
Higby, Lawrence, 197; FBI and, 208
Hobler, Herbert W., 73
Hoffman, Nicholas von, 45; rank, 140; style, 142, 147
Holmes, Oliver Wendell, 32; laissez-faire and, 8
Holsti, Ole R., 87
Hoover, Herbert, 55
Hoover, J. Edgar, 209; wiretapping by, 221
Hunt, E. Howard, 223
Huntley, Chet, 43-44
hysteria: anti-Communist, 22; anti-radical, 22

Ickes, Harold, 47
I. F. Stone's Weekly, 196
Indian Affairs, Bureau of, 220
Information Agency, U.S., 224
Ingle, Robert D., 73
International Federation of Newspaper Publishers, 196
International Telegraphic Convention, 35
Interstate Commerce Act, 35
intimidation, blandness by, 130-32

jackal syndrome, 47
Johnson, Lyndon, 158; media relations, 56
journalism: First Amendment and, 170-71; interpretive, 43-44; tradition, 251

Kaltenborn, H. V., 39; radio commentary, 48
Karnow, Stanley, 210
Keith, Hastings, 207
Kellogg, Ansel, Nash, 48
Kennedy, John F., 46, 158; David Halberstam and, 56; press relations, 46
Kilpatrick, James, 5-6, rank, 140; style, 142
Kirk, Russel, 139
Kissinger, Henry, 86, 225
Kittross, John M., 36
Klein, Herbert, 187; Catherine Mackin and, 217; Chet Huntley and, 197; criminal network commentary, 190; media criticism, 191
Klein, Lewis, 74
Kleindienst, Richard G., 219-20
Knappmann, Edward, 93
KNBC-TV, 189
Knops, Mark, 199-200
Kohlmeier, Louis, 139
Kraft, Joseph, 5-6, 138; and foreign newspapers, 47; ranking, 140; style, 142, 148
Krasnow, Erwin G., 133
Kuhn, Thomas S., 172

laissez-faire: vs. government licensing, 9; libertarian theory and, 7-8
Lashner, Marilyn A., 93
Lasswell, Harold, 39, 41
Lawrence, Bill, 139
Lawrence, John F., 219
Lee, Robert E., 176
Leonard, Richard H., 74
Lewis, Anthony, 214; rank, 141; style, 142, 145
licensing, government vs. laissez-faire, 10-11
Liddy, G. Gordon, 223
Life, 190
Ling, James J., 194

Lippmann, Walter, 46
Lisagor, Peter, 215
Longly, Lawrence D., 133
Longworth, Alice Roosevelt, 229
Los Angeles Times, 209
Lower, Elmer W., 74
"Loyal Opposition, The," 197

McCardle, Dorothy, 218-19
McCarthy, Joseph, 218
McCloskey, Robert J., 208
McCrea, W. Sloan, 192
McGovern, George, 77
McIntyre, Thomas J., 192
McLaren, Richard W., 188
MacNeil, Robert, 215
Macy, John W., Jr., 74, 215
Madison, James, 54
Magruder, Jeb: David Brinkley and, 193; "Shot-gun vs. the Rifle," 189; *Washington Post* and, 195-96
Maines, Patrick D., 96
Mardian, Robert C., 204
Martin, Judith, 203-4
Maynard, Robert C., 62
media, and Nixon policy, 56-59
media executives and WHAMA, 104-5
Meiklejohn, Alexander, 165
Miami Herald v. *Tornillo*, 30-31
Mitchell, John: Pentagon study and, 206; and subpoenas, 194, 198
Mollenhoff, Clark R., 191
Monroe, Bill, 39
Mundt-Nixon Bill, 57
Muskie, Edmund, 64

National Association of Broadcasters, 197
National Association of Manufacturers, 226
National Broadcasting Company (NBC): Haldeman censoring of, 169; news analysts, 150-51
National Broadcasting Company v. *United States*, 27
National Press Club, 57
National Public Radio, 210
NBC News, 190
Near v. *Minnesota*, 25, 35
Nelson, Jack, 220
network executives, 155
New England Society of Newspaper Editors, 218
newspapers vs. television, 109-11
Newsweek, 190
New York Daily News, 198
New York Times, Spiro Agnew and, 191
Nixon, Richard: anti-media efforts, 13, 56-59; criminal violations, 60; and First Amendment, 5; Indochina policy, 197; political milestones, 56-57
nonissues, 252
North, Robert C., 87
Novak, Robert, 47; rank, 140; style, 142

Officials Secrets Act, 221
Oliphant, Thomas, 222
Osborne, John, 61
"Other Prisoners, The," 231-33
Ottinger, John C., 96

Paine, Thomas, 45
Paley, William S.: Charles Colson and, 199; Richard Nixon and, 202; Stanton, Frank and, 221; Watergate report and, 157
paradigm, 252
Pastore, John, 188
Pearson, Drew, 48
Pegler, Westbrook, 47
Pentagon Papers: Daniel Ellsberg and, 224; Nixon administration and, 60; Supreme Court and, 23;

WHAMA and, 107
Personal Attack Rules: commentaries and, 48; Communications Act and, 28-29
Porter, William, 56
potency dimension, 252
Powledge, Fred, 63
president(s): criticism of, 118; and the press, 55-56
press: -government relationship, 167-68; presidents and, 55-56; pressure on, 166-67; requirements of, 42
Press, Royal Commission on the, 42
pressure, on press, 166-67
Prime Time Access Rule, 227; FCC and, 196
private ownership vs. public-trustee principle, 11
public: Elmer Davis, and, 39; TV influence on, 182-84
public affairs columnist, primary impact of, 46
public policy, 252; First Amendment and, 32
public-trustee principle, 252; vs. private ownership, 11
Pulitzer Prize, 213

Radio Act: of 1912, 26; of 1927, 26
Radio-Television News Directors Association, 29; Frank Shakespeare and, 189
Raspberry, William, 146; rank, 141; style, 143
Rather, Dan, 61; ranking, 139
Reasoner, Harry, 6, 76; rank, 141; style, 143, 149
Rebozo, Bebe, 192, 209
Red Lion v. *FCC*, 2, 27-28
Republican National Committee, 189
resource allocation, market controls

vs. government decision, 10
Reston, James: influence of, 46-47; rank, 140; style, 142; vs. television, 32; Watergate and, 138; White House affairs and, 5-6
reverse chilling effect, 129-30
Reynolds, Frank, 6, 76; rank, 141; style, 143
Richardson, Elliot, 101
Richmond Times Dispatch, 200
Roosevelt, Franklin D., 46; press relations, 55
Rosenblatt v. *Baer*, 92
Roth v. *United States*, 16

Safire, William: rank, 140; style, 142, 145
St. Louis Post-Dispatch, 220
Salant, Richard S., 74; John Erlichman and, 202
Schenck v. *United States*, 34
Schorr, Daniel, 72; Nixon and, 207
Schram, Martin, 212
Sedition Act, 21
Select Committee (Senate), 224
"Selling of the Pentagon, The," 107, 198
Sevareid, Eric: Nixon and, 76; rank, 140; style, 142, 149; Vietnam and, 83; White House and, 6
Shakespeare, Frank, 189
Sheehan, Neil, 224
Sheehan, William, 74
"Shot-gun versus the Rifle, The," 189
Sigelman, Lee, 161
"single market rule," 195
"60 Minutes," 192-93
Small, William J., 53-54; Watergate and, 62
Smith, Howard K., 76; rank, 140; style, 142; White House and, 6
Soderlund, Walter C., 161

Southern Christian Leadership Conference, 200
Staggers, Harley O., 213; broadcasting regulation and, 188; CBS and, 202
standardized attitude object, 253
Stanford Political Dictionary, 87-88, 253
Stans, Maurice, 64
Stanton, Frank, 199; CBS and, 157; Charles Colson and, 209; "Selling of the Pentagon" and, 206
Star Stations, Inc., 200-1
Strout, Stanley L., 139
Students for a Democratic Society, 193
Supreme Court (U.S.), First Amendment and, 23
Swing, Raymond Gram, 39
syndicated political columns, vigorousness index, 113
Szulc, Tad, 224

Taylor, Arthur R., 74; John Erlichman and,, 222
Telecommunications Policy, Office of, 58
telegraphy, regulation, 26
television: blandness quotient, 116-17; firmament, 148-50; government intimidation of, 71; manipulation of, 7; vs. newspapers, 109-11; timidity, 70-71, 121-22; vigorousness quotient, 116-17
thesis statement, 253; George Estey and, 80
Thimmesch, Nick: rank, 140, style, 142
Thompson, Dorothy, 48
Thurmond, Strom, 59
Time, 190
timidity: shape of, 121-22; television's, 70-71
Tooke, Franklin A., 74

Tornillo, Patrick, 30
Tornillo v. *Miami Herald*, 30-31
Truman, Harry, 56
Turner, Wallace, 232
Twentieth Century Fund, 212; task force, 54

Udwin, Gerald E., 74
Underground Press Syndicate, 209
United States v. *Carolene Products Co.*, 35
unlimited resources, vs. doctrine of scarcity, 10

Vanocur, Sander, 215
Vietnam war, 13; Charles Colson and, 200
vigorousness: anatomy of, 145-48; defined, 77, 79; dimension of, 112; index, 112-14
vigorousness quotient, 112-14; of news analysis, 139-45; of presidential criticism, 120; of TV subjects, 116-17; of Watergate, 119
Violence, National Commission on the Cause and Prevention of, 192

Wagenberg, Ronald H., 161
Wallace, Mike, 195
Wamsley, Gary L., 94
Warren, Gerald, 226
Washington Evening Star, 197
Washington Free Press, 187
Washington, George, 55
Washington Post Company, 189
Washington Star-News, 228
"Washington Week in Review," 215
Wasilewski, Vincent T., 74
Water Committee (Senate), 225-26
Watergate, 59-62
Weathermen, 190, 193
Weicker, Lowell, 227

Weiner, Richard, 46

Weiss, Fredric A., 17

WHAMA. *See* White House Anti-Media Assault

Whitehead, Clay T., 193; White House and, 194

White House: David Brinkley and, 6; Timothy Crouse and, 61; press secretary, 58

White House Anti-Media Assault (WHAMA): attitude object, 84-85; chilling effect analysis, 128-29; collision course, 124-28; content analysis, 77-78; frequency count, 103; index of, 99-100; media response to, 7; questionnaire, 71-75; reverse chilling effect, 129-30; sample selection, 76-77; storms of state, 103-8; thesis statement, 78-90

Whitney v. *California*, 34

Whitten, Les, 72; Bureau of Indian Affairs and, 220

Wicker, Tom: foreign newspapers and, 47; "The Other Prisoners," 231;
ranking, 140, 144, 145; style, 142; Watergate and, 138; White House and, 5-6

Wilkins, Roy, 139

Will, George F., 139

Wills, Garry, 139

Wilson, Donald, 210

Winchell, Walter: Franklin D. Roosevelt and, 46; public opinion and, 48

Wireless Ship Act, 35

WJXT-TV, 220

WLBW-TV, 192

Woodward, Bob, 61

Wounded Knee Indian uprising, 108

WPLG-TV, 192

Wright, Charles R., 45; and commentary style, 47-48

WTOP-AM, 189

WTOP-TV, 189

WUHY-FM, 195

Zeigler, Ronald, 58; *Boston Globe* and, 212; commentary response, 190

ABOUT THE AUTHOR

Marilyn A. Lashner holds a Ph.D. in communications. Formerly on the faculties of Pennsylvania State and Temple universities, she is founder and president of the Institute for News Media Analysis, a nonprofit corporation formed for the purpose of analyzing the news media with regard to their responsibilities under the First Amendment.